THE RUNNER'S BUCKET LIST

THE 500 MOST EPIC RUNS, RACES AND ADVENTURES AROUND THE WORLD

First published in Australia and New Zealand by
Pier 9, an imprint of Murdoch Books, in 2021

Copyright © 2021 Quarto Publishing plc

All rights reserved. No part of this book may be reproduced or transmitted in any form or by any means, electronic or mechanical, including photocopying, recording or by any information storage and retrieval system, without prior permission in writing from the publisher. The Australian *Copyright Act 1968* (the Act) allows a maximum of one chapter or 10 per cent of this book, whichever is the greater, to be photocopied by any educational institution for its educational purposes provided that the educational institution (or body that administers it) has given a remuneration notice to the Copyright Agency (Australia) under the Act.

10 9 8 7 6 5 4 3 2 1

ISBN: 978-1-92235-118-0

Murdoch Books Australia
83 Alexander Street
Crows Nest NSW 2065
Phone: (61 2) 8425 0100
www.murdochbooks.com.au
info@murdochbooks.com.au

Murdoch Books UK
Ormond House
26-27 Boswell Street
London WC1N 3JZ
Phone: (44 0) 20 8785 5995
www.murdochbooks.co.uk
info@murdochbooks.co.uk

Conceived, designed, and produced by
The Bright Press, an imprint of the Quarto Group
The Old Brewery
6 Blundell Street
London N7 9BH
United Kingdom
T 00 44 20 7700 6700
www.QuartoKnows.com
Publisher: James Evans
Art Director: James Lawrence
Senior Designer: Katherine Radcliffe
Designer: Paul Sloman
Editorial Director: Isheeta Mustafi
Managing Editor: Jacqui Sayers
Project Editor: Katie Crous
Senior Editor: Caroline Elliker
Editorial Assistant: Chloe Porter
Picture Researcher: Katie Crous

 A catalogue record for this book is available from the National Library of Australia

Printed and bound in Singapore

All trademarks or trade names referred to herein are the property of their respective owners, none of whom are affiliated with this book, and are used solely for identification and informational purposes. This book is a publication of The Bright Press, and has not been licensed, authorised, approved, sponsored or endorsed by any of the respective trademark owners or any other person or entity. The publisher is not associated with any product, service, or vendor mentioned in this book, and does not endorse the products or services of any vendor mentioned in this book.

THE RUNNER'S BUCKET LIST

THE 500 MOST EPIC RUNS, RACES AND ADVENTURES AROUND THE WORLD

JOHN BREWER **FOREWORD BY DAVE BEDFORD**

CONTENTS

	FOREWORD	5
	INTRODUCTION	6
	HOW TO USE THIS BOOK	8
	MONTH-BY-MONTH CALENDAR	9
1	**USA AND CANADA**	20
2	**MEXICO, CENTRAL AND SOUTH AMERICA**	88
3	**EUROPE**	112
4	**AFRICA AND THE MIDDLE EAST**	210
5	**ASIA, AUSTRALASIA AND THE SOUTH PACIFIC**	240
6	**POLES AND BEYOND**	296
	BIOGRAPHIES	313
	INDEX	314
	PICTURE CREDITS	319
	ACKNOWLEDGEMENTS	320

FOREWORD

As a former world record holder for 10,000 m, often running 320 km (200 miles) each week, and later as race director of the London Marathon and chairman of World Athletics (IAAF) Road Running Commission, I think it is fair to say that I know a little bit about training, running and racing!

One of the joys of my own training, often three times a day, was finding new routes in unusual and exciting locations that would stimulate my mind and help me to forget some of the drudgery of training. I was lucky to be living in North London, with its spectacular Hampstead Heath and Totteridge Valley just a mile from home, but a race or training run in a new location would always inspire. During my running career I've enjoyed the loneliness and beauty of the lakes and forests of Finland and Sweden, running with friends on Auckland Domain, the beaches of New Zealand, the mountains of the Pyrenees and Alps, the English Canals, Kenya's Rift Valley and morning runs to the Equator and back in Nyahururu.

John Brewer is a running expert whom I have known for many years. Unlike me, he still enjoys regular runs and races, and he now brings us this sumptuous guide to the world of running. Looking at the photographs in *The Runner's Bucket List* certainly gets the running juices going again. So many exciting races and training opportunities – 500 in all – that provide plenty of fodder for my dreams. Finding a race with a few days' training in a spectacular environment will be easy with this book, which will help you plan your next running adventure. This perfect bucket-list guide makes a great gift – the hard part is deciding where to go next!

David Bedford, OBE

INTRODUCTION

When I first started to run, it was long enough ago for running to be a sport that was quite niche, dominated by men in vests running races around a track, on roads or across muddy fields. Female participation was limited and sadly not encouraged (the first female Olympic Marathon was not held until 1984, almost 90 years after the males first raced in the Olympic Games over the same distance), and there were none of the mass participation events that now take place around the world. Today, running has grown to become a global sport and pastime that enriches the lives of runners of all abilities, offering them the chance to make friends, explore different places and enhance their physical and mental well-being.

I am often asked if I find running boring. The answer is a definite 'no', and to show why this is I have compiled a collection of races, places, distances and surfaces that make running the sport that is loved by so many millions of people because it offers choice, freedom, variety and excitement that, in my view, is hard to beat.

My early running career was very much focused on racing, and any run that wasn't a race was a training run to prepare for my next race. Today, while I still race, I enjoy running for the sheer pleasure of being out in the fresh air, exploring a landscape that is often familiar but sometimes new. I have been fortunate that over the years my work and holidays have taken me to many parts of the world that I never thought I would see. When I am on a tight timescale, cramming meetings or a conference into a busy day, I am always grateful that I can pull on my running shoes and often be back in my hotel before breakfast, invigorated by the sights that I have seen and the city and landscape I have just explored. This book is, in many ways, a tribute to 'tourist running' – it's not a surprise that many of the world's best runs are also in great cities or places that would be worth a visit even if you were not a runner.

Runners, and running psychologists, often refer to the 'runner's high', when running feels effortless and runners feel part of the environment in which they are running. I have run in many of the races and at many of the places that feature in this book, and I know from my own experiences that many of them have provided me with adventures that I will never forget. So, in compiling this list of runs, I have been mindful that the book can be used as a means of finding a route or race to run simply because you find yourself in that place, or it can be used proactively to choose a place to visit with the specific goal of taking part in a run. I hope readers will agree that either way works.

Much of this book was written while the Covid-19 pandemic swept around the world, so at the time of writing many of the races featured in the book had been cancelled. As the world slowly recovers, I hope that all the featured races will be staged again, but sadly, of course, this may not always be the case. So before heading off to a distant country, please do first check that the race you are going to enter is still taking place.

Happy running!

HOW TO USE THIS BOOK

This book is organised by the continents of the world. Within each chapter you will then find entries organised under individual countries – or in the case of the USA and Canada, states, provinces and territories. If you have a specific run or race in mind, simply turn to page 314 to search for it in the index. If you want to create your own running schedule for the year, or to easily check which events are on when, use the calendar starting opposite or the continent-specific calendars at the start of each chapter. The book features a mixture of organised races – big and small – at specific times of the year in specific places, and recommended running routes that are free to access mostly all year round.

A NOTE ABOUT CATEGORIES

Location details appear at the start of each entry, followed by one or two categories that best describe the route or race. Some races would happily fit into numerous categories – always check the finer details of the event itself.

WHEN TO RUN

Some countries/routes, particularly those with extreme temperatures/terrain, will be best done at certain times of year, so, where relevant, this has been noted in the heading information, although you should always check before organising and travelling.

DISTANCE

Where relevant, all distances have been noted in the headings, and in both kilometres and miles in the main description. It's worth noting that many of the larger organised events around the world have multiple distances/routes available, maximising their appeal and suitability, and for some running routes the choice of distance is yours to make, so these instances are categorised as 'Various' in the headings.

MONTH-BY-MONTH CALENDAR

JANUARY

USA & CANADA
- 65   Freeze Your Half Off, Tennessee
- 70   Walt Disney World Marathon Weekend, Florida
- 74   Miami Marathon, Florida

MEXICO, CENTRAL & SOUTH AMERICA
- 115   Marathon Bahamas Race Weekend, Bahamas

EUROPE
- 161   Sugar Loaf 10K, Ireland
- 175   Falkirk Epic Trail 10K, Scotland
- 181   Worms Head 10K, Wales
- 222   Cliveden Cross Country 10K, England
- 234   Polar Night Half-marathon, Norway
- 287   Swiss Snow Run, Switzerland

AFRICA & THE MIDDLE EAST
- 339   Egyptian Marathon, Egypt

ASIA, AUSTRALASIA & SOUTH PACIFIC
- 390   Hong Kong 100 Ultra Trail Race, Hong Kong
- 402   Khon Kaen Marathon, Thailand
- 405   Ultra Trail Angkor, Cambodia
- 409   Ho Chi Minh City Marathon, Vietnam
- 449   North Shore Run Series, New Zealand
- 457   Tussock Traverse, New Zealand
- 461   Wine Run, New Zealand

POLES & BEYOND
- 476   White Continent 50K, Antarctic

FEBRUARY

USA & CANADA
- 35   Zion Half-marathon, Utah
- 39   Run Sedona, Arizona
- 73   Paradise Coast Half-marathon, Florida

MEXICO, CENTRAL & SOUTH AMERICA
- 119   Tropikal Half-marathon, Puerto Rico
- 134   Jungle Marathon, Brazil
- 148   El Cruce Columbia, Argentina to Chile

EUROPE
- 167   Armagh 5K, Northern Ireland
- 186   The National, UK
- 205   Tough Guy, England
- 218   Portsmouth Coastal Half-marathon, England
- 321   Milestii Mici Wine Run, Moldova

[CONTINUED OVER PAGE]

AFRICA & THE MIDDLE EAST
- 334 Sahara Marathon, Algeria
- 347 Rwamagana Marathon, Rwanda

ASIA, AUSTRALASIA & SOUTH PACIFIC
- 446 Cradle Mountain, Australia
- 455 Tarawera Ultra, New Zealand
- 464 Shotover Moonlight Adventure Run, New Zealand

MARCH

USA & CANADA
- 7 Chuckanut 50K, Washington
- 24 Badger Cove Half-marathon, California
- 31 San Diego Half-marathon, California
- 64 Music City Half-marathon, Tennessee
- 66 Barkley Marathons, Tennessee
- 75 Bridge Run, Florida
- 97 Umstead 100-mile Ultra, North Carolina
- 106 Around the Bay Road Race, Ontario
- 108 Chilly Half-marathon, Ontario

MEXICO, CENTRAL & SOUTH AMERICA
- 114 Carrera D Teotihuacan Trail Race, Mexico
- 141 Rock 'n' Roll Santiago, Chile

EUROPE
- 157 Ballyliffin Coastal Challenge, Ireland
- 168 Isle of Man Easter Festival, Isle of Man
- 211 Cambridge Half-marathon, England
- 231 Orion 15, England
- 266 Loop Den Haag Half-marathon, The Netherlands
- 279 Survival Run, Switzerland
- 290 Malta Marathon, Malta
- 298 Prague Half-marathon, Czech Republic
- 305 Presov Night Run, Slovakia
- 307 Lake Balaton 26, Hungary
- 312 Paphos Marathon, Cyprus

AFRICA & THE MIDDLE EAST
- 340 Jerusalem Marathon, Israel
- 354 Kilimanjaro Marathon, Tanzania
- 365 Two Oceans Marathon, South Africa

ASIA, AUSTRALASIA & SOUTH PACIFIC
- 393 Nagoya City Marathon, Japan
- 398 Tokyo Marathon, Japan
- 404 Vientiane Half-marathon, Laos
- 433 Six Foot Track Marathon, Australia
- 437 Australian Alpine Ascent, Australia
- 463 Macpac Motatapu, New Zealand

POLES & BEYOND
- 477 Antarctica Marathon, Antarctica
- 489 Eiffel Tower Vertical Race, France

APRIL

USA & CANADA
- 3   Hapalua Half-marathon, Hawaii
- 18 Diablo Trails Challenge, California
- 22 Big Sur Marathon, California
- 66 Barkley Marathons, Tennessee
- 72 Florida Coast 2 Coast Relay, Florida
- 81 Boston Marathon, Massachusetts
- 93 Cherry Blossom Ten Mile, Washington, D.C.
- 95 Parkway Classic, Virginia
- 96 Ukrop's Monument Avenue 10K, Virginia

MEXICO, CENTRAL & SOUTH AMERICA
- 150 Stanley Marathon, Falkland Islands

EUROPE
- 157 Ballyliffin Coastal Challenge, Ireland
- 158 Connemarathon, Ireland
- 163 Valentia Island Half-marathon, Ireland
- 168 Isle of Man Easter Festival, Isle of Man
- 180 Coastal Trail Series, Wales
- 201 Manchester Marathon, England
- 203 Mersey Tunnel 10K, England
- 210 Shakespeare Marathon, England
- 226 London Marathon, England
- 254 Paris Marathon, France
- 267 Rotterdam Marathon, The Netherlands
- 272 Airport Night Run, Germany
- 273 Kreissparkassen Trail, Germany
- 289 Lema Trail, Switzerland
- 299 Brno Half-marathon, Czech Republic

AFRICA & THE MIDDLE EAST
- 323 Madeira Island Ultra-Trail, Madeira
- 330 Marathon des Sables, Morocco
- 336 Sfax International Half-marathon, Tunisia
- 342 Dead Sea Ultra, Jordan
- 345 Great Gambia Run, The Gambia
- 355 Heart Half-marathon, Tanzania
- 365 Two Oceans Marathon, South Africa

ASIA, AUSTRALASIA & SOUTH PACIFIC
- 394 Sakura Michi Nature Run, Japan
- 410 2XU Compression Run, Singapore
- 415 Moon Shadow Night Run, Australia
- 420 Kangaroo Island Marathon, Australia
- 424 Five Peaks SA Trail Running Festival, Australia
- 427 Gold Coast Running Festival, Australia

MAY

USA & CANADA
- 15   Bay to Breakers, California
- 47   Bolder Boulder, Colorado
- 51   Fargo Marathon and Festival, North Dakota
- 62   Chicago Spring Half-marathon, Illinois
- 89   Brooklyn Half-marathon, New York
- 111 Ottawa Race Weekend, Ontario

MEXICO, CENTRAL & SOUTH AMERICA
- 142 Circuito Trail Running Races, Chile

[CONTINUED OVER PAGE]

MONTH-BY-MONTH CALENDAR

EUROPE
- 165　Cork City Marathon, Ireland
- 170　Tiree, Scotland
- 171　Cape Wrath Ultra, Scotland
- 193　Grasmere Gallop, England
- 195　Keswick Mountain Festival, England
- 198　Mad Dog 10K, England
- 200　Great Manchester 10K, England
- 202　Run for the 96, England
- 224　RunFestRun, England
- 236　Arctic Triple Lofoten Trail, Norway
- 239　Sundsvall Trail Races, Sweden
- 240　Göteborgsvarvet Half-marathon, Sweden
- 246　Helsinki City Running Day, Finland
- 262　The National Centre for Altitude Training, France
- 263　Brussels 20K, Belgium
- 264　Bütgenbach Half-marathon, Belgium
- 278　Grand Prix of Bern, Switzerland
- 293　Jesolo Moonlight Half-marathon, Italy
- 311　Skiathos 10K Trail Run, Greece
- 316　Warsaw Half-marathon, Poland
- 322　Moscow Half-marathon, Russia

AFRICA & THE MIDDLE EAST
- 324　Madeira Sky Race, Madeira
- 326　Transvulcania, Canary Islands
- 367　Ultra Trail des ô Plateaux, Madagascar

ASIA, AUSTRALASIA & SOUTH PACIFIC
- 379　Everest Marathon, Nepal
- 381　Thunder Dragon Marathon, Bhutan
- 386　Great Wall Marathon, China
- 434　SMH Half-marathon, Australia
- 441　Puffing Billy Running Festival, Australia
- 452　Waiheke Half-marathon, New Zealand
- 458　Hawke's Bay Marathon, New Zealand

POLES & BEYOND
- 478　Wings for Life World Runs, Worldwide
- 491　International Vertical Marathon, China
- 492　Menara Tower Night Towerthon, Malaysia

JUNE

USA & CANADA
- 11　Western States Endurance Run, California
- 12　Dipsea Run, California
- 40　Madison River Run 5K, Montana
- 58　WW (Wounded Warrior) Military Miles, Texas
- 80　Covered Bridges Half-marathon, Vermont
- 83　Resurgence Half-marathon, New York
- 90　Sri Chinmoy Self-Transcendence 3100 Mile Race, New York
- 91　Bridgehampton Half, New York

MEXICO, CENTRAL & SOUTH AMERICA
- 133　Inca Trail Marathon, Peru
- 139　Marathon Rapa Nui, Easter Island

EUROPE
- 185　Rabbit Run, Wales
- 190　Hutton Roof Fell Race, England
- 204　Round Sheffield Run, England
- 213　Jurassic Coast Challenge, England
- 232　Spitsbergen Marathon, Norway
- 233　Midnight Sun Marathon, Norway

MONTH-BY-MONTH CALENDAR

EUROPE (CONTD)
- 237 Palace Park, Norway
- 243 Cross Lapland Marathon/Half-marathon, Finland
- 262 The National Centre for Altitude Training, France
- 302 Bled Night Run, Slovenia
- 313 Vitosha 100K, Bulgaria

AFRICA & THE MIDDLE EAST
- 327 Tenerife Blue Trail Night Challenge, Canary Islands
- 356 Citidash 5K and 10K, Namibia
- 360 4Peaks Mountain Challenge, South Africa
- 362 Comrades Marathon, South Africa

ASIA, AUSTRALASIA & SOUTH PACIFIC
- 384 Lanzhou Marathon, China
- 396 Ohme Road Race, Japan
- 412 Borneo Marathon, Malaysia
- 465 Mount Difficulty Ascent, New Zealand
- 471 Aitutaki Pursuit in Paradise Marathon, Cook Islands

POLES & BEYOND
- 473 North Pole Marathon, North Pole

JULY

USA & CANADA
- 14   Dirty Dozen and Half Dozen, California
- 17   Bad Bass Half-marathon, California
- 23   Badwater 135, California
- 30   Surfing Madonna Beach Run, California
- 43   Hardrock 100, Colorado
- 53   Honey Radger 100-mile Ultra, Kansas
- 76   Peachtree Road Race, Georgia

MEXICO, CENTRAL & SOUTH AMERICA
- 113 Half-marathon Mexico City, Mexico
- 128 Bogotá Half-marathon, Colombia

EUROPE
- 155 Laugavegur Ultramarathon, Iceland
- 178 Snowdonia Race, Wales
- 182 Love Trails, Wales
- 192 Lakeland 50 or 100, England
- 207 Heckington 10, England
- 225 Down Tow Up Flow Half-marathon, England
- 241 Kustmaran and Kristianopel Runt, Sweden
- 242 NUTS Ylläs Pallas, Finland
- 253 Skyrace Comapedrosa, Andorra
- 274 Bavaria Run, Germany
- 276 Tour du Lac de Joux, Switzerland
- 284 Eiger Ultra Trail, Switzerland
- 288 Swissalpine Race Weekend, Switzerland
- 291 Ortler Sky Trails, Italy
- 292 Brixen Dolomiten Marathon, Italy
- 294 Ecomaratona del Ventasso, Italy
- 300 Silvrettarun 3000, Austria
- 301 Ossiacher See Nachthalbmarathon, Austria

[CONTINUED OVER PAGE]

MONTH-BY-MONTH CALENDAR

AFRICA & THE MIDDLE EAST
- 335 Zriba Night Trail, Tunisia
- 357 Victoria Falls Marathon, Zimbabwe
- 363 Durban 10K, South Africa
- 368 Mauritius Marathon, Mauritius

ASIA, AUSTRALASIA & SOUTH PACIFIC
- 371 The Great Tibetan Marathon, India
- 378 Longrun Marathon, Maldives
- 395 Fuji Mountain Race, Japan
- 417 Australian Outback Marathon, Australia
- 470 Savai'i Marathon, Samoa
- 472 Tahiti-Moorea Marathon, French Polynesia

AUGUST

USA & CANADA
- 5 Spartan Race Hawaii, Hawaii
- 8 Hood to Coast, Oregon
- 41 Bridger Ridge Run, Montana
- 45 Leadville 100, Colorado
- 46 Transrockies Run, Colorado
- 48 Pikes Peak Ascent & Marathon, Colorado
- 102 Sea Wheeze Half-marathon, British Columbia
- 109 Hungry Hollow 5K, Ontario
- 110 Toronto Women's Run Series, Ontario

MEXICO, CENTRAL & SOUTH AMERICA
- 128 Bogotá Half-marathon, Colombia
- 131 Galapagos Marathon, Galapagos Islands
- 132 Pisco 30K, Peru
- 144 Snow Running, Chile

EUROPE
- 156 Extreme North, Ireland
- 179 Race the Train, Wales
- 194 Hawkshead 16K, England
- 223 Beat the Boat, England
- 228 Midnight 2 Midnight, England
- 235 Tromsø Mountain Challenge, Norway
- 259 Ultra-Trail du Mont-Blanc, France/Italy/Switzerland
- 285 Sierre-Zinal, Switzerland
- 319 Kuldiga Half-marathon, Latvia

AFRICA & THE MIDDLE EAST
- 358 Skukuza Half-marathon, South Africa
- 361 Mandela Day Marathon, South Africa

ASIA, AUSTRALASIA & SOUTH PACIFIC
- 377 Arugam Bay Half-marathon, Sri Lanka
- 383 Mongolia Sunrise to Sunset, Mongolia
- 408 Da Nang Marathon, Vietnam
- 416 City to Surf, Australia
- 419 Alice Springs Running Festival, Australia
- 426 Challenge the Mountain, Australia
- 431 Dubbo Stampede, Australia
- 435 City2Surf, Sydney, Australia
- 445 Flinders Island Running Festival, Australia
- 453 Mount Maunganui Half-marathon, New Zealand

POLES & BEYOND
- 494 Sydney Tower Stair Challenge, Australia

MONTH-BY-MONTH CALENDAR 15

SEPTEMBER

USA & CANADA
- 10 Oregon Fall Half-marathon, Oregon
- 42 Jackson Hole Marathon, Wyoming
- 57 Texas Trail Festival, Texas
- 67 Run Woodstock Festival, Michigan
- 88 Fifth Avenue Mile, New York
- 91 Hamptons Marathon, New York
- 100 Handloggers Half-marathon, British Columbia

MEXICO, CENTRAL & SOUTH AMERICA
- 118 Santo Domingo Marathon, Dominican Republic
- 140 The Atacama Crossing, Chile
- 145 Patagonian International Marathon, Chile
- 149 Buenos Aires Marathon, Argentina

EUROPE
- 172 Ring of Steall Skyrace, Scotland
- 188 Great North Run, England
- 227 London Color Run, England
- 244 Nakukymppi, Finland
- 255 Paris to Versailles 16 km, France
- 256 Marathon du Medoc, France
- 265 Amsterdam Marathon, The Netherlands
- 269 Serengeti Park Run, Germany
- 270 Berlin Marathon, Germany
- 280 Ultra Tour Du Monte Rosa, Switzerland/Italy
- 283 Jungfrau Marathon, Switzerland
- 304 Bratislava Half-marathon, Slovakia
- 306 Budapest Half-marathon, Hungary
- 317 Beskidy Ultra, Poland

AFRICA & THE MIDDLE EAST
- 325 Fanals Vertical Kilometre, Madeira

ASIA, AUSTRALASIA & SOUTH PACIFIC
- 372 Ladakh Ultra, India
- 375 Satara Hill Half-marathon, India
- 382 The Gobi March, Mongolia
- 422 Adelaide City to Bay, Australia
- 432 Backyard Blister, Australia
- 438 Surf Coast Century, Australia
- 442 Phillip Island Running Festival, Australia
- 462 4 Paws Marathon, New Zealand

POLES & BEYOND
- 490 Pyramidenkogel Tower Run, Austria

OCTOBER

USA & CANADA
- 36 Escalante Canyons Marathon, Utah
- 49 Emma Crawford Coffin Races, Colorado
- 52 Run Crazy Horse Marathon, South Dakota
- 54 Tulsa Run, Oklahoma
- 59 Shannon Monster 5K, Texas
- 60 Fort Smith Marathon, Arkansas
- 63 Chicago Marathon, Illinois
- 77 Mount Desert Island Marathon, Maine
- 84 Niagara Falls International Marathon, New York to Canada
- 92 HoBOOken Halloween 5K, New Jersey
- 94 Marine Corps Marathon, Washington, D.C.

[CONTINUED OVER PAGE]

MEXICO, CENTRAL & SOUTH AMERICA
- 112 Copper Canyon 100-mile Ultra, Mexico
- 131 Galapagos Marathon, Galapagos Islands
- 137 Rio de Janeiro Marathon, Brazil
- 138 Florianópolis Marathon, Brazil
- 151 The Stone Run Half-marathon, Falkland Islands

EUROPE
- 159 Dublin Marathon, Ireland
- 164 Great Limerick Run, Ireland
- 217 Great South 10-mile, England
- 219 Ridgeway Run, England
- 249 Bilbao Night Marathon, Spain
- 250 Ultra Pirineu, Spain
- 252 World's Fastest Marathon, Spain
- 261 Grand Trail des Templiers, France
- 271 The Great 10K, Germany
- 286 Spartacus Run, Switzerland
- 296 Roma by Night, Italy
- 308 Brasov Half-marathon, Romania
- 309 Tirana Half-marathon, Albania

AFRICA & THE MIDDLE EAST
- 369 Avalon Trail, Mauritius

ASIA, AUSTRALASIA & SOUTH PACIFIC
- 373 Delhi Half-marathon, India
- 376 Himalaya 100-mile Stage Race, India
- 385 Beijing Marathon, China
- 430 Byron Bay Lighthouse Run, Australia
- 439 Melbourne Marathon Festival, Australia
- 448 Great Barrier Island Wharf to Wharf, New Zealand
- 450 Auckland Marathon, New Zealand
- 456 Taupo Ultra, New Zealand
- 459 Abel Tasman Coastal Classic, New Zealand
- 460 Aoraki Mount Cook Marathon, New Zealand

POLES & BEYOND
- 475 Polar Circle Marathon, Greenland
- 487 Empire State Building Run-Up, New York

NOVEMBER

USA & CANADA
- 21 Monterey Bay Half-marathon, California
- 27 Malibu Half-marathon, California
- 32 Silver Strand Veterans Day Half-marathon, California
- 33 Rock 'n' Roll Las Vegas Marathon, Nevada
- 55 Route 66 Marathon, Oklahoma
- 56 Trans-Pecos Ultra, Texas
- 69 Pensacola Women's Half-marathon Weekend, Florida
- 86 New York City Marathon, New York

MEXICO, CENTRAL & SOUTH AMERICA
- 124 Costa Rica Ultra Trail, Costa Rica
- 127 Salento Trail Challenge, Colombia

EUROPE
- 169 OMM, UK
- 191 Brampton to Carlisle 10, England
- 197 Blackpool 10, England
- 209 Silverstone Half-marathon, England
- 257 Lyon Urban, France
- 310 Athens Classic Marathon, Greece

MONTH-BY-MONTH CALENDAR **17**

AFRICA & THE MIDDLE EAST
- 338 Pharaonic Race 100K, Egypt
- 346 Great Ethiopian Run, Ethiopia
- 348 Rift Marathon, Uganda
- 352 Masai Mara Half-marathon, Kenya
- 353 Serengeti Safari Marathon, Tanzania

ASIA, AUSTRALASIA & SOUTH PACIFIC
- 373 Delhi Half-marathon, India
- 376 Himalaya 100-mile Stage Race, India
- 380 Everest Trail Race, Nepal
- 400 Bagan Temple Marathon, Myanmar
- 407 Halong Bay Heritage Marathon, Vietnam
- 428 Ultra Trail Gold Coast, Australia
- 444 Summit Survivor, Australia
- 447 Point to Pinnacle Half-marathon, Australia
- 454 Rotorua Running Festival, New Zealand
- 468 Queenstown Marathon, New Zealand

POLES & BEYOND
- 493 Eureka Stair Climb, Australia

DECEMBER

USA & CANADA
- 6   Honolulu Marathon, Hawaii
- 13   California International Marathon, California
- 20   Summit Rock Half-marathon, California
- 85   Caroler 5K, New York
- 98   Kiawah Island Marathon, South Carolina

MEXICO, CENTRAL & SOUTH AMERICA
- 117 Reggae Marathon, Jamaica
- 121 End of the World Marathon, Belize
- 123 Trinidad and Tobago International Marathon, Trinidad and Tobago
- 143 Vulcano Ultra Trail, Chile

EUROPE
- 258 La SaintéLyon, France
- 277 Christmas Midnight Run, Switzerland
- 281 Silvesterlauf, Switzerland
- 295 Pisa Marathon, Italy
- 318 Vilnius Christmas Runs, Lithuania

AFRICA & THE MIDDLE EAST
- 329 Lanzarote Marathon, Canary Islands
- 351 Baringo Half-marathon, Kenya

ASIA, AUSTRALASIA & SOUTH PACIFIC
- 391 Fukuoka Marathon, Japan
- 469 Kepler Challenge 60 km, New Zealand

POLES & BEYOND
- 488 Colpatria Tower Ascent, Colombia

ALL YEAR ROUND

USA & CANADA

1	Bird to Gird Pathway, Alaska (summer)
2	Tony Knowles Trail, Alaska (spring, summer, autumn)
4	Diamond Head, Hawaii
9	Pre's Trail, Oregon
16	Golden Gate Bridge, San Francisco
19	Yosemite Valley Loop, California
25	Santa Barbara Waterfront, California
26	Runyon Canyon Park, California
28	The Strand, California
29	Joshua Tree National Park, California
34	The Strip, Nevada
37	Monument Valley Wildcat Trail, Utah (spring, summer, autumn)
38	Rim to Rim to Rim, Arizona
44	Lost Man Loop, Colorado
50	Dale Ball Trails, New Mexico
61	New Orleans, Louisiana
68	Gulf Shores Beaches, Alabama
71	Space Coast Beaches, Florida
78	Maine Coast, Maine
79	Reach the Beach, New Hampshire (autumn)
82	Charles River, Massachusetts
87	Central Park, New York
99	5 Peaks Trail Running Series BC, British Columbia (autumn)
101	Vancouver, British Columbia
103	Wild Pacific Trail, British Columbia
104	Moose Mountain Trail, Alberta
105	Itijjagiaq Trail, Nunavut (spring, summer, autumn)
107	Foxtail Hundred, Ontario (summer)

MEXICO, CENTRAL & SOUTH AMERICA

116	Seven Mile Beach, Cayman Islands
120	El Yunque National Forest, Puerto Rico
122	Barbados Boardwalk, Barbados
125	Ciclovía Cinta Costera Path, Panama
126	Grand Tour of Cartagena, Colombia
129	Parque Metropolitano Guangüiltagua, Ecuador
130	Quilotoa Loop, Ecuador (spring, summer, autumn)
135	Ibirapuera Park, Brazil
136	Rio de Janeiro Beachfront, Brazil
146	Costanera Promenade, Paraguay
147	Rambla Waterfront, Uruguay
152	Tierra del Fuego National Park, Tierra del Fuego

EUROPE

153	Grímsey Island, Iceland (spring, summer, autumn)
154	Ölfusá River, Iceland (spring, summer, autumn)
160	Phoenix Park Circular, Ireland
162	Cliffs of Moher, Ireland
166	Giant's Causeway, Northern Ireland
173	South Loch Ness Trail, Scotland
174	West Highland Way, Scotland (spring, summer)
176	Water of Leith Walkway, Scotland
177	Arthur's Seat, Scotland
183	The Black Mountains, Wales
184	Taff Trail, Wales
187	Gilsland Chase, England
189	Durham Heritage Coast Trail, England
196	Pikes Peak, England
199	Rivington Pike, England
206	The Wrekin, England
208	Burghley House, England
212	South West Coastal Path, England
214	Teignmouth Seafront, England
215	Exmoor Fells, England
216	Jamaica Inn, England
220	Oxford River Running, England
221	Oxford University's Iffley Road Track, England
229	Greenwich Foot Tunnel & Park, England
230	Brighton Beach, England
238	Parks and Lakes, Denmark
245	Myrskylä, Finland (spring, summer, autumn)
247	Peniche, Portugal
248	The Rock, Gibraltar
251	Seville, Spain
260	Chamonix, France (summer)
268	Bambésch Forest, Luxembourg

275	Hochstaufen/Bad Reichenhall, Germany	429	Snapper Rocks, Australia
282	Bisse du Torrent Neuf, Switzerland	436	Bondi Beach, Australia
297	Sentiero degli Dei, Italy	440	Albert Park, Australia
303	Lokrum Island, Croatia	443	Portsea, Australia
314	Istanbul, Turkey	451	One Tree Hill, New Zealand
315	Pirita Path, Estonia	466	Routeburn Track, New Zealand (summer)
320	Velodorozhka, Belarus	467	Milford Track, New Zealand (summer)

AFRICA & THE MIDDLE EAST

328	Jinama Trail, Canary Islands
331	Toubkal Circuit, Morocco
332	Casablanca Waterfront, Morocco
333	Menara Gardens, Morocco
337	Gezira Island, Egypt
341	Timna National Park, Israel
343	Yas Marina Circuit, United Arab Emirates
344	Dubai Marina, United Arab Emirates
349	Nangili Road, Kenya
350	Iten, Kenya
359	Faire Glen Nature Reserve, South Africa
364	Table Mountain, South Africa
366	Tsitsikamma Trail, South Africa

POLES & BEYOND

474	Arctic Circle Trail, Greenland
479	Ragnar Challenges, Worldwide
480	Midnight Runners, Worldwide

VIRTUAL RUNS

481	Route 66, USA
482	Appalachian Trail, USA
483	ODDyssey Half-marathon, USA
484	John O'Groats to Land's End Annual Challenge, UK
485	Run Down Under, Australia
486	Run New Zealand, New Zealand

PARKRUNS

495	Canyon Rim Trail Parkrun, Idaho
496	Cape Pembroke Lighthouse Parkrun, Falklands Islands
497	Haga Parkrun, Sweden
498	Bushy Parkrun, England
499	East Coast Parkrun, Singapore
500	Cloncurry Parkrun, Australia

ASIA, AUSTRALASIA & SOUTH PACIFIC

370	Baku Boulevard, Azerbaijan
374	Mumbai, India
387	The Bund, China
388	Sai Van Lake, Macau
389	Victoria Peak Circle Run, Hong Kong
392	Kyoto, Japan
397	Imperial Palace Loop, Japan
399	Arakawa Trail, Japan
401	Lumpini Park, Thailand
403	Patong Beach to Kalim Hill, Thailand
406	Hoang Lien National Park, Vietnam
411	Lambir Hills National Park Summit Trail, Malaysia
413	Manila Baywalk, Philippines
414	Kokoda Trail, Papua New Guinea
418	Uluru Base Trail, Australia
421	Elder Park, Australia
423	Mount Lofty Climb, Australia
425	Cairns, Australia

USA AND CANADA

22 USA AND CANADA

SEE PAGE 25 FOR **CALIFORNIA** AND **HAWAII**

USA AND CANADA: ENTRY LIST

JANUARY
- 65 Freeze Your Half Off, Tennessee
- 70 Walt Disney World Marathon Weekend, Florida
- 74 Miami Marathon, Florida

FEBRUARY
- 35 Zion Half-marathon, Utah
- 39 Run Sedona, Arizona
- 73 Paradise Coast Half-marathon, Florida

MARCH
- 7 Chuckanut 50K, Washington
- 24 Badger Cove Half-marathon, California
- 31 San Diego Half-marathon, California
- 64 Music City Half-marathon, Tennessee
- 66 Barkley Marathons, Tennessee
- 75 Bridge Run, Florida
- 97 Umstead 100-mile Ultra, North Carolina
- 106 Around the Bay Road Race, Ontario
- 108 Chilly Half-marathon, Ontario

APRIL
- 3 Hapalua Half-marathon, Hawaii
- 18 Diablo Trails Challenge, California
- 22 Big Sur Marathon, California
- 66 Barkley Marathons, Tennessee
- 72 Florida Coast 2 Coast Relay, Florida
- 81 Boston Marathon, Massachusetts
- 93 Cherry Blossom Ten Mile, Washington, D.C.
- 95 Parkway Classic, Virginia
- 96 Ukrop's Monument Avenue 10K, Virginia

MAY
- 15 Bay to Breakers, California
- 47 Bolder Boulder, Colorado
- 51 Fargo Marathon and Festival, North Dakota
- 62 Chicago Spring Half-marathon, Illinois
- 89 Brooklyn Half-marathon, New York
- 111 Ottawa Race Weekend, Ontario

JUNE
- 11 Western States Endurance Run, California
- 12 Dipsea Run, California
- 40 Madison River Run 5K, Montana
- 58 WW (Wounded Warrior) Military Miles, Texas
- 80 Covered Bridges Half-marathon, Vermont
- 83 Resurgence Half-marathon, New York
- 90 Sri Chinmoy Self-Transcendence 3100 Mile Race, New York
- 91 Bridgehampton Half, New York

JULY
- 14 Dirty Dozen and Half Dozen, California
- 17 Bad Bass Half-marathon, California
- 23 Badwater 135, California
- 30 Surfing Madonna Beach Run, California
- 43 Hardrock 100, Colorado
- 53 Honey Badger 100-mile Ultra, Kansas
- 76 Peachtree Road Race, Georgia

AUGUST
- 5 Spartan Race Hawaii, Hawaii
- 8 Hood to Coast, Oregon
- 41 Bridger Ridge Run, Montana
- 45 Leadville 100, Colorado
- 46 Transrockies Run, Colorado
- 48 Pikes Peak Ascent & Marathon, Colorado
- 102 Sea Wheeze Half-marathon, British Columbia
- 109 Hungry Hollow 5K, Ontario
- 110 Toronto Women's Run Series, Ontario

SEPTEMBER
- 10 Oregon Fall Half-marathon, Oregon
- 42 Jackson Hole Marathon, Wyoming
- 57 Texas Trail Festival, Texas
- 67 Run Woodstock Festival, Michigan
- 88 Fifth Avenue Mile, New York
- 91 Hamptons Marathon, New York
- 100 Handloggers Half-marathon, British Columbia

USA AND CANADA

OCTOBER
- 36 Escalante Canyons Marathon, Utah
- 49 Emma Crawford Coffin Races, Colorado
- 52 Run Crazy Horse Marathon, South Dakota
- 54 Tulsa Run, Oklahoma
- 59 Shannon Monster 5K, Texas
- 60 Fort Smith Marathon, Arkansas
- 63 Chicago Marathon, Illinois
- 77 Mount Desert Island Marathon, Maine
- 84 Niagara Falls International Marathon, New York to Canada
- 92 HoBOOken Halloween 5K, New Jersey
- 94 Marine Corps Marathon, Washington, D.C.

NOVEMBER
- 21 Monterey Bay Half-marathon, California
- 27 Malibu Half-marathon, California
- 32 Silver Strand Veterans Day Half-marathon, California
- 33 Rock 'n' Roll Las Vegas Marathon, Nevada
- 55 Route 66 Marathon, Oklahoma
- 56 Trans-Pecos Ultra, Texas
- 69 Pensacola Women's Half-marathon Weekend, Florida
- 86 New York City Marathon, New York

DECEMBER
- 6   Honolulu Marathon, Hawaii
- 13 California International Marathon, California
- 20 Summit Rock Half-marathon, California
- 85 Caroler 5K, New York
- 98 Kiawah Island Marathon, South Carolina

ALL YEAR ROUND
- 1   Bird to Gird Pathway, Alaska (summer)
- 2   Tony Knowles Trail, Alaska (spring, summer, autumn)
- 4   Diamond Head, Hawaii
- 9   Pre's Trail, Oregon
- 16   Golden Gate Bridge, San Francisco
- 19   Yosemite Valley Loop, California
- 25   Santa Barbara Waterfront, California
- 26   Runyon Canyon Park, California
- 28   The Strand, California
- 29   Joshua Tree National Park, California
- 34   The Strip, Nevada
- 37   Monument Valley Wildcat Trail, Utah (spring, summer, autumn)
- 38   Rim to Rim to Rim, Arizona
- 44   Lost Man Loop, Colorado
- 50   Dale Ball Trails, New Mexico
- 61   New Orleans, Louisiana
- 68   Gulf Shores Beaches, Alabama
- 71   Space Coast Beaches, Florida
- 78   Maine Coast, Maine
- 79   Reach the Beach, New Hampshire (autumn)
- 82   Charles River, Massachusetts
- 87   Central Park, New York
- 99   5 Peaks Trail Running Series BC, British Columbia (summer)
- 101 Vancouver, British Columbia
- 103 Wild Pacific Trail, British Columbia
- 104 Moose Mountain Trail, Alberta
- 105 Itijjagiaq Trail, Nunavut (spring, summer, autumn)
- 107 Foxtail Hundred, Ontario (summer)

USA AND CANADA **25**

CALIFORNIA AND **HAWAII**

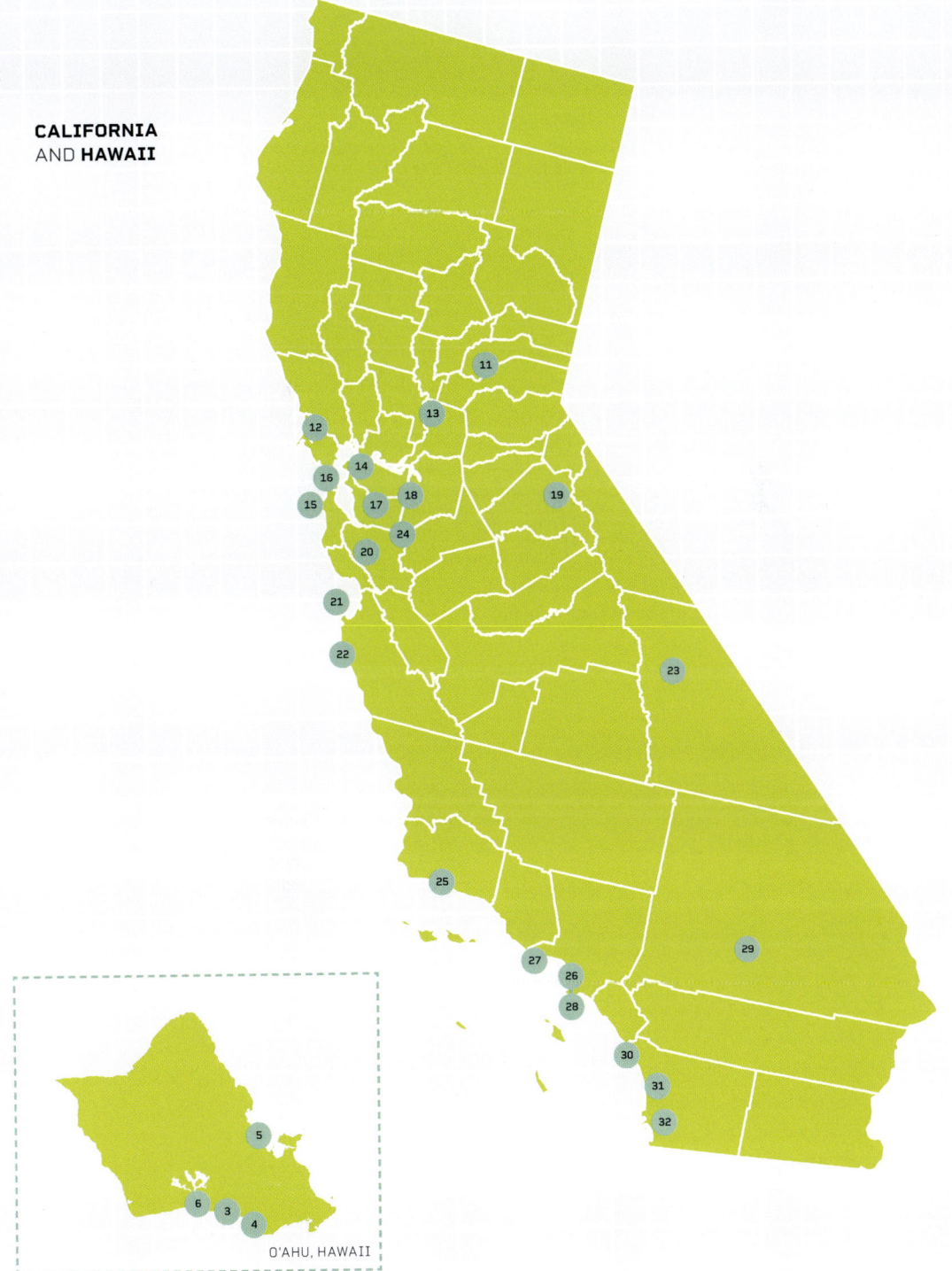

O'AHU, HAWAII

1 | **Spectacular glacial scenery on the Bird to Gird Pathway**

1

BIRD TO GIRD PATHWAY
ANCHORAGE, ALASKA
Running route/Trail
Summer/21 km

Alaska, America's biggest state, is the definition of unspoiled beauty. People travel here to get away from it all, explore the outdoors and switch off from modern life. The Bird to Gird Pathway runs alongside the Alaska railroad, with the gulf by your side for 21 km (13 miles). The path is a must for the nature enthusiast. Chances to spot incredible wildlife are high, and glacier views are absolutely guaranteed. Run the path in the summer months to make the most of the magical light nights.

2

TONY KNOWLES TRAIL
ANCHORAGE, ALASKA
Running route/Trail
Spring, Summer, Autumn/18 km

The Tony Knowles Trail is a popular path that runs for 18 km (11 miles) along the Alaskan coast from Anchorage to Kincaid Park. The route is predominantly flat and fully paved, and can be joined in many different places to offer a variety of distances. Runners share the trail with rollerbladers, walkers and cyclists, and in the winter it is often snow-covered, so popular with cross-country skiers. Anyone looking for something longer can add on the connecting 6 km (4 miles) of the Chester Creek Trail.

3
HAPALUA HALF-MARATHON
WAIKIKI, HAWAII
Coastal/Festival
April/21 km

The largest half-marathon in Hawaii starts beside the iconic Waikiki Beach and regularly attracts more than 10,000 runners. The course includes downtown Honolulu and loops around Diamond Head hill, before finishing in Kapiolani Park, where finishers will be rewarded with a concert and plenty of traditional Hawaiian food to kickstart the all-important refuelling process.

4
DIAMOND HEAD
O'AHU, HAWAII
Running route/Coastal
All year round/6 km

Other than beaches and incredible surf, Hawaii is known for its volcanoes – some of which are active! Diamond Head, a crater formed from a singular eruption, is now deemed a national landmark and makes for a unique run. Six kilometres (4 miles) will take you around the perimeter of the crater, which includes some climbs, giving you incredible views of the island and coast. If you feel energetic, take the stairs to the very top to visit the monument.

3 | **Waikiki Beach is the backdrop for the Hapalua Half-marathon**

5

SPARTAN RACE HAWAII
VARIOUS, HAWAII
Obstacle course race
August/5–50 km

Picture an ultra in soaring temperatures. Now picture the same race but with 2.5-m (8-ft) walls, monkey bars, rope climbs, barbed-wire and fire loops to tackle on the course. This is a Spartan Race! Choose from the Sprint, Super, Beast or Ultra, and get geared up for a race that is all about agility, speed, endurance and incredible mental toughness. If you're really crazy, aim to become a Trifecta Spartan by completing three in one season! Spartans return year after year, so expect to take on experienced racers.

6
HONOLULU MARATHON
HAWAII
Road/Coastal
December/10 & 42 km

As the fireworks light up the sky in Honolulu, 30,000 runners speed off down the coast to start their race. If you don't fancy a full marathon, but love the crowds and atmosphere, the Honolulu Start to Park 10K is perfect. Join the masses as you race through the beautiful city and along the famous Waikiki Beach, completing the first 10 km (6.2 miles) of the marathon course and finishing at Kapiolani Park.

7
CHUCKANUT 50K
BELLINGHAM, WASHINGTON
Trail
March/50 km

This friendly event has a relatively easy first and last 10 km (6.2 miles), but in between there are 30 km (19 miles) of climbing. The terrain is technical and challenging in places, particularly on the 30-km (19-mile) loop that includes a total ascent and descent of 1,524 m (5,000 ft) within the Chuckanut mountain range. The two 10-km (6.2-mile) stretches at the start and finish on the Interurban Trail provide some welcome respite to weary legs, which need to cross the finish line within the eight-hour time limit.

8
HOOD TO COAST
MOUNT HOOD, OREGON
Relay
August/320 km

'The mother of all relays' takes runners (in teams of eight to twelve, with approximately 1,000 teams taking part) from Mount Hood's Timberline Lodge, through Portland, and on to the Pacific-coast town of Seaside, some 320 km (199 miles) away. The HTC franchise has expanded into other markets since the event's debut in 1982, but this one is the original.

9
PRE'S TRAIL
EUGENE, OREGON
Running route/Trail
All year round/6.5 km

Named after the University of Oregon's Olympic long-distance runner Steve Prefontaine, who was tragically killed in a car crash at the age of 24, the trail is located to the north of the Willamette River in Oregon. It is a 6.5-km (4-mile) mix of woodchip and bark, especially designed for runners and walkers. The trail passes through woods and parkland, and contains three loops of different distances, all of which connect with interlinking paths.

10

OREGON FALL HALF-MARATHON
CANBY, OREGON
Road
September/21 km

The Willamette Valley is well known for its wine, with more than 500 vineyards in the region. In the running community, it is also known for its races, with three of the four chip-timed races of the renowned Half Marathon Series held here. The autumn race is held at St Josef's winery on one of the finest routes of them all. Go out hard on this flat course and be sure to reward yourself afterwards with a glass of that world-famous Pinot Noir.

11

WESTERN STATES ENDURANCE RUN
OLYMPIC VALLEY, CALIFORNIA
Ultra/Trail
June/161 km

More commonly known as the Western Sates 100, this is reputed to be the world's oldest 100-mile trail run, having started in 1960. The race – for which participants must qualify – climbs over 5,500 m (18,000 ft), with runners often experiencing snow on the course, even though temperatures can be incredibly hot. Starting at 5 a.m., there is a 30-hour cut-off time, and finishing runners receive a belt buckle, which is bronze if the finishing time is under 30 hours, silver if under 24 hours.

11 | **Most of the Western States trail passes through remote and rugged territory**

12

DIPSEA RUN

MARIN COUNTY, CALIFORNIA
Trail
June/12 km

Boasting to be 'the oldest trail run in America', these 12 km (7.4 miles) promise to be beautiful, gruelling and treacherous. There are sections where you can carve your own way through the landscape, and the course includes ascents and descents named 'Cardiac' and 'Suicide'. The handicap system allows anyone (masters, kids, older participants) the chance to win, and enables generations of families to compete.

13

CALIFORNIA INTERNATIONAL MARATHON

SACREMENTO, CALIFORNIA
Marathon/Road
December/42 km

First held in 1983, the race starts from the impressive setting of Folsom Dam, before heading towards the suburbs of Sacramento. The mainly flat and slightly downhill course offers an opportunity for fast times, and the finish in front of the State Capitol in the heart of Sacramento is lower than the start. The cool, late autumnal conditions normally offer ideal conditions for marathon running, which helps to explain why this race has become popular with runners from all over the world.

15 | A pageant of colour flows through the streets of San Francisco

14
DIRTY DOZEN AND HALF DOZEN
POINT PINOLE, CALIFORNIA
Trail/Novelty
July/6–12 hours

A test of both mental and physical endurance for runners who complete the same 5.4-km (3.37-mile) loop, largely on trails, for either 6 hours (the Half Dozen) or 12 hours (the Dozen). A shorter 1-km (0.6-mile) loop is used for the last hour of each race. Views of the nearby bay and neighbouring counties are splendid, but become quite familiar as the races progress!

15
BAY TO BREAKERS
SAN FRANCISCO, CALIFORNIA
Novelty/Coastal
May/12 km

Is Bay to Breakers a race or a party? In truth, it's both, from the elite field toeing the start line to the thousands of walkers, many unregistered, who follow the enormous field. The 12-km (7.5-mile) course, which begins at San Francisco Bay and cuts westward to Ocean Beach, is as much a parade as anything, with many runners in costumes – and some without any clothes at all!

16

GOLDEN GATE BRIDGE
SAN FRANCISCO, CALIFORNIA
Running route
All year round/7 km

Take the 7-km (4.4-mile) California Coastal trail to cross this architectural wonder, with 10,000 pedestrians doing so on an average day. From the Welcome Center at one end to the Vista Point at the other, you'll be joined by a rollerblading, cycling and strolling throng, but there's still plenty of opportunity to take in the impressive views – if you can stop running, that is.

17
BAD BASS HALF-MARATHON
CASTRO VALLEY, CALIFORNIA
Multi-terrain
July/21 km

Offering three choices of distance, and routes that are a mix of paved and dirt trails, the Bad Bass has become popular with runners of all abilities. All the courses are undulating, and the climb up Live Oak is more conducive to walking than running. The 5K and 10K are out-and-back routes, while the half-marathon is a loop, and the half-marathoners need to reach aid stations within cut-off times if they are to finish.

18
DIABLO TRAILS CHALLENGE
WALNUT CREEK, CALIFORNIA
Trail/Multi-distance
April/Various

Get ready for an early start if you choose the 50K, as it starts at 6.30 a.m. and has a cut-off time of 11 hours. The courses (also 5K, 10K and half-marathon) are all at Mount Diablo State Park, and are run on dirt trails, with some small sections that are single track. The 50K runners reach the summit of Mount Diablo, and all of the races have plenty of drink stations. The views are fantastic, but the undulating nature of all of the distances makes fast times unlikely.

19
YOSEMITE VALLEY LOOP
YOSEMITE NATIONAL PARK, CALIFORNIA
Running route/Multi-terrain
All year round/11.6 & 18.5 km

With a choice of either an 18.5-km (11.5-mile) full loop or an 11.6-km (7.2-mile) half loop, it is hard to beat the spectacular setting of this trail. As both loops follow the valley floor they are fairly level, and can be accessed from a variety of points throughout the valley. Although well marked, it is best to take a map, as route finding can be tricky in places. Surfaces are a mix of road, track, trail and sand. The run is never short of incredible views, including the magnificent El Capitan and Half Dome.

20
SUMMIT ROCK HALF-MARATHON
SARATOGA, CALIFORNIA
Multi-terrain
December/21 km

All of the distances take place in the redwood groves of the Santa Cruz mountains, close to Silicon Valley. The longer 10K and half-marathon races provide steep ascents, but runners are rewarded with spectacular views from the summit. The courses are a mixture of roads and single tracks, and the half-marathon has a cut-off time of 4.5 hours. Runners will face climbs of just under 200 m (700 ft) for the 5K, 460 m (1,500 ft) for the 10K, and a leg-burning 880 m (2,900 ft) for the half-marathon.

22 | Hurricane Point on the Big Sur Marathon route

21
MONTEREY BAY HALF-MARATHON
CALIFORNIA
Coastal
November/21 km

This stunning area of California is visited by thousands of tourists daily, and for good reason. Its charming town is full of quaint shops mixed with trendy eateries that sit within areas of outstanding natural beauty. The route takes it all in, heading from downtown, through historic Cannery Row, then along the coast to finish at Fisherman's Wharf. Many say the course has the perfect amount of elevation to make it both exciting and rewarding.

22
BIG SUR MARATHON
CALIFORNIA
Marathon/Road
April/42 km

This point-to-point event heads north from Big Sur, along the iconic and spectacular Highway 1, to Carmel. The route hugs the rugged coastline, and runners are treated to views of crashing waves rolling in from the Pacific Ocean, coastal mountains and giant redwood trees. The undulating course means a climb of over 640 m (2,100 ft) during the race, including a 150-m (500-ft) climb between 16 and 19 km (10 and 12 miles) to Hurricane Point. Halfway, on Bixby Bridge, there is a tradition for runners to be entertained by a tuxedo-wearing pianist playing a grand piano.

23
BADWATER 135
FURNACE CREEK AND LONE PINE, CALIFORNIA

Ultra/Mountain
July/217 km

Badwater is extreme, with 217 km (135 miles) of tortuous terrain. From Death Valley to Mount Whitney, runners start at the lowest elevation in North America, 85 m (280 ft) below sea level, and aim to finish at the highest point, 2,530 m (8,300 ft). In between, there are three mountain ranges to battle, inflicting many highs and lows.

24

BADGER COVE HALF-MARATHON
LIVERMORE, CALIFORNIA
Trail
March/21 km

The organisers of these races (10K and 5K included) are certainly honest. Their statement that 'if you are looking for a super-fast, flat, easy course, you are probably in the wrong place' is almost certainly true. What these races do offer is the chance to run off-road on trails through Del Valle Regional Park, with great scenery, lots of support and post-race t-shirts and awards for finishers.

26 | **Panoramic views of Los Angeles from Runyon Canyon Park**

25

SANTA BARBARA WATERFRONT
CALIFORNIA
Running route/Coastal
All year round/8 km

This classic, palm-lined coastal run is from Shoreline Park in the north to East Beach in the south, or vice versa. Taking in the best of the Santa Barbara scenery – from mountains and marinas to piers and parks – this 8-km (5-mile) flat route is easy on the legs and a treat to the eyes. Add in Point Castillo for a fantastic harbour viewpoint, and Montecito Loop for spectacular mansions and the beautiful Butterfly Beach.

26

RUNYON CANYON PARK
LOS ANGELES, CALIFORNIA
Running route/Trail
All year round/Various

The 310-acre (125-hectare) Runyon Canyon Park is a popular place for runners, located near Hollywood. The park is at the east end of the Santa Monica Mountains, with a range of undulating loops of different distances. The majority of the trails are paved or dirt roads, but runners who want to get away from the crowds can find plenty of single-track trails that thread up into the hills. Runners beware: this is a 'dog free' park, where dogs are permitted to run free off their leads.

27
MALIBU HALF-MARATHON
CALIFORNIA
Coastal
November/5 & 21 km

If you want a race to take your mind off the pain of 21 km (13.1 miles), this is just the one. Starting and finishing at the expansive Zuma Beach, this is a great out-and-back scenic course along the Pacific coast. En route, runners will pass huge beachfront mansions, many of which are owned by Hollywood's most famous stars. All finishers receive an obligatory race medal and a beach towel, which comes in handy when the enticing ocean is mere steps away from the finish line.

28
THE STRAND
MANHATTAN BEACH, CALIFORNIA
Running route/Coastal
All year round/6 km

Recognised as the beach volleyball capital of the world, there is a pedestrian walkway and cycle path known as the Strand, which starts in northern Manhattan Beach. Over the next 6 km (3.5 miles) to the Redondo Beach Pier, you will pass locals playing beach volleyball and multi-million-dollar beachfront homes that look out to the Pacific Ocean. It's possible to extend the run beyond Redondo Beach, and, if the mood takes you, alternate some stretches of sandy-beach running with the walkway.

USA AND CANADA

29

JOSHUA TREE NATIONAL PARK
CALIFORNIA

Running route/Desert
All year round/Various

Crossing a vast expanse of the Mojave and Colorado deserts, the Joshua Tree National Park offers runners a wide range of trails of varying difficulty and length. As nights can be chilly and the days distinctly hot, the best times for running are mid-morning and late afternoon. Keep an eye out for climbers enjoying their sport on the many rocky outcrops that are an intrinsic part of the scenery, and consider using one of the many campsites or driving from nearby Palm Springs.

30

SURFING MADONNA BEACH RUN
ENCINITAS, CALIFORNIA

Coastal
July/1–12 km

Starting and finishing on Moonlight Beach, the entire race is completed on hardpacked sand at low tide, with crashing surf to one side and steep cliffs to the other. Runners loop around flags to retrace their steps to the finish, according to the distance they choose, and potential spectators include sea lions and dolphins. The distances range from 1 to 12 km (0.6 to 7.5 miles), to cater to runners of all abilities, and each runner receives a large medal.

30 | **Sand, sea and sun at the Surfing Madonna Beach Run**

31 | Running along Harbor Drive in the San Diego Half-marathon

31

SAN DIEGO HALF-MARATHON
CALIFORNIA
Urban
March/21 km

The route is scenic and takes in all the main features of one of the United States' most vibrant cities. Starting close to the San Diego Convention Center, runners head along the palm-tree-lined Harbor Drive, with views of San Diego Bay and the city's spectacular skyline. After passing through Washington Street, the last few kilometres offer runners some welcome relief with a gradual descent and the reward of a fantastic finish inside Petco Park, home to Major League Baseball's San Diego Padres.

32

SILVER STRAND VETERANS DAY HALF-MARATHON
CORONADO, CALIFORNIA
Coastal
November/21 km

The courses are all fast and flat, starting in Sunset Park in Coronado, and running alongside the Silver Strand State Beach. The races offer discount entry fees for armed-forces veterans, and raise money for charities linked to those who have served their country. The out-and-back courses along the narrow Silver Strand peninsula offer runners the choice of viewing the Pacific Ocean on one side, or the San Diego Bay on the other. Start times are early, with the 5K runners heading off at 7 a.m., followed by the half-marathoners and 10-milers at 7.20 a.m.

33

ROCK 'N' ROLL LAS VEGAS MARATHON
NEVADA
Marathon/Night
November/42 km

This highly enjoyable race actually closes the world-famous strip, and starts as the sun sets and the city lights up. It has everything you need for the perfect weekend, from a range of distances (from 5K up to the marathon), music, entertainment, great food and a setting that can't fail to get your engine revving. Plus, the course is more or less flat, so it's super-quick.

35 | Impressive cliffs line the route of the Zion Half-marathon

34
THE STRIP
LAS VEGAS, NEVADA
Running route/Novelty
All year round/5 km

One thing you can bet on is that at whatever time of the day or night you decide to run the Las Vegas Strip, it will not be a peaceful or solitary experience! Las Vegas Boulevard, as it is more correctly (but seldom) known is just over 5 km (3 miles) long, and passes larger-than-life hotels such as Caesars Palace, the Stratosphere, Circus Circus and the MGM Grand. Watch out for mini Eiffel Towers, pirate ships and huge waterfalls and fountains. A run to remember, and one that is best tackled in the early morning to avoid the heat of the desert and the crowds.

35
ZION HALF-MARATHON
VIRGIN, UTAH
Mountain
February/21 km

A popular race that often sells out well in advance of race day, this half-marathon follows the road into the beautiful Zion Canyon from the start point in the town of Virgin. The race is point to point, with much of it following a steady climb from the start and into the canyon. Surrounded by steep cliffs and spectacular mountain scenery, runners stay on the road while following the path of the Virgin River, before finishing in the town of Springdale.

USA AND CANADA   45

37 | **Large buttes on the Monument Valley Wildcat Trail**

36
ESCALANTE CANYONS MARATHON
BOULDER, UTAH
Marathon/Mountain
October/42 km

You might benefit from some altitude training for this one! Held in the impressive canyons of Utah, the courses (also 5K and a half-marathon) covers some elevation. An easy pace is recommended to start with, before you exhaust yourself on the multitude of inclines ahead. Luckily there is plenty of downhill, too. The course follows the Byway 12, which means your supporters can drive and stop along the way. Make sure they get those race snaps, as the vistas are incredible.

37
MONUMENT VALLEY WILDCAT TRAIL
MEXICAN HAT, UTAH
Running route/Trail
Spring, Summer, Autumn/6.4 km

This run of just under 6.4 km (4 miles) takes runners past many of the most famous rock buttes in Monument Valley and deep into the heart of territory synonymous with many well-known Hollywood westerns. Start and finish the trail by the sign at the north-west corner of the Monument Valley visitor centre, with most of this mainly flat run completed on loose sandy trails.

38 | A tough descent and climb awaits Rim runners

38
RIM TO RIM TO RIM
GRAND CANYON, ARIZONA
Running route/Mountain
All year round/35 km

This route requires planning and preparation, but given the spectacular location it's well worth it. Start on the north rim on the South Kaibab Trail, perhaps in the snow, then drop down the base of the canyon and its stifling heat. Next, climb relentlessly to the summit of the south rim and its Mediterranean climate, before returning. Or have someone waiting for you there – the choice is yours. It's not far one way – 35 km (22 miles) or so – but with 3,200 m (10,550 ft) of elevation difference, and a huge temperature change, it's a challenge!

39
RUN SEDONA
SEDONA, ARIZONA
Road/Trail
February/Various

Modestly claiming to be the most beautiful place on Earth, it is fair to say that the Sedona scenery is as good as it gets for any run, anywhere. The course takes runners through the Coconino National Forest, famous for spectacular rock formations that are reddened by deposits of iron. The half-marathon, 10K and 5K courses are undulating, but largely on road and trail.

40
MADISON RIVER RUN 5K
ENNIS, MONTANA

Road/Festival

June/5 km

This is a family-friendly event that tends to focus more on fun-runners than elites. Starting above the Madison River (halfway across a bridge), the route finishes at the local distillery, which lays on food and festivities for runners and spectators. Faster finishers will need to be patient, as the festivities only start when the last runner has crossed the finishing line.

42 | **The Grand Teton Range looms large in the Jackson Hole Marathon**

41
BRIDGER RIDGE RUN
BOZEMAN, MONTANA

Trail

August/32 km

Although not a full marathon, at 32 km (20 miles), this race is tougher than many that are. The unpredictable weather, very steep ascents and descents, and unstable terrain mean that it is not a race for the fainthearted. Limited to 250 entrants but always greatly oversubscribed, the race is a test of endurance and physiology, as the start near Fairy Lake is at 2,300 m (7,600 ft), with a high point at Sacagawea Peak of almost 2,900 m (9,600 ft), before runners descend to the finish.

42
JACKSON HOLE MARATHON
WYOMING

Marathon/Road

September/21 & 42 km

The Jackson Hole marathon and half-marathon showcase much of the incredible natural landscape of the state of Wyoming, while the high altitude will add to the challenge of the distances. Both races start in Jackson Hole Valley before crossing the Snake River and finishing in Teton Village, near the base of the spectacular Teton Range. Runners may even catch a glimpse of the local wildlife that includes bear, buffalo and moose.

43

HARDROCK 100
SILVERTON, COLORADO
Ultra/Trail
July/160 km

Rated as one of the toughest races of its kind in the world, this ultra is limited to a field of just 140 runners who are selected using a lottery in which they have to demonstrate both their running ability and mountaineering skills. The race starts in Silverton in the Colorado Mountains, and, as well as the 160-km (100-mile) distance, runners have to climb no less than 10,000 m (33,000 ft) before they reach the finish line. Much of the race is held at an altitude of over 3,400 m (11,000 ft), with the rarified air providing an additional physiological challenge. With a start time of 6 a.m. and a cut-off time of 48 hours, most runners will see the sun set twice before reaching the finish line.

45 | **Cooling off in the Leadville 100**

44
LOST MAN LOOP
ASPEN, COLORADO
Running route/Trail
All year round/14 km

Though the name suggests otherwise, this trail is not a loop. In fact, the route is a 14-km (8.8-mile) one-way trail across alpine meadow and mountainous terrain. However, for a return route, many suggest running from Independence Pass up to the lake and back. The trail is beautiful year-round, but it is best run in the summer months, when it is filled with alpine flowers, lush forests and plenty of flowing creeks to help you cool off.

45
LEADVILLE 100
COLORADO
Ultra
August/160 km

In an ever-competitive world, one or two races stand out head and shoulders above all others: Leadville, run through the spectacular Rockies, is such an event. More than 3,000 m (10,000 ft) and 160 km (100 miles) await competitors, who have been drawn to this sleepy mining town since 1983. The race starts at high altitude and heads even higher. Famously, the barefoot runners of Mexico, the Tarahumara, first came to the fore here in the early 1990s. Finishers receive a coveted belt buckle.

46
TRANSROCKIES RUN
BUENA VISTA, COLORADO

Multiday adventure/Mountain
August/193 km

Held over six days and seven stages (stage seven is 'The Party'), this ultra starts in Buena Vista and finishes in Beaver Creek. Along the 193-km (120-mile) route competitors have to spend four nights under canvas camping, and climb a total of 6,000 m (20,000 ft). The organisers claim that the race will leave competitors breathless, which is not surprising as much of it is held at a low-oxygen, lung-burning altitude of over 2,700 m (9,000 ft). The legendary post-race party features a gondola ride to Spruce Saddle Lodge, before heading back down to Beaver Creek Village for a night of dancing and well-deserved celebration.

47 | Runners making a splash in Bolder Boulder

47
BOLDER BOULDER
BOULDER, COLORADO
Urban
May/10 km

This tremendous 10K loops around the iconic running town, home to Olympic-winning marathoner Frank Shorter and other celebrated US runners. At the start, you will know it's at a high altitude, 1,624 m (5,328 ft), but you'll soon forget as you charge off at high speed. Then, at around 6 km (4 miles), you'll whack into 'the wall' and run out of oxygen. It's all worthwhile as you finish in the stadium, with wave after wave of finishers sitting down with a Coke to cheer you on.

48
PIKES PEAK ASCENT & MARATHON
MANITOU SPRINGS, COLORADO
Marathon/Mountain
August/21 & 42 km

This weekend double-header offers runners the chance to qualify for one or both races: those that complete both are known as 'doublers', but it is a title that certainly has to be earned the hard way. The 21-km (13-mile) Ascent held on Saturday involves a climb of over 2,800 m (9,200 ft) to the summit of Pikes Peak, at a lung-busting altitude of 4,300 m (14,000 ft). The marathon on Sunday follows the same ascent route, then turns around to make the descent to the finish. The route is narrow, winding and tricky underfoot.

49
EMMA CRAWFORD COFFIN RACES
MANITOU SPRINGS, COLORADO
Novelty
October/178 m

Emma Crawford moved to Manitou Springs in 1889 in the hope that the mountain air would cure her tuberculosis. It didn't, and she died two years later. She was buried at the top of nearby Red Mountain until 1929 when, following heavy rain, she made an unexpected reappearance after her coffin was washed down the mountain. The first coffin race in her memory was launched in 1995. Today teams of four runners, dressed appropriately, carry or push a homemade coffin containing a real-life 'Emma' through the streets of the town, racing one another in heats and ultimately the final, for the honour of winning the Coffin Cup.

50
DALE BALL TRAILS
SANTA FE, NEW MEXICO
Running route/Trail
All year round/Various

Situated in the foothills of the Sangre de Cristo Mountains, and close to Santa Fe, the Dale Ball Trails provide runners with a 35-km (22-mile) network of routes that range in length and degree of difficulty. The trails use a numbering system that helps to make navigation easy, and there are connections with other local trails that can be used to add variety and distance. The trails are popular with cyclists and hikers, but runners will be pleased to know that dogs must be kept on a lead.

52 | **The Crazy Horse Memorial in the Black Hills**

51

FARGO MARATHON AND FESTIVAL
NORTH DAKOTA
Marathon/Festival
May/Various

This week-long festival offers a 5K, 10K, half-marathon and the showpiece event, the marathon. There is even a FurGo Dog Run over 2.4 km (1.5 miles) for dogs and their owners, and a four-person relay option for the marathon. Runners also have the chance to double up in the Go Far Challenge by competing in the 5K on Friday evening and then choosing to run the 10K, half-marathon or marathon the following day. Expect a great atmosphere at the start and finish of all the main races as they are indoors, within the huge Fargodome arena.

52

RUN CRAZY HORSE MARATHON
HILL CITY, SOUTH DAKOTA
Marathon/Road
October/5 & 42 km

Held in the Black Hills, the marathon starts beneath what is planned to be the world's largest mountain carving – the giant Crazy Horse Memorial, a 152-m (500-ft) monument carved into a mountain that is dedicated to the Oglala Lakota warrior who took up arms against the government. The 5K also starts at the memorial, with the marathon passing through the appropriately named town of Custer, before both races finish in Hill City.

53
HONEY BADGER 100-MILE ULTRA
CHENEY, KANSAS
Ultra/Road
July/160 km

This is a tough race and not one for novices. Competitors need to supply their own support team and vehicle, food and drink. Around 150 km (93 miles) are run on road, and the race is appropriately named after the honey badger, cited by the organisers as 'the toughest animal on Earth'. Starting at 6 a.m., there is a 36-hour time limit, and competitors must have reached the halfway point within 16 hours to avoid disqualification.

54
TULSA RUN
OKLAHOMA
Urban
October/15 km

This race offers a spectacularly fast 15 km (9.3 miles) that starts downtown before heading out for an out-and-back course along the Arkansas River. Over the years (since the late 1970s), this quick course has seen world record holders, world champions and Olympians battle it out, while there's a cherished mug on offer for any man who can crack an hour (70 minutes for women); fast running indeed.

53 | **An interested spectator at the Honey Badger 100**

55 | Running for the highway on Route 66

55

ROUTE 66 MARATHON
TULSA, OKLAHOMA

Marathon
November/42 km

This is a flat, fast marathon, which has a few memorable sections as part of the course – you'll hit Route 66 several times! It starts in downtown Tulsa, home of the largest concentration of Art Deco architecture outside of Miami, before heading out to the iconic Route 66. The marathon has a lively atmosphere, with cheering crowds, music and beer stations, as you run on this classic highway that links Chicago to Los Angeles.

56

TRANS-PECOS ULTRA
BIG BEND, TEXAS

Ultra/Multiday adventure
November/163 km

Big Bend is a geographical area of Texas, renowned for its river, valley and mountains, and this 163-km (101-mile) ultra takes in most of it. Runners complete a total of six stages over seven days, running through remote rugged countryside and staying at campsites each night. Finishers receive a buckle, which may be useful for those who have lost weight completing the course.

57
TEXAS TRAIL FESTIVAL
SPICEWOOD, TEXAS
Festival/Multi-terrain
September/Various

Texas is famous for its big grills, soaring temperatures and captivating live music. It's worth a visit, and if you travel in September you'll also get your running fix. The festival, held at Krause Springs, has all of the above, and more. Spend your time playing games, relaxing at the swimming hole, listening to music – and running, of course! You can sign up to as many as three races in a day, all covering various distances and terrain.

58
WW (WOUNDED WARRIOR) MILITARY MILES
IRVING, TEXAS
Road/Trail
June/Various

This Texan event is one of a series of Wounded Warrior runs held throughout North America in honour of the men and women of the military, and to raise funds for military charities. The Texas races (5K, 10K and half-marathon) are held on the Campion Trail, which offers a mix of urban and natural views as it passes through the Dallas suburb of Irving.

59
SHANNON MONSTER 5K
KELLER, TEXAS
Novelty
October/5 km

Held annually on the closest weekend to Halloween, runners are encouraged to wear fancy dress that is appropriate for the time of the year. The less than serious atmosphere is enhanced by a post-race party, music and pancakes, along with copious quantities of beer from the local brewery that sponsors the event. Not surprisingly, there are also awards for the best male and female costumes.

60
FORT SMITH MARATHON
ARKANSAS
Marathon
October/21 & 42 km

The best way to see the historic frontier town of Fort Smith is to run the town's marathon. The combination of climbs, descents, trail and road running don't make for a fast course, but they do make this a unique and memorable race. Along with the half-marathon, there is also the option of running in the marathon as part of a relay team, with the courses for both races covering ground that was at the heart of the Wild West in the nineteenth century.

61 | Tree-lined Audubon Park at sunset

61
NEW ORLEANS
LOUISIANA
Running route/Urban
All year round/Various

Think enchanting architecture, energising jazz, tempting cuisine, thriving festival seasons and a surprisingly good running scene. Yes, New Orleans' leafy suburbs, flat river trails and lakeside pavements make it somewhat of a runner's paradise all year round. Take a day to explore the city on one of your long runs in one of the many parks, or, alternatively, take the 35-km (22-mile) Levee Path, which has sunset views over the Mississippi River.

62
CHICAGO SPRING HALF-MARATHON
ILLINOIS
Urban
May/10 & 21 km

These springtime races celebrate Chicago's emergence from the winter, with 4,000 runners taking part in both the half-marathon and the 10K. The races combine an urban setting with a lakeside course, and finishers are rewarded with a hot gourmet breakfast buffet, as well as a lively Spring Market.

63
CHICAGO MARATHON
ILLINOIS

Marathon/Urban
October/42 km

A spot in this Marathon Major, and the fourth-largest race worldwide, is increasingly difficult to come by. Should you by chance find a golden ticket, prepare for the race of your life. Records have been broken at this event and there is huge potential for a PB. The course is superflat, extremely well supported and has good weather conditions, usually.

USA AND CANADA

64 | Stepping in time at the Music City Half-marathon

64
MUSIC CITY HALF-MARATHON
NASHVILLE, TENNESSEE
Multi-terrain
March/21 km

Where better to run a music-themed race than in the home of country and western music, Nashville? The races (there's also a 5K and 10K) follow the route of the Cumberland River, so the courses are flat and fast. The route is out and back, starting at the city's football stadium, and is a mix of paved road and trails. The event is held as close to St Patrick's Day as possible, so inevitably there is a strong Irish theme to the on-course entertainment.

65
FREEZE YOUR HALF OFF
CHATTANOOGA, TENNESSEE
Road
January/21 km

This race is all about getting out on a crisp January morning to enjoy yourself with like-minded people. A great choice for your first ever half-marathon, with a gentle, flat and multi-loop course, so you can easily identify where you're up to. The 'all you can eat' station at the finish line is a well-deserved perk.

BARKLEY MARATHONS
FROZEN HEAD STATE PARK, TENNESSEE
Ultra/Novelty
March or April/160+ km

No (roughly) 160-km (100-mile) ultra is ever easy, but the Barkley stands out as one of the toughest ultras in the world. Only 40 competitors are allowed to take part each year, and fewer than 20 of the 1,000 who started the race have ever finished inside the 60-hour cut-off time – and there have even been years where there were no finishers at all. Starting between midnight and noon, the five laps of 32 km (20 miles) include an ascent of around 16,500 m (54,000 ft) – almost twice the height of Mount Everest – and runners have to complete at least two of the laps in the dark. To add to the difficulty, runners must find between nine and fourteen books on the course and tear out the page relating to their number, before receiving a new number for the next lap.

68 | The inviting vista of a Gulf Shores beach

67

RUN WOODSTOCK FESTIVAL
PINCKNEY, MICHIGAN

Festival/Trail
September/Various

This three-day event offers a running choice for most, including the Flower Power 8 km (5 miles), the Hippie Half, the Mellow Marathon, the Freak 50K, the Peace and Love 80 km (50 miles), the Happening 100K and the Hallucination 160 km (100 miles). There is plenty of musical entertainment on each day, as well as the chance to take part in other slightly more relaxing activities such as meditation and yoga.

68

GULF SHORES BEACHES
ALABAMA

Running route/Coastal
All year round/Various

With more than 64 km (40 miles) of coastal beaches that offer great running, you're spoilt for choice when exploring this part of the Gulf of Mexico. You can soak in the sights and sounds of the area on a number of beaches, including Orange Beach, Perdido Beach and Gulf Shores Beach – these have good running conditions and are generally not too crowded. Just check the forecast before venturing out, as the weather can be variable, often windy, and the region is prone to hurricanes.

USA AND CANADA

70 | Running in Florida, Disney style

69
PENSACOLA WOMEN'S HALF-MARATHON WEEKEND
FLORIDA
Festival
November/21 km

An unusual event in that it is held for women only; men can run, but they won't receive a finishers' medal. The organisers emphasise the social nature of the race, encouraging runners to base themselves in the town for the entire weekend. With the options of a 5K and mile-dash, as well as the half-marathon, the race is held on the Gulf Coast, with a cut-off time of 3.5 hours for the half-marathon.

70
WALT DISNEY WORLD MARATHON WEEKEND
ORLANDO, FLORIDA
Novelty
January/42 km

This race weekend is a must for lovers of all things Disney, so it is not surprising that runners are encouraged to wear appropriate Disney-themed costumes. As a result, there are plenty of Mickey Mouses, Donald Ducks and Cinderellas among the starters, and all of the finishers' medals have an appropriate Disney theme. The Disney runs start early to ensure runners finish and are out of the parks before the gates open to the public – marathoners should be prepared to start as early as 3.30 a.m.!

71 | **Time for blast off on the Space Coast Beaches**

71

SPACE COAST BEACHES
CAPE CANAVERAL, FLORIDA
Running route/Coastal
All year round/Various

If you want to run in a location that is synonymous with the race to the moon and space exploration, there is nowhere better than the golden sands of the Space Coast Beaches. Close to the site of numerous rocket launches and Launchpad 39A, which was used to send *Apollo 11* to the moon and back, the Space Coast provides a 116-km (72-mile) stretch of beaches that are firm enough to be run on themselves, or that can be enjoyed from the boardwalks and pavements set back from the surf.

72

FLORIDA COAST 2 COAST RELAY
TITUSVILLE, FLORIDA
Relay
April/320 km

This exciting, twelve-leg relay race covers 320 km (200 miles) cross-state, running day and night. Choose your team wisely, as prizes are up for grabs. Categories are all male, all female or mixed. It is possible to accompany your teammate on bikes in sections of the course to get involved. The race starts at Titusville and ends in Tarpon Springs, also known as Little Greece.

73

PARADISE COAST HALF-MARATHON
NAPLES, FLORIDA
Forest/Coastal
February/5 & 21 km

This is a great multi-loop course in the unspoilt North Collier Regional Park. The paved course winds its way round lakes and forest, offering plenty of spots for family and friends to support. Temperatures can soar during the day, so runners can be thankful of the early start – which means finishers can enjoy the post-race buzz all day long.

74
MIAMI MARATHON
FLORIDA
Urban/Road
January/21 & 42 km

Almost 20,000 participants gather for this event (which includes a half-marathon option) every year as the sun rises at 6 a.m. over the famous city of Miami. The course is run mainly on road at sea level, with just a couple of small climbs over bridges on the way. Despite the early start, there is a carnival atmosphere, with music pumping through the streets to keep runners moving. Of course, everyone looks forward to a fabulous Miami-style after-party at the finish.

76 | Join the crowds at the Peachtree Road Race

75

BRIDGE RUN
MARATHON, FLORIDA

Road

March/11 km

This 11-km (6.8-mile) event from Knights Key in the city of Marathon to Little Duck Key is run on a bridge, meaning you'll be surrounded by water for the entire race. Plus, of course, you'll be in the amazing resort of Key West, home to Ernest Hemingway, pelicans and endless days of sunshine.

76

PEACHTREE ROAD RACE
ATLANTA, GEORGIA

Road

July/10 km

Since 1970, this enormously popular race has been held each year on Independence Day. Today the Peachtree Road Race claims to be the largest 10K in the world, attracting more than 60,000 runners and walkers. The largely flat course starts in the streets of Buckhead, before heading south to finish in Piedmont Park. The race focuses on encouraging fitness and fun, and since it is on the fourth of July, it's guaranteed that the route will be lined with thousands of spectators.

77
MOUNT DESERT ISLAND MARATHON
BAR HARBOR, MAINE

Marathon/Road
October/21 & 42 km

This race takes in a splendid mix of lakes, villages and forest, but along with the great vistas there are plenty of ups and downs, although none are too steep. Runners will also run alongside Somes Sound, the only fjord on the Eastern Seaboard of the United States. As the race is held in the autumn, expect to see some spectacular colours from the changing foliage. The marathon starts in the resort town of Bar Harbor, while the half-marathon starts in Northeast Harbor, with both races finishing in the lobster fishing village of Southwest Harbor.

78
MAINE COAST
MAINE

Running route/Coastal
All year round/Various

This spectacular stretch of coast on the US Eastern Seaboard, from Kittery in the south to Bar Harbor in the north, offers runners a vast choice of running routes and experiences. Wells, Popham and Old Orchard beaches offer vast expanses of flat, firm sand, while waterfront trails can be found in many of the coastal towns and harbours. The Wells Reserve and Camden Hills State Park have many kilometres of trails through woodlands and grassland, and the Nubble Lighthouse can be reached from Cape Neddick.

79
REACH THE BEACH
BRETTON WOODS, NEW HAMPSHIRE

Relay
Autumn/322 km

The oldest relay race on the East Coast, Reach the Beach is also one of the most popular. It's easy to see why. New England is charming and picturesque at any time of the year, but in September it erupts with autumnal foliage. Not a bad backdrop for a 322-km (200-mile) run with friends.

80
COVERED BRIDGES HALF-MARATHON
POMFRET, VERMONT

Road/Novelty
June/21 km

Covered Bridges are, quite simply, wooden structures that are completely enclosed, and this race takes in four of Vermont's unique covered bridges along its route. The race has been held since 1992, and starts in the town of Pomfret, but runners need to arrive at the finish in Quechee Gorge Village first, from where they are taken by bus to the start. This popular race has an entry limit of just over 2,000 runners and is frequently oversubscribed.

81
BOSTON MARATHON
MASSACHUSETTS

Marathon/Urban
April/42 km

Begun in 1897, Boston is the oldest annual marathon in the world. It's also, arguably, the most prestigious – runners must earn a spot by meeting a stringent qualifying time, adjusted for age and gender. The course overall is fairly narrow for a city marathon, with notable sections that include Wellesley College's 'Scream Tunnel' (see below) at 19 km (12 miles) (block your ears to guard them from the unbroken wall of sound the students create), 'Heartbreak Hill' – the fourth in a row of hills from 29–34 km (18–21 miles), and the finish line at Copley Square. If you're looking for a race steeped in history, with serious bragging rights, Boston is hard to beat – as is the record four wins by famed runner Bill Rodgers.

USA AND CANADA

82 | Training alongside the Charles River

82
CHARLES RIVER
BOSTON, MASSACHUSETTS
Running route/Urban
All year round/Various

The Charles River is a popular place for runners of all abilities, and the pavements are full with people running at almost all times of the day. The city of Boston has long been associated with running because of its historic and high-profile marathon, but the pavement alongside the river shows that recreational running also plays a major part in the city's culture. Don't be surprised if you catch sight of plenty of wildlife, as squirrels, falcons and turtles are all part of the river's ecosystem.

83
RESURGENCE HALF-MARATHON
BUFFALO, NEW YORK
Urban
June/21 km

The races (there's also a 10K and 5K) all start and finish at the Resurgence Brewing Company in Buffalo, close to the mouth of the Niagara River. All of the courses run alongside the spectacular shore of Lake Erie and so are predominantly flat and fast, but be prepared for a breeze that will either help or hinder, depending on the direction of travel. The post-race finish party is hosted by the brewery, and promises to rehydrate runners in a way that only a brewery can.

USA AND CANADA

84 | Celebrating completion of the Niagara Falls Marathon

84
NIAGARA FALLS INTERNATIONAL MARATHON
NEW YORK TO CANADA
Marathon
October/42 km

This race is run in two countries: it starts in Buffalo, USA, and finishes at the epic setting of Canada's Niagara Falls. Fortunately, there is no need for runners to carry their passports, as the course crosses the Peace Bridge over the Niagara River before reaching the finish line in Niagara Park, next to the incredible spectacle of the mighty falls.

85
CAROLER 5K
EAST AURORA, NEW YORK
Novelty/Road
December/5 km

This festive race encourages runners to 'carol all the k's', which may be harder as the race progresses and breath is needed for energy, not singing! A largely flat course held on roads, there are a few twists and turns as runners make their way through the town. Before the race, runners are encouraged to donate food or toys to local charities, and the first 500 finishers receive a festive hat and a pint glass.

86

NEW YORK CITY MARATHON
NEW YORK

Marathon/Urban
November/42 km

This Marathon Major is the largest in the world and arguably the most famous. The iconic race dates back to 1970, and despite its tough course, has seen several world records broken. The race begins on Staten Island, just before the Verrazzano-Narrows Bridge, where you can feel the adrenaline pulsing through the 50,000-strong crowd of ambitious runners. The course then winds its way through Brooklyn, Queens and finally into Manhattan, to finish in Central Park. It's easy to get swept up in the atmosphere of New York, but keep your cool, enjoy the moment and stay focused, so that you can finish strong.

87

CENTRAL PARK

MANHATTAN, NEW YORK

Running route
All year round/Various

The global phenomenon of park running is huge in the United States, and New York has the perfect venue in Central Park, with its variety of terrain and excellent scenery. Best run in the early morning or late evening to avoid the crowds, a full loop covers just over 9.5 km (6 miles), but the network of paths make it possible to extend or shorten the run to any chosen distance. The Jacqueline Kennedy Onassis Reservoir is highly recommended, to follow in the footsteps of Dustin Hoffman in the 1976 movie *Marathon Man*. It's just 2.6 km (1.6 miles) around.

USA AND CANADA

89 | The kids' race at Brooklyn

88
FIFTH AVENUE MILE
MANHATTAN, NEW YORK

Road/Urban

September/1.6 km

If you want to run a race in New York but the marathon is too far, this could be the event to choose. Starting on 80th Street, the race heads twenty blocks south on Fifth Avenue to 60th Street, and regularly attracts big prize money for the winners, and a world-class field. The elite races are held separately to the mass-participation events, which include a Youth Mile and the George Sheehan Memorial Mile for runners aged 60 and over.

89
BROOKLYN HALF-MARATHON
NEW YORK

Urban

May/21 km

The largest half-marathon in the United States is a race for early risers, as the start near the Brooklyn Museum is at 7 a.m. Due to the race's popularity, runners are set off in waves to avoid congestion, and run past the Brooklyn Botanic Garden and then around the Grand Army Plaza. After a long loop around Prospect Park, runners head along Ocean Parkway towards the iconic Coney Island, before finishing on the boardwalk and collecting their medal.

90 | Sri Chinmoy is a true test of endurance

90
SRI CHINMOY SELF-TRANSCENDENCE 3100 MILE RACE
QUEENS, NEW YORK
Ultra/Urban
June, July, August/4,989 km

This super-endurance ultra is a test for even the most resilient of runners, testing both mental and physical stamina. Claiming to be the world's longest road race, runners have to circle the same city block in Queens, running on 52 consecutive days between 6 a.m. and midnight each day. The course is just 883 m (966 yards) long, so finishers must complete 5,649 loops, and need to average just under 97 km (60 miles) each day. Perhaps it is no surprise that there is a high drop-out rate and only a small number of those who start go the distance.

91
BRIDGEHAMPTON HALF OR HAMPTONS MARATHON
THE HAMPTONS, NEW YORK
Coastal/Urban
June/September/21 & 42 km

The Hamptons are a group of cute seaside towns with white sandy beaches usually frequented by affluent New Yorkers. These two events take place in the towns of Sagaponack and Bridgehampton, where there is plenty to distract you from the pain. The towns are full of trendy cafes, upmarket restaurants and designer boutiques you can check out as you run by. The Hamptons Marathon, and its half-marathon event, are mostly run along the beach in Southampton. For all race options, you'll also pass farms and stunning estates as you run on the beautiful terrain of Long Island.

93 | Cherry blossom trees flower for runners in Washington

92
HOBOOKEN HALLOWEEN 5K
HOBOKEN, NEW JERSEY
Novelty
October/5 km

As the leaves are turning golden and the pumpkins line the streets, residents of New Jersey come to the city of Hoboken to take on this cheerfully spooky race in aid of the local homeless shelter. Boasting views of the Manhattan skyline and the Hudson River, runners will not be disappointed with the scenic course. It should be mentioned that fancy dress is more than encouraged – it's rewarded!

93
CHERRY BLOSSOM TEN MILE
WASHINGTON, D.C.
Road
April/16 km

Held each year on the first Sunday in April to coincide with the peak cherry blossom season, this popular race attracts more than 15,000 runners, who are started in waves of 2,500 to reduce congestion. The race starts and finishes close to the spectacular Washington Memorial, and is fast and flat, running alongside Washington's historic Tidal Basin and the Potomac River, and passing famous sights such as the Watergate Building, the Arlington National Cemetery, the Lincoln Memorial and the Jefferson Memorial.

94

MARINE CORPS MARATHON
WASHINGTON, D.C.
Road
October/10–50 km

The Marine Corps Marathon Organization hosts a series of events that are held to honour those who have served their country in the US armed forces. Their most popular events are the ultra, marathon and 10K held in Arlington. The marathon offers a rolling course and is known as beginner- and spectator-friendly. When you reach the final hill, a group of Marines encourage you up to the finish. Runners from more than 60 nations compete in this 'People's Marathon'.

95

PARKWAY CLASSIC
ALEXANDRIA, VIRGINIA
Road
April/5 & 16 km

This 16-km (10-mile) race is held on a point-to-point course that starts at George Washington's Mount Vernon Estate, before heading through the wide streets of Alexandria, and then alongside the banks of the Potomac River. The race finishes in Oronoco Bay Park, from where a 5K starts and finishes. The wide and largely flat, tree-lined routes make these very popular races, and there is a free shuttle bus service to take the 16-km finishers back to the start.

96

UKROP'S MONUMENT AVENUE 10K
RICHMOND, VIRGINIA
Road
April/10 km

This popular race attracts up to 30,000 entrants, and mixes crazy costumes with elite running. Runners start in almost 40 waves according to their ability, and the flat and fast route is packed with plenty of on-course entertainment, including thousands of spectators who line the route. Designated cheer zones, live bands and entertainment guarantee an electric atmosphere.

USA AND CANADA

97 | **Forest trails on the Umstead Ultra**

97

UMSTEAD 100-MILE ULTRA
RALEIGH, NORTH CAROLINA
Ultra/Trail
March/160 km

First held in 1994, runners have 30 hours to complete this 160-km (100-mile) race that takes place in William B. Umstead State Park. Don't be fooled: this is no ordinary run in the park. Conditions underfoot are mainly dirt track and road, and the setting offers pleasant but undulating woodland on a course that consists of five laps. Runners can be supported by their own crew and are allowed to have their crew member run with them for the final lap. This is seen as an entry-level 100 (a 50-miler/80-km is also available) – certainly not easy but a good one to try if tackling the distance for the first time.

98

KIAWAH ISLAND MARATHON
SOUTH CAROLINA
Marathon/Road
December/21 & 42 km

Technically not an island, but nevertheless this is a spectacular setting for both the marathon and half-marathon. Since it was first held in 1978, runners have had fantastic views of woodland, opulent homes and marshes. The largely flat course means that quick times are achievable, and pacers are on hand to help runners hit their target times. There is a cut-off time of 6.5 hours for both the marathon and the half.

Tricky footing in British Columbia

99
5 PEAKS TRAIL RUNNING SERIES BC
WHISTLER, BRITISH COLUMBIA
Mountain
Summer/Various

This series is held throughout the summer months on various mountain trails across the province. The Whistler event is extremely popular and allows you to race on the mountain rather than up it! Thanks to the impressive ski infrastructure, your legs will benefit from taking the gondola up Whistler, then on to Blackcombe to the start line, where there is plenty of work to do. Runners can opt for the longer scenic course or the short sports course. Don't leave the kids behind as there are plenty of events for them too, making this a perfect choice for families of all ages.

100
HANDLOGGERS HALF-MARATHON
BOWEN ISLAND, BRITISH COLUMBIA
Trail
September/21 km

Once a year, Bowen Island, off the coast of Vancouver, welcomes long-distance runners to its shores to take on the challenging half-marathon trail run. The relatively intimate race is superbly organised and is growing in capacity each year. Runners can take the ferry from Horseshoe Bay directly to the start line to commence a literally breathtaking loop of the island.

101

VANCOUVER

BRITISH COLUMBIA

Running route/Urban

All year round/Various

Where else in the world can you find a city with beaches, forests, mountain trail and impressive urban skylines? Vancouver is made for runners. To the west you will find the university parkland and the beaches; to the north you'll find mountain trails, the Lions Gate Bridge and the must-run Stanley Park. If you want a longer run, challenge yourself to the famous Seawall, a 27-km (17-mile) continuous waterside path taking in much of the above.

102

SEA WHEEZE HALF-MARATHON

VANCOUVER, BRITISH COLUMBIA

Festival/Road

August/21 km

This is a half-marathon route to remember, with a mix of noisy city, running through the streets of the vibrant and eclectic Vancouver, and a magnificent 11 km (7 miles) spent running alongside beaches and the Pacific Ocean. With more than 10,000 runners, the race is the highlight of a west-coast party weekend that includes yoga sessions, a Pre-Wheeze party and a post-race music festival in Stanley Park.

101 | **Fantastic autumnal scenery in Vancouver**

103
WILD PACIFIC TRAIL
VANCOUVER ISLAND, BRITISH COLUMBIA
Running route/Coastal
All year round/8.6 km

This famous trail on Vancouver Island can be run at any time of the year, and each season brings a spectacularly different running experience. Be prepared to see bears, eagles, sea lions and whales, which are around from March to November. The trail is split into two main sections – the 2.6-km (1.6-mile) Lighthouse Loop and a longer 6-km (3.7-mile) section – which can be enjoyed all at once or individually. Expect rugged outcrops, rough seas, ancient forest and beautiful beaches, not to mention some of the best sunsets you'll ever see.

104
MOOSE MOUNTAIN TRAIL
KANANASKIS IMPROVEMENT, ALBERTA
Running route/Trail
All year round/13.8 km

The Moose Mountain Trail is a 13.8-km (8.6-mile) rocky trail in Kananaskis Country. The mountain gets its name from its moose-like appearance rather than an abundance of moose. Hikers use the trail from spring to autumn, and in colder months snowshoes and/or spikes may be required. Start at the end of Moose Mountain Road and follow the trail towards the summit. The first peak is Moose Dome, and the trail continues upwards to the lookout before you can claim victory.

103 | Admire the wildlife on the Wild Pacific Trail

USA AND CANADA

105 | Basic accommodation on the Itijjagiaq Trail

106 | Running around the bay in Hamilton

105
ITIJJAGIAQ TRAIL
KATANNILIK, NUNAVUT

Running route/Multiday adventure
Spring, Summer, Autumn/177 km

Ever fancied running in the Arctic? Take yourself north to Baffin Island and discover Katannilik Territorial Park, where it's easy to imagine dramatic events that led to the formation of the Earth's surface. Hikers tend to cover this 177-km (110-mile) rocky trail in seven days, staying in shelters along the way, but it is possible to run it much faster. To benefit from the beauty of the Arctic tundra in bloom, visit towards the end of summer.

106
AROUND THE BAY ROAD RACE
HAMILTON, ONTARIO

Coastal/Relay
March/30 km

This is the oldest race in North America, which takes runners on a challenging 30-km (19-mile) course around the natural harbour of Hamilton. Runners who complete the course for two consecutive years get a free entry for their third year, and there are also options to complete the course as part of a three-person relay, with each runner completing 10 km (6.2 miles), or a two-person relay, with each runner completing 15 km (9.3 miles).

108 | **Wrap up warm for the Chilly Half**

107
FOXTAIL HUNDRED
DUNDAS, ONTARIO

Ultra/Trail

Summer/up to 161 km

This epic race takes place in the lush Canadian forest during the warmer summer months. There are various distances, with each event using a flat 53-km (33-mile) loop. Pacers are allowed after runners complete the first loop, jumping in at the race headquarters where there will be aid stations, supportive campers and a big bonfire to enjoy afterwards. All competitors look forward to receiving the Foxtail Hundred straw hat, and those who complete the 100-mile race also get the sought-after belt buckle.

108
CHILLY HALF-MARATHON
LAKE ONTARIO, ONTARIO

Road

March/21 km

As the name suggests, this race can take place in freezing temperatures, but prepare well and you could be on track for a good time. The out-and-back half-marathon course runs alongside the shores of Lake Ontario and, as such, is very flat. The race is popular with locals, and there is a fantastic atmosphere at the end with food, beer and an awards ceremony. If the half-marathon is not your distance, there is the option of the Frigid 5K or Frosty 10K instead.

109
HUNGRY HOLLOW 5K
HALTON HILLS, ONTARIO

Multi-terrain

August/5 km

Georgetown is a charming small town located in Halton Hills, not too far from Toronto, and the scenic Hungry Hollow trail lies in a valley to the south of the town. This chip-timed race is a friendly local run open for all abilities and children. Runners take on two laps of the Hungry Hollow ravine, which is made up of bridges, boardwalks, forest path and meadows. You'll pass ponds and beautiful marshes as you race along the Silver Creek branch of the Credit River.

USA AND CANADA

111 | **Poised and ready in Ottawa**

110
TORONTO WOMEN'S RUN SERIES
ONTARIO

Trail

August/5 & 10 km

Summer is the perfect time of the year to visit Canada's biggest city. This all-female event takes place in Sunnybrook Park, downtown Toronto. Put your training to the test as you blitz round this paved course with more than 1,500 women of varying abilities and goals. Post-race, use those endorphins to explore the city, try the food and dance the night away in one of Toronto's bars.

111
OTTAWA RACE WEEKEND
ONTARIO

Road/Festival

May/Various

This two-day running festival includes seven races, all of which start and finish at Ottawa City Hall. The shortest distance is a 1.2-km (0.7-mile) children's race; the longest is a full marathon; distances in between that include a 5K, a 10K wheelchair event and a half-marathon. More than 40,000 runners take part and the marathon has become the largest marathon event in Canada.

MEXICO, CENTRAL AND SOUTH AMERICA

MEXICO, CENTRAL AND SOUTH AMERICA: ENTRY LIST

JANUARY
115 Marathon Bahamas Race Weekend, Bahamas

FEBRUARY
119 Tropikal Half-marathon, Puerto Rico
134 Jungle Marathon, Brazil
148 El Cruce Columbia, Argentina to Chile

MARCH
114 Carrera D Teotihuacan Trail Race, Mexico
141 Rock 'n' Roll Santiago, Chile

APRIL
150 Stanley Marathon, Falkland Islands

MAY
142 Circuito Trail Running Races, Chile

JUNE
133 Inca Trail Marathon, Peru
139 Marathon Rapa Nui, Easter Island

JULY
113 Half-marathon Mexico City, Mexico
128 Bogotá Half-marathon, Colombia

AUGUST
128 Bogotá Half-marathon, Colombia
131 Galapagos Marathon, Galapagos Islands
132 Pisco 30K, Peru
144 Snow Running, Chile

SEPTEMBER
118 Santo Domingo Marathon, Dominican Republic
140 The Atacama Crossing, Chile
145 Patagonian International Marathon, Chile
149 Buenos Aires Marathon, Argentina

OCTOBER
112 Copper Canyon 100-mile Ultra, Mexico
131 Galapagos Marathon, Galapagos Islands
137 Rio de Janeiro Marathon, Brazil
138 Florianópolis Marathon, Brazil
151 The Stone Run Half-marathon, Falkland Islands

NOVEMBER
124 Costa Rica Ultra Trail, Costa Rica
127 Salento Trail Challenge, Colombia

DECEMBER
117 Reggae Marathon, Jamaica
121 End of the World Marathon, Belize
123 Trinidad and Tobago International Marathon, Trinidad and Tobago
143 Vulcano Ultra Trail, Chile

ALL YEAR ROUND
116 Seven Mile Beach, Cayman Islands
120 El Yunque National Forest, Puerto Rico
122 Barbados Boardwalk, Barbados
125 Ciclovía Cinta Costera Path, Panama
126 Grand Tour of Cartagena, Colombia
129 Parque Metropolitano Guangüiltagua, Ecuador
130 Quilotoa Loop, Ecuador (spring, summer, autumn)
135 Ibirapuera Park, Brazil
136 Rio de Janeiro Beachfront, Brazil
146 Costanera Promenade, Paraguay
147 Rambla Waterfront, Uruguay
152 Tierra del Fuego National Park, Tierra del Fuego

MEXICO, CENTRAL AND SOUTH AMERICA

112
COPPER CANYON 100-MILE ULTRA
MEXICO
Ultra/Trail
October/161 km

'Rarámuri' means 'those who run fast', and long-distance running has been part of this so-called local group of indigenous people's heritage and culture. Today it is possible to run with them in a series of races that take place within the Copper Canyon's valleys and fertile plains, running along trails that have been used by the Rarámuri (also known as Tarahumara) for thousands of years as running routes between villages.

113
HALF-MARATHON MEXICO CITY
MEXICO
Road/Urban
July/21 km

Featuring a mixture of road running and paths through a park, this race regularly receives praise from runners who have completed the course. Finishing next to the Angel of Independence, you'll take in many of the city's famous sights and landmarks. While the course is relatively flat, don't expect a PB, as the high altitude can place an extra strain on oxygen uptake capacity.

112 | Run with the Tarahumara on ancient trails

History and heritage combine on the Carrera D Teotihuacan

114
CARRERA D TEOTIHUACAN (ANCIENT ROUTES) TRAIL RACE
MEXICO
Trail
March/Various

Although the start is close to the centre of Mexico City, the Ancient Routes trail races (5K, 10K, 21 km/13 miles) give you the chance to experience spectacular scenery and the spirit of the ancient gods. The route goes through the Teotihuacan UNESCO Heritage site, where you'll pass the pyramids, the largest of which is the Pyramid of the Sun, reputedly built over 2,000 years ago and now one of the most popular tourist attractions in Mexico.

115
MARATHON BAHAMAS RACE WEEKEND
NASSAU, BAHAMAS
Festival
January/Various

Held in Nassau, the capital of the Bahamas, this race weekend attracts runners from all over the world. The two-day festival starts with the 5K on Saturday, followed by the marathon, half-marathon and relay on Sunday. The courses are predominantly fast and flat, and offer many kilometres of ocean views. The 6 a.m. start time for the marathon makes the most of the cool winter weather, and, as a result, fast times are a common feature of the weekend.

116 | Golden sand and the Caribbean Sea

116
SEVEN MILE BEACH
CAYMAN ISLANDS

Running route/Coastal
All year round/9 km

You'll have a choice of either a wide concrete pavement or the reasonably firm sand of the beach. Despite the beach's name, the run stretches for 5.5 miles (9 km), not 7, but you can double up if you run it out and back. The ever-present highlight of the flat route is the fantastic views over the Caribbean Sea, but if you decide to run along the sand, it is worth checking the tide times before setting out, as the firmest sand can be covered at high tide.

117
REGGAE MARATHON
NEGRIL, JAMAICA

Coastal
December/42 km

In a country known more for its world-class sprinters, the Reggae Marathon, half-marathon and 10K provide an opportunity for Jamaica to embrace endurance running. Not surprisingly, runners are continually motivated by pulsating reggae music at every mile, but the marathon does have to be completed inside 6 hours. The races start and finish at Long Bay Beach Park in Negril, alongside the town's famous 11-km (7-mile) white-sand beach.

118
SANTO DOMINGO MARATHON
DOMINICAN REPUBLIC
Road/Coastal
September/21 & 42 km

You'll run the first few kilometres of these races in the dark, as they start at the early time of 5 a.m. (marathon) and 5.30 a.m. (half-marathon) to avoid the worst of the Caribbean heat and humidity. You'll have a choice of completing a single loop for the half-marathon or two loops for the marathon. The loop combines the city streets of Santo Domingo with a long out-and-back section along the coast.

119
TROPIKAL HALF-MARATHON
PUERTO RICO
Coastal/Road
February/21 km

This is a well-organised, spectator-friendly event on a Caribbean island that offers the chance to combine the race with a holiday. The course is a series of loops around the island's ancient capital city, San Juan, with a height gain of just over 122 m (400 ft). Held entirely on road, the race offers great views of the city, nearby beaches and harbour.

120
EL YUNQUE NATIONAL FOREST
PUERTO RICO
Road/Trail
All year round/Various

You are certain to get wet on this run through the rainforest in Puerto Rico, but it will be worth it. Just an hour outside the city of San Juan, you'll experience waterfalls and rich vegetation while shaded from the heat under a canopy of trees. Almost constantly running through a cooling mist and rain, perhaps surprisingly, much of the trail through the rainforest is made of concrete, offering very little off-road running.

MEXICO, CENTRAL AND SOUTH AMERICA

121
END OF THE WORLD MARATHON
PLACENCIA, BELIZE
Road/Festival
December/21 & 42 km

First held in 2012, just before a December date that local tradition thought would signal the end of the world, the marathon and half-marathon races wind through the local towns and villages of Placencia, Seine Bight and Maya Beach. Fortunately, the world did not end in December 2012, so the festival has been held ever since and has become a regular feature in the sporting calendar of Belize.

122
BARBADOS BOARDWALK
BARBADOS
Running route/Coastal
All year round/1.6 km

Stretching 1.6 km (1 mile) between Camelot and Accra beach, this solid structure set into the sand has become popular with runners and walkers alike, despite the controversy when first built (due to its perceived impact on the environment). The route is flat and edges the sands and the Caribbean Sea along the south coast of Barbados. Expect to see lovely beach and ocean views as you make your way along.

123
TRINIDAD AND TOBAGO INTERNATIONAL MARATHON
TRINIDAD AND TOBAGO
Marathon/Coastal
December/42 km

The Caribbean's oldest marathon is not a mass participation event; despite the name, it normally only attracts around 100 runners. The action kicks off at 5 a.m., before the heat of the Caribbean sun builds up, and runners race from Freeport to the capital, Port of Spain. You'll enjoy plenty of local music and hospitality – just make sure you beat the 6.5-hour cut-off time.

124 | The mountains and jungle of the Costa Rica Ultra Trail

124
COSTA RICA ULTRA TRAIL
COSTA RICA
Ultra/Mountain
November/120 & 200 km

This trail comprises two routes: the 'Adventure' is a shorter 120-km (75-mile) run, while the longer 'Extreme' is 200 km (125 miles). Both are tough and involve a series of five stages and an overnight stay in a bivouac. Starting at the Pacific Ocean on the west coast, runners cross Costa Rica to the Caribbean, and in between have to cope with the mountains and jungle of the Central Valley. Daily stages are between 38 and 48 km (24 and 30 miles) for the Extreme, with a total elevation gain of 9,300 m (30,500 ft). Those completing the Adventure climb 5,300 m (17,500 ft), with daily stages of between 20 and 30 km (12 and 19 miles).

125
CICLOVÍA CINTA COSTERA PATH
PANAMA CITY, PANAMA
Running route/Coastal
All year round/8 km

Claiming to be one of the best waterfront running routes in South America, this path was built in 2009. Since then it has been extended to provide runners with an 8-km (5-mile) route from Estadio Maracaña in the south to Democracy Plaza in the north. The route offers great views of the Gulf of Panama and Panama City's skyline, and includes plenty of on-course exercise stations for those who want to add in a spot of resistance training.

126

GRAND TOUR OF CARTAGENA
COLOMBIA

Running route/Coastal
All year round/8 km

A series of shorter runs around the historic seaside city of Cartagena can be combined to create a longer 18-km (11-mile) route that provides a circuit of the entire city. The highlight is the Old Town and the Clock Tower, which is the best place to start the tour. Then head out along the waterfront and follow the ancient walls to the seafront, into the Castillogrande neighbourhood, before returning to the Clock Tower via either the seafront or the walls. Take a map and prepare to get lost!

127

SALENTO TRAIL CHALLENGE
COLOMBIA

Marathon/Trail
November/Various

The three distances – marathon, half-marathon, 10K – offer a mix of trails and road running through the picturesque Cocora Valley. Mountains, forests and bridge crossings of fast-flowing rivers are all part of the races, and the half-marathon and marathon runners will face the additional challenge of high-altitude running as they climb to 3,000 m (9,850 ft), where the lack of oxygen will cause additional fatigue.

127 | **Run through the valleys of the Salento Trail**

128 | The streets of Bogotá fill with runners for the half-marathon

128
BOGOTÁ HALF-MARATHON
COLOMBIA
Road/Urban
July or August/10 & 21 km

The largest running event in Colombia with 45,000 runners, the half-marathon starts in Bolívar Square, the main square of Bogotá, and finishes at the main gates of Bolívar Park. Also featuring a 10K, the event is seen as a celebration of life and encourages runners of all abilities to take part, enjoy running and complete the distance.

129
PARQUE METROPOLITANO GUANGÜILTAGUA
QUITO, ECUADOR
Running route/Park
All year round/8 km

This large park in the centre of the city of Quito is popular with runners of all ages and abilities. A gravel and stone road circles the park for 8 km (5 miles), offering great views of the nearby mountains. Plenty of interconnecting paths enable the total distance to be lengthened or shortened, and watch out for wildlife that could include hummingbirds and the park's herd of llamas.

130

QUILOTOA LOOP
ANDES, ECUADOR

Running route/Multiday adventure
Spring, Summer, Autumn/40 km

The Quilotoa Loop is a self-guided multiday run that should be started from the stunning Quilotoa Lake in the Cotopaxi region, connecting remote Andes villages at altitudes that often exceed 3,700 m (12,000 ft). The total loop is approximately 40 km (25 miles), but the altitude and ascents and descents mean that it is advisable to schedule at least one overnight stay in a local hostel or hotel. Steep gorges and towering cliffs are a constant feature of the loop, which is also popular with hikers.

131

GALAPAGOS MARATHON
GALAPAGOS ISLANDS

Marathon/Coastal
August & October/42 km

Who knows what Darwin would make of the species collectively known as 'marathon runner' had he been alive today and visited the Galapagos Islands on marathon day? Unusually, the marathon is held twice – once in August, at the height of the tourist season, when the weather is cool, and again in October, as a means of stimulating the local economy. Each runner is allocated their own 'caddy', whose job is to help the runner reach the finishing line, including providing navigational support and offering drinks every 2 km (1.2 miles).

130 | **Quilotoa Lake on the popular Quilotoa Loop**

133 | Immerse yourself in the ancient history of the Inca

132
PISCO 30K
CORDILLERA BLANCA, PERU

Mountain

August/30 km

This challenging race offers steep ascents and descents, high alpine terrain and fantastic Peruvian mountain scenery. Held in the Huascarán National Park, the race challenges runners both physically and physiologically, since it includes a high point of 4,900 m (16,000 ft), and over 5 km (3 miles) of the 30-km (19-mile) distance take place in oxygen-deprived air at an altitude of over 4,600 m (15,000 ft).

133
INCA TRAIL MARATHON
PERU

Marathon/Mountain

June/42 km

As the name suggests, the Inca Trail Marathon runs along the famous Inca Trail that leads to the iconic Machu Picchu ruins, a global tourist attraction. Claiming to be one of the most difficult marathons in the world, it includes the crossing of a lung-busting 4,200-m (13,800-ft) mountain pass. A comfortable campground is provided for before/after the race, and porters carry your gear.

134
JUNGLE MARATHON
AMAZON, BRAZIL
Ultra/Multiday adventure
February/Various

Set in the Brazilian Amazon jungle, this extreme test of endurance offers participants a choice of the marathon distance, a four-stage 127 km (79 miles) or a six-stage 254 km (158 miles). The courses include steep climbs and descents, swamps, river crossings and beaches, as well as high temperatures and humidity. Runners must be self-sufficient, and compulsory kit includes a hammock, food, water and a mosquito net. Runners are also warned by the event organisers that they may be exposed to snakes, wild animals and poisonous plants.

135
IBIRAPUERA PARK
SÃO PAULO, BRAZIL
Running route/Park
All year round/Various

This popular park in the very heart of São Paolo is a haven for runners looking to escape the noisy streets of the city. The park is open from 5 a.m. until midnight, so there is no excuse not to find time to fit it into your diary. There are plenty of running tracks to choose from, ranging in terrain and distance, so you can create your own route, which might pass through wooded areas or past the large lake in the centre.

136
RIO DE JANEIRO BEACHFRONT
BRAZIL
Running route/Coastal
All year round/5 km

Sport is synonymous with Rio, and there is no better place to run than along the beaches that face out to the Atlantic Ocean. There is a beachside path that gives runners the option of covering their choice of distance – Leblon Beach to Ipanema Beach is just under 5 km (3 miles), and a longer run can be had by continuing to the famous Copacabana Beach, where you'll enjoy views to the ocean on one side and mountains to the other.

137
RIO DE JANEIRO MARATHON
BRAZIL
Marathon/Coastal
October/42 km

Starting in Flamengo Park, runners pass through areas of Rio that include Leblon, Copacabana and Botafogo. The race is guaranteed to have a carnival atmosphere, with crowds of more than 100,000 regularly turning out to cheer on the runners. The combination of mountains and sea makes this a picturesque route, and other sights include Sugarloaf Mountain and Christ the Redeemer on top of Corcovado Mountain.

137 | **Expect a carnival atmosphere near the finish line in Rio**

138

FLORIANÓPOLIS MARATHON
BRAZIL
Road/Coastal
October/42 km

This annual road race is held in the Brazilian city of Florianópolis, a city that is unusually situated on a small island. As a result, the courses are flat and at sea level – perfect for fast times. There are also half-marathon and 10K race options. You'll have great views of the ocean, and the marathon's popularity is such that more than 10,000 people normally take part. The organisers encourage runners to base their post-race recovery on one of the city's 42 beaches.

139

MARATHON RAPA NUI
HANGA ROA, EASTER ISLAND
Marathon/Coastal
June/42 km

Getting to the start line for this marathon is a challenge in itself, as Easter Island lies 3,700 km (2,300 miles) from the nearest land mass. Those who do make the journey will be rewarded with a race that takes them from the start at Hanga Roa on the west coast, followed by a steady climb to 18 km (11 miles), then a steep descent to Anakena on the north coast, passing the island's famous stone statues, known as Moai. Anakena is the halfway point, where you'll turn to retrace your steps back to Hanga Roa. Leave plenty of luggage space for the flight home, as finishers receive a cap, medal, t-shirt – and a windbreak.

140
THE ATACAMA CROSSING
CHILE

Multiday adventure
September/250 km

Billed as one of the toughest running races in the world, this epic race covers 250 km (155 miles) over six separate stages in seven days, all of which are within the infamous Atacama Desert. The course is marked with flags that runners must follow in temperatures of over 40°C (100°F), and reaching a high point of 3,500 m (11,500 ft). Racers carry everything they need for the week – except tents and water – in their backpacks. Thankfully, it is possible to walk the entire course, and about a third of racers are doing an event of this sort for the first time.

MEXICO, CENTRAL AND SOUTH AMERICA 105

141

ROCK 'N' ROLL SANTIAGO
CHILE

Festival

March/Various

One of the several races in the 'Rock 'n' Roll' series, the Santiago event combines a carnival atmosphere with music, sound and exercise. Runners will experience the cosmopolitan city that Santiago has become in recent years, combining history with vibrant parks and buildings. Starting in the Avenue del Condor and finishing amid the sounds of a music concert, entrants can choose from a range of distances – 5K, 10K, half-marathon – that will give them an experience to remember.

142

CIRCUITO TRAIL RUNNING RACES
CHILE

Trail

May/Various

Starting from the town of Alhué, a 150-km (93-mile) drive from the Chilean capital, Santiago, these are challenging races along dirt tracks, with plenty of tough ascents and descents. The 34-km (21-mile) race involves four distinct summits and a total climb of over 2,100 m (6,890 ft), while the shorter 14 km (9 miles) still has a climb of 500 m (1,640 ft) and three summits. The scenery is spectacular, and the race has become a popular feature of the Chilean trail-running calendar.

143

VULCANO ULTRA TRAIL
PATAGONIA, CHILE
Trail/Ultra
December/100 km

Offering a range of distances from 2 to 100 km (1.2 to 62 miles), the Vulcano Ultra Trail (or VUT) is held within the imposing Osorno Volcano in Chilean Patagonia. The shorter distances cater to children, fun-runners and families, while the longer distances provide ever-increasing challenges and ascents over tough and rugged terrain that includes volcanic sand, riverbeds, sandy beaches and mountain roads.

144

SNOW RUNNING
PATAGONIA, CHILE
Snow
August/10 & 20 km

These 10K and 20K races are held entirely on snow at the southern tip of the South American continent. Runners must dress for the cold and will have to ditch their normal running shoes for snow shoes. It's certainly not a course for those who prefer the warm or who are after a PB. Be prepared for tired legs at the end, especially if the snow is soft.

143 | **The Osorno Volcano dominates the Vulcano Ultra Trail**

145

PATAGONIAN INTERNATIONAL MARATHON
CHILE

Marathon/Mountain
September/42 km

With spectacular views of mountains, these races (also a half-marathon and 10K) are held at the southern tip of the South American continent, and attract runners from all over the world. Conditions can be unpredictable but often cold, and the courses contain climbs of between 170 and 700 m (560 and 2,300 ft). You'll be running on roads, but these can be twisty as well as undulating, in the surrounding area of the Torres del Paine National Park.

146
COSTANERA PROMENADE
ASUNCIÓN, PARAGUAY

Running route/Coastal
All year round/8 km

Asunción is one of the oldest cities in South America, and while many of the city's streets are not a good home for runners, the Costanera Promenade runs along the waterfront that sits alongside the Paraguay River. An out-and-back route makes it possible to run approximately 8 km (5 miles) along this relatively flat and easy-to-follow path.

147
RAMBLA WATERFRONT
COLONIA DEL SACRAMENTO, URUGUAY

Running route/Coastal
All year round/8 km

Colonia del Sacramento is a former Portuguese settlement in southern Uruguay, famous for its historic streets and an ancient lighthouse. A wide 4-km (2.5-mile) path follows the waterfront, and is popular with runners. Many of the beaches alongside the path have sand that is firm enough for running on, and an out-and-back run, starting from the city centre, offers around 8 km (5 miles) of flat running with great views.

147 | Take a breather at the Rambla Waterfront

149 | Runners tour the city in the Buenos Aires Marathon

148
EL CRUCE COLUMBIA
ARGENTINA TO CHILE
Multiday adventure/Mountain
February/100 km

This tough 100-km (62-mile) mountain race crosses the Andes, with competitors having to cope with low oxygen levels as a result of the high altitude that they encounter. The race is held over three days and three stages, and runners compete in teams of two to help with navigation and safety. The race is extreme and requires intense prior training, but runners are rewarded by volcanoes, snow-capped mountains, forests, immaculate lakes and refuelling barbecues.

149
BUENOS AIRES MARATHON
ARGENTINA
Road/Marathon
September/42 km

First held in 1984, the Buenos Aires Marathon has become a popular event for both domestic and international runners, frequently attracting more than 10,000 entrants. The course passes the famous River Plate stadium before entering the Palermo and Gardel neighbourhoods. You'll start and finish in the city centre, and while it's mainly flat, there is an early climb between 3 and 5 km (2 and 3 miles), and a smaller but fatigue-inducing climb between 19 and 21 km (12 and 13 miles).

MEXICO, CENTRAL AND SOUTH AMERICA 111

150
STANLEY MARATHON
FALKLAND ISLANDS
Road/Marathon
April/42 km

Be prepared for a tough time if you enter the world's most southerly AIMS-certified marathon. Held since 2005, a combination of uphill sections, strong winds and the constant threat of bad weather makes this a particularly strenuous marathon course. For those looking to ease the challenge, you can buddy up with your running companions to make a relay team of four.

151 | **A unique half-marathon in the remote Falkland Islands**

151
THE STONE RUN HALF-MARATHON
FALKLAND ISLANDS
Coastal
October/21 km

If you enjoy a friendly atmosphere in a unique location, then the Stone Run offers something that is genuinely special. There is a certain beauty to the rugged landscape, and the route passes close to many 'stone runs', vast features of boulders that have eroded over millions of years to resemble rivers of rocks. The race, organised by the Falklands Island Running Club, is undulating and can be breezy.

152
TIERRA DEL FUEGO NATIONAL PARK
TIERRA DEL FUEGO
Running route/Trail
All year round/Various

Situated 12 km (7.5 miles) from the city of Ushuaia, the Tierra del Fuego National Park has a 35-km (22-mile) network of trails that pass through marine, forest and mountain environments. This combination of coastal and mountain terrain makes it a great place to run, with the added bonus of an abundance of wildlife both on the ground and in the air. Albatross, oystercatchers and foxes are regular sights, and all of the trails are well marked.

EUROPE

114 EUROPE

SEE PAGE 117 FOR MORE OF **EUROPE**

EUROPE: ENTRY LIST

JANUARY
- 161 Sugar Loaf 10K, Ireland
- 175 Falkirk Epic Trail 10K, Scotland
- 181 Worms Head 10K, Wales
- 222 Cliveden Cross Country 10K, England
- 234 Polar Night Half marathon, Norway
- 287 Swiss Snow Run, Switzerland

FEBRUARY
- 167 Armagh 5K, Northern Ireland
- 186 The National, UK
- 205 Tough Guy, England
- 218 Portsmouth Coastal Half-marathon, England
- 321 Milestii Mici Wine Run, Moldova

MARCH
- 157 Ballyliffin Coastal Challenge, Ireland
- 168 Isle of Man Easter Festival, Isle of Man
- 211 Cambridge Half-marathon, England
- 231 Orion 15, England
- 266 Loop Den Haag Half-marathon, The Netherlands
- 279 Survival Run, Switzerland
- 290 Malta Marathon, Malta
- 298 Prague Half-marathon, Czech Republic
- 305 Presov Night Run, Slovakia
- 307 Lake Balaton 26, Hungary
- 312 Paphos Marathon, Cyprus

APRIL
- 157 Ballyliffin Coastal Challenge, Ireland
- 158 Connemarathon, Ireland
- 163 Valentia Island Half-marathon, Ireland
- 168 Isle of Man Easter Festival, Isle of Man
- 180 Coastal Trail Series, Wales
- 201 Manchester Marathon, England
- 203 Mersey Tunnel 10K, England
- 210 Shakespeare Marathon, England
- 226 London Marathon, England
- 254 Paris Marathon, France
- 267 Rotterdam Marathon, The Netherlands
- 272 Airport Night Run, Germany
- 273 Kreissparkassen Trail, Germany
- 289 Lema Trail, Switzerland
- 299 Brno Half-marathon, Czech Republic

MAY
- 165 Cork City Marathon, Ireland
- 170 Tiree, Scotland
- 171 Cape Wrath Ultra, Scotland
- 193 Grasmere Gallop, England
- 195 Keswick Mountain Festival, England
- 198 Mad Dog 10K, England
- 200 Great Manchester 10K, England
- 202 Run for the 96, England
- 224 RunFestRun, England
- 236 Arctic Triple Lofoten Trail, Norway
- 239 Sundsvall Trail Races, Sweden
- 240 Göteborgsvarvet Half-marathon, Sweden
- 246 Helsinki City Running Day, Finland
- 262 National Centre for Altitude Training, France
- 263 Brussels 20K, Belgium
- 264 Bütgenbach Half-marathon, Belgium
- 278 Grand Prix of Bern, Switzerland
- 293 Jesolo Moonlight Half-marathon, Italy
- 311 Skiathos 10K Trail Run, Greece
- 316 Warsaw Half-marathon, Poland
- 322 Moscow Half-marathon, Russia

JUNE
- 185 Rabbit Run, Wales
- 190 Hutton Roof Fell Race, England
- 204 Round Sheffield Run, England
- 213 Jurassic Coast Challenge, England
- 232 Spitsbergen Marathon, Norway
- 233 Midnight Sun Marathon, Norway
- 237 Palace Park, Norway
- 243 Cross Lapland Marathon/Half-marathon, Finland
- 262 National Centre for Altitude Training, France
- 302 Bled Night Run, Slovenia
- 313 Vitosha 100K, Bulgaria

JULY
- 155 Laugavegur Ultramarathon, Iceland
- 178 Snowdonia Race, Wales
- 182 Love Trails, Wales
- 192 Lakeland 50 or 100, England
- 207 Heckington 10, England
- 225 Down Tow Up Flow Half-marathon, England
- 241 Kustmaran and Kristianopel Runt, Sweden
- 242 NUTS Ylläs Pallas, Finland
- 253 Skyrace Comapedrosa, Andorra
- 274 Bavaria Run, Germany
- 276 Tour du Lac de Joux, Switzerland
- 284 Eiger Ultra Trail, Switzerland
- 288 Swissalpine Race Weekend, Switzerland
- 291 Ortler Sky Trails, Italy
- 292 Brixen Dolomiten Marathon, Italy
- 294 Ecomaratona del Ventasso, Italy
- 300 Silvrettarun 3000, Austria
- 301 Ossiacher See Nachthalbmarathon, Austria

AUGUST
- 156 Extreme North, Ireland
- 179 Race the Train, Wales
- 194 Hawkshead 16K, England
- 223 Beat the Boat, England
- 228 Midnight 2 Midnight, England
- 235 Tromsø Mountain Challenge, Norway
- 259 Ultra-Trail du Mont-Blanc, France/Italy/Switzerland
- 285 Sierre-Zinal, Switzerland
- 319 Kuldiga Half-marathon, Latvia

SEPTEMBER
- 172 Ring of Steall Skyrace, Scotland
- 188 Great North Run, England
- 227 London Color Run, England
- 244 Nakukymppi, Finland
- 255 Paris to Versailles 16 km, France
- 256 Marathon du Medoc, France
- 265 Amsterdam Marathon, The Netherlands
- 269 Serengeti Park Run, Germany
- 270 Berlin Marathon, Germany
- 280 Ultra Tour Du Monte Rosa, Switzerland/Italy
- 283 Jungfrau Marathon, Switzerland
- 304 Bratislava Half-marathon, Slovakia
- 306 Budapest Half-marathon, Hungary
- 317 Beskidy Ultra, Poland

OCTOBER
- 159 Dublin Marathon, Ireland
- 164 Great Limerick Run, Ireland
- 217 Great South 10-mile, England
- 219 Ridgeway Run, England
- 249 Bilbao Night Marathon, Spain
- 250 Ultra Pirineu, Spain
- 252 World's Fastest Marathon, Spain
- 261 Grand Trail des Templiers, France
- 271 The Great 10K, Germany
- 286 Spartacus Run, Switzerland
- 296 Roma By Night, Italy
- 308 Brasov Half-marathon, Romania
- 309 Tirana Half-marathon, Albania

NOVEMBER
- 169 OMM, UK
- 191 Brampton to Carlisle 10, England
- 197 Blackpool 10, England
- 209 Silverstone Half-marathon, England
- 257 Lyon Urban, France
- 310 Athens Classic Marathon, Greece

DECEMBER
- 258 La SaintéLyon, France
- 277 Christmas Midnight Run, Switzerland
- 281 Silvesterlauf, Switzerland
- 295 Pisa Marathon, Italy
- 318 Vilnius Christmas Runs, Lithuania

ALL YEAR ROUND
- 153 Grímsey Island, Iceland (spring, summer, autumn)
- 154 Ölfusá River, Iceland (spring, summer, autumn)
- 160 Phoenix Park Circular, Ireland
- 162 Cliffs of Moher, Ireland
- 166 Giant's Causeway, Northern Ireland
- 173 South Loch Ness Trail, Scotland
- 174 West Highland Way, Scotland (spring, summer)
- 176 Water of Leith Walkway, Scotland
- 177 Arthur's Seat, Scotland
- 183 The Black Mountains, Wales
- 184 Taff Trail, Wales
- 187 Gilsland Chase, England
- 189 Durham Heritage Coast Trail, England
- 196 Pikes Peak, England
- 199 Rivington Pike, England
- 206 The Wrekin, England
- 208 Burghley House, England
- 212 South West Coastal Path, England
- 214 Teignmouth Seafront, England
- 215 Exmoor Fells, England
- 216 Jamaica Inn, England
- 220 Oxford River Running, England
- 221 Oxford University's Iffley Road Track, England
- 229 Greenwich Foot Tunnel & Park, England
- 230 Brighton Beach, England
- 238 Parks and Lakes, Denmark
- 245 Myrskylä, Finland (spring, summer, autumn)
- 247 Peniche, Portugal
- 248 The Rock, Gibraltar
- 251 Seville, Spain
- 260 Chamonix, France (summer)
- 268 Bambésch Forest, Luxembourg
- 275 Hochstaufen/Bad Reichenhall, Germany
- 282 Bisse du Torrent Neuf, Switzerland
- 297 Sentiero degli Dei, Italy
- 303 Lokrum Island, Croatia
- 314 Istanbul, Turkey
- 315 Pirita Path, Estonia
- 320 Velodorozhka, Belarus

154 | Gullfoss Falls are the highlight of a run along the Ölfusá River

153
GRÍMSEY ISLAND
AKUREYRI, ICELAND
Running route/Coastal
Spring, Summer, Autumn/10 km

This tiny island off the north coast of Iceland is the only part of the country that lies, partially, within the Arctic Circle. So for a run that takes you into the Arctic – and back out again – there is no better route than the 10-km (6.1-mile) path that circumnavigates the island. The path overlooks rugged cliffs and basalt columns, and is a mix of dirt tracks and trails. Local wildlife includes puffins and sheep, and there is a stone monument that marks the line of the Arctic Circle.

154
ÖLFUSÁ RIVER
REYKJAVÍK, ICELAND
Running route/Trail
Spring, Summer, Autumn/Various

Iceland is a country that is different from almost any other, with glaciers, geysers, mountains and waterfalls aplenty. A short drive from Reykjavík, the capital city, is the spectacular Gullfoss Falls, but before you arrive, find a spot to stop the car and run along the path adjacent to the Ölfusá River to reach the falls themselves. Expect to see millions of tonnes of water cascading over the falls, with accompanying mist, noise and spray. The track descends down to the falls for a closer view of the torrent.

155 | Volcanic landscape dominates the Laugavegur Ultramarathon

155
LAUGAVEGUR ULTRAMARATHON
ICELAND
Ultra/Trail
July/55 km

If you're an experienced runner who fancies heading out into the southern highlands of Iceland, open to visitors for just a few weeks a year, then this 55-km (34-mile) ultra is for you. Remote, demanding, cold and wet (you'll have to cross plenty of rivers), this is an amazing adventure that few Icelanders will ever experience, let alone anyone else. It requires preparation, but the outstanding scenic beauty is well worth the effort. Don't forget your camera.

156
EXTREME NORTH
DONEGAL, IRELAND
Multiday adventure/Coastal
August/Various

This event is more than a race, it's an adventure. Held over four days in the summer, participants will get to know fellow competitors and enjoy a wonderful, fulfilling experience as they race four marathons or half-marathons on the Wild Atlantic Way together. The scenery is nothing short of spectacular, with the vast Atlantic Ocean to your right side most of the way. The four marathons are mostly run on country roads, but there are some trail and beach sections – and expect lots and lots of hills.

157

BALLYLIFFIN COASTAL CHALLENGE

DONEGAL, IRELAND

Coastal

March or April/11 & 16 km

Held over Easter in the beautiful county of Donegal, this 11- or 16-km (7- or 10-mile) race is popular among the locals and the odd international runner alike. The course starts in the small town of Ballyliffin, and winds through the scenic country roads to finish on a 3-km (2-mile) stretch of Pollan Beach. In the distance you will see Malin Head, one of the filming locations for *Star Wars* and the most northern point of Ireland. It can be windy and exposed in parts, all helping to make the race that little bit tougher. Look forward to a congratulatory Easter egg at the end!

158

CONNEMARATHON

CONNEMARA, IRELAND

Coastal

April/Various

Each year, thousands of runners take on western Ireland's Connemarathon in spring. Runners can choose from one of three distances – half-marathon, marathon and a 63.2-km (39.3-mile) ultra – with each race finishing at Maam Cross. Runners of all distances are treated to endless mountain views, sparkling lakes and peat-bog countryside.

159

DUBLIN MARATHON

IRELAND

Marathon/Urban

October/42 km

The atmosphere the Dublin Marathon brings to the city is huge – it's one of the iconic marathons, and thousands come to cheer on the runners making their way round the loop of the city. Some say it's the world's friendliest marathon, and the crowd's cheerful ambience just adds to the endorphin surge that runners experience as they cross the finish line. It's probably not a course for PBs as there is quite a bit of elevation, but that certainly keeps things interesting.

160

PHOENIX PARK CIRCULAR

DUBLIN, IRELAND

Running route/Park

All year round/5.8 km

Rolling and green. The paths are superb, but like anything in Dublin, this 5.8 km (3.6 miles) is all about the quiet calm the city (and its parks) provides. Home to many a fine race, including the Great Ireland Run, this is best experienced as part of a long, easy run where you can enjoy the deer and surprisingly exotic fauna.

161
SUGAR LOAF 10K
WICKLOW, IRELAND
Trail
January/10 km

When competitors who have finished this trail event describe it as 'the race you all love (to hate!)', you know it's something special. It's going to be wet, and it's almost certainly going to be windy, but nonetheless the lap around this spectacular mountain is also going to be memorable. There are plenty of tough climbs, more than the odd stretch of technical terrain, but there's also a downhill finish.

162
CLIFFS OF MOHER
COUNTY CLARE, IRELAND
Running route/Coastal
All year round/5 & 8 km

Set on the west coast of Ireland, the trail across the top of the cliffs is over 200 m (655 ft) above sea level, offering runners breathtaking views of rugged rock and the powerful Atlantic Ocean. Starting at the Cliffs' visitor centre, runners can chose either a 5-km (3-mile) run to Hags Head, or an 8-km (5-mile) run to Doolin, both of which provide views of the Aran Islands and Galway Bay.

162 | **Keeping to the path is important along the Cliffs of Moher**

164 | **The Great Limerick Run is popular with runners of all ages**

163

VALENTIA ISLAND HALF-MARATHON
IRELAND
Coastal
April/10 & 21 km

Located off the west coast of Ireland, Valentia Island was the location for the first transatlantic telegraph cable running from Newfoundland in 1858. Its rugged coastline, sandy beaches, undulating roads and pretty little fishing villages make it a perfect spot to run a half-marathon (or 10K). The island is used to tourism, and there aren't many other places in the world you'll get such a warm and friendly welcome.

164

GREAT LIMERICK RUN
IRELAND
Festival
October/Various

This is a popular event that aims to promote inclusiveness through its wide range of distances: marathon, half-marathon, 9.5 km (6 miles) and relay marathon. All routes pass through the medieval city of Limerick and its picturesque countryside and riverside locations. More than 15,000 people of all abilities take part. Families are encouraged to run together over the shorter distances, and the races are now recognised as one of the biggest festivals of running in Ireland.

165
CORK CITY MARATHON
IRELAND
Marathon/Relay
May/42 km

It's an 8.30 a.m. start for this race around the historic streets of Cork, which is largely flat but includes a nasty steep incline just after 29 km (18 miles), the point at which marathon runners start to feel the effects of fatigue, even without the presence of a hill. The unusual team relay option enables the marathon to be covered in five legs of differing distances, with runners able to run one leg each, or a maximum of two consecutive legs.

167 | Flat, fast running in the Armagh 5K

166
GIANT'S CAUSEWAY
BUSHMILLS, NORTHERN IRELAND
Running route/Coastal
All year round/Various

The causeway consists of 40,000 interlocking basalt columns, but the mythical story goes that giant Finn MacCool was challenged to a fight by the Scottish giant Benandonner. Finn accepted the challenge and built the causeway across the North Channel so that the two giants could meet. It's a wonderfully rolling run along the coastline that takes in the causeway, views of Scotland and a celebratory whiskey at nearby Old Bushmills Distillery.

167
ARMAGH 5K
ULSTER, NORTHERN IRELAND
Road/Park
February/5 km

This unassuming market town plays host to the fastest 5K in the world every February. With more than 140 runners cracking the 15-minute barrier, there's no arguing that when it comes to a high-quality field, this race is far superior than anything else more exotic locations might offer. Basically, it's five laps around a small town park known as The Mall – flat and fast.

168
ISLE OF MAN EASTER FESTIVAL
PORT ERIN, ISLE OF MAN

Road/Trail

March/April/Various

A mix of students and dedicated club runners make this a memorable long weekend. You'll run a 10K road race, the infamous and very tough Peel Hill race, and end it all with a quick 5K spin along Douglas Promenade. Traditionally a favourite with spring-break students, there is always plenty of beer involved, but there is also a serious side, with good prizes and fast times on offer.

169
OMM
SOMEWHERE IN THE NORTH, UK

Multiday adventure

November/Surprise distance

The OMM (Original Mountain Marathon) takes place every year somewhere in the North of Britain and involves teams of two taking two days to self-navigate over demanding winter countryside. Runners carry everything they need and camp out overnight. The route is not revealed until the week before, to make sure participants can't plan their journey beforehand.

170
TIREE
HEBRIDES, SCOTLAND

Multi-terrain

May/10 & 21 km

This popular 10K and half-marathon event is held on a remote Hebrides island renowned for its clear blue water, stunning landscape and sandy beaches. The races start and finish on the hard-packed sand of Sorobaidh beach, and in between there is a mix of trail and road that passes through picturesque villages. The course is mainly flat, with superb views, and the post-race dance party is known as the island's 'best dance of the year'.

171
CAPE WRATH ULTRA
HIGHLANDS, SCOTLAND

Multiday adventure

May/400 km

This is a 400-km (250-mile) eight-day epic through the Scottish Highlands, from Fort William to Cape Wrath at the most north-westerly tip of the UK. The event is run every year and sells out very quickly. It's a test of planning, training and, perhaps most of all, mental tenacity. Teamwork, camaraderie and an ability to smile in poor weather are all requirements.

It's a test of endurance for Cape Wrath runners

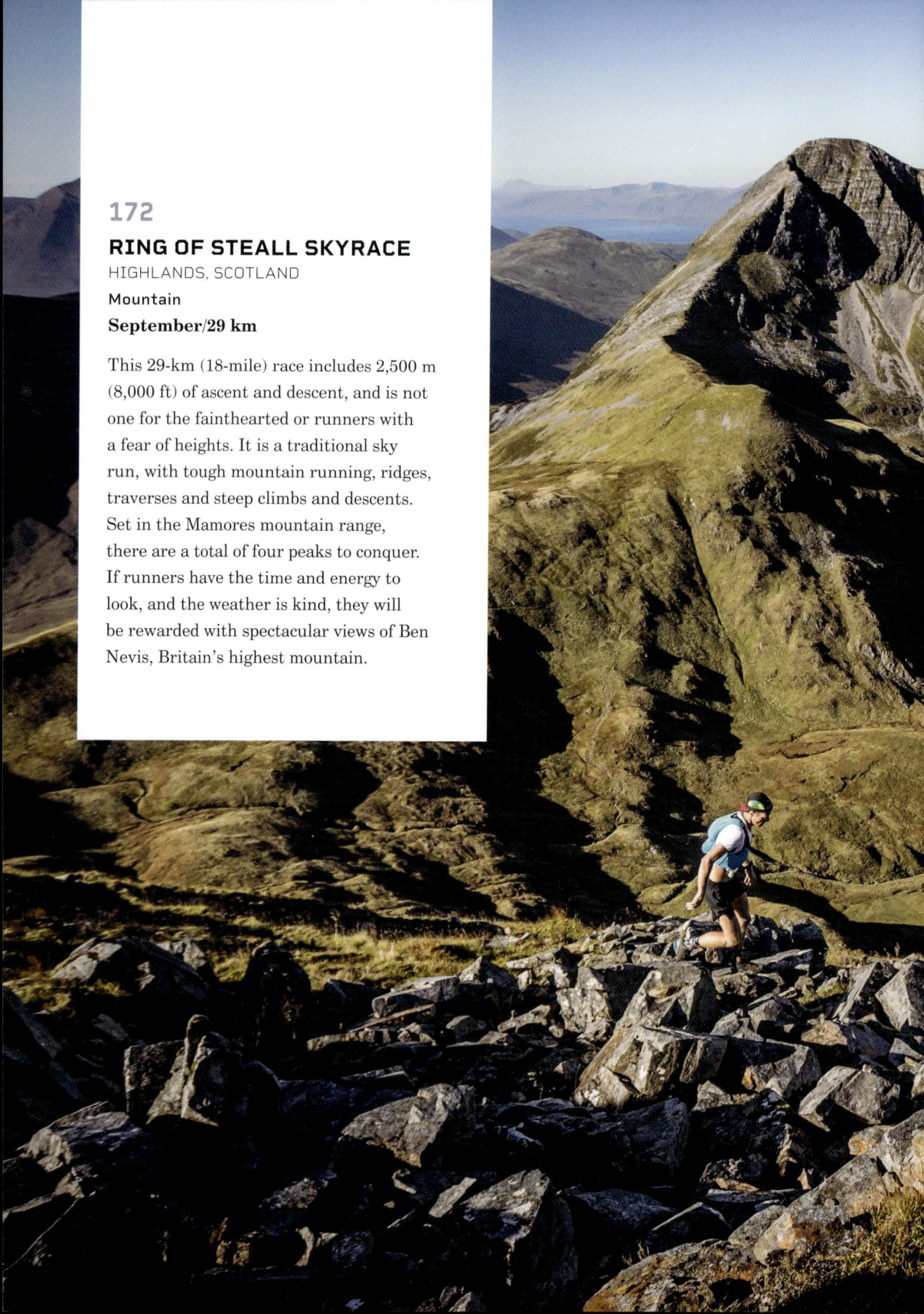

172

RING OF STEALL SKYRACE
HIGHLANDS, SCOTLAND

Mountain

September/29 km

This 29-km (18-mile) race includes 2,500 m (8,000 ft) of ascent and descent, and is not one for the fainthearted or runners with a fear of heights. It is a traditional sky run, with tough mountain running, ridges, traverses and steep climbs and descents. Set in the Mamores mountain range, there are a total of four peaks to conquer. If runners have the time and energy to look, and the weather is kind, they will be rewarded with spectacular views of Ben Nevis, Britain's highest mountain.

173 | **Monster spotting is part of the South Loch Ness Trail**

173
SOUTH LOCH NESS TRAIL
HIGHLANDS, SCOTLAND
Running route/Trail
All year round/58 km

Try spotting Nessie on this run, the mythical creature 'living' for years in the depths of this vast loch. The 58-km (36-mile) trail is a stunningly beautiful path through the Scottish Highlands running from Fort Augustus to the city of Inverness, and you can pick up the route at any point. The trail takes in some steep inclines in sections, but you are rewarded with spectacular scenery at the peaks. Arguably the best part of the trail is at Fair Haired Lad's Pass, with uninterrupted views over Loch Ness and beyond.

174
WEST HIGHLAND WAY
SCOTLAND
Running route/Multiday adventure
Spring, Summer/154 km

A stunningly beautiful and adventurous 154-km (96-mile) path takes ancient drover and coach routes through the mountains from Glasgow to Fort William. Runners can choose to run a section or can aim to complete the entire route, staying along the way in B&Bs or by camping wild. The best time to tackle the route is in the spring and summer months, but be aware the weather can still turn quickly. Keep an eye out for some amazing wildlife, including golden eagles, red deer and the occasional mountain hare.

174 | The stunning scenery of the West Highland Way

176
WATER OF LEITH WALKWAY
EDINBURGH, SCOTLAND

Multi-terrain
All year round/21 km

This 21-km (13-mile) footpath is popular with runners and cyclists, crossing the Scottish capital along the side of the River Leith, with a short stretch that heads into the city centre while running beside the Union Canal, before reaching the river for a second time. A splendid mix of trail, track and urban running, this route is one to do at any time of the year, starting and finishing in Leith.

175
FALKIRK EPIC TRAIL 10K
SCOTLAND

Trail/Park
January/10 km

This winter race really helps to put New Year resolutions in motion and work off those festive puddings. This fun but challenging event is held in the grounds of the fourteenth-century château-styled Callendar House, which includes both woodland and park trails, and a section of the Roman Antonine Wall, a UNESCO World Heritage site. All abilities are welcome, and everyone gets a medal.

177
ARTHUR'S SEAT
EDINBURGH, SCOTLAND

Running route
All year round/Various

This is all about the perfect mix where geology meets history, with a bit of running tradition thrown in to make it a must for all runners. In simple numbers it doesn't sound too taxing, as the climb is just 251 m (823 ft). But running up Arthur's Seat is about more than height: the rocks date back 341 million years, to when it was a volcano, while the view of the city from the summit is as impressive, with Edinburgh Castle looking magnificent. The venue has also played host to some amazing cross-country races, and the Edinburgh Marathon finishes at its base.

178

SNOWDONIA RACE
WALES

Trail/Mountain
July/15.5 km

A must-do for all serious mountain runners, the Snowdon Race is a classic but gruelling 15.5 km (9.6 miles) out and back from the centre of Llanberis, up the main Snowdon track, to the summit at 1,085 m (3,560 ft). The route follows a well-defined stony path, frequently running alongside the railway line, meaning runners have to take care around walkers and train tracks, especially in the second half, where an average gradient of 13.4 per cent makes for high-speed descents – and occasional spectacular falls. For those who get down safely, the 32 per cent gradient in places means that, as well as the satisfaction of running up the highest mountain in Wales, most will have stiff and sore legs for a few days after.

EUROPE 131

179 | **It's easy to run out of puff when racing a train**

179
RACE THE TRAIN
TYWYN, WALES
Trail/Novelty
August/22.5 km

There's a fair chance here of achieving the seemingly impossible task of beating the train. That's because you're taking on a steam train, and its speed is slow enough to allow elite runners to cover the 22.5 km (14 miles) quicker than it can. Plus, the train stops in various locations to take on water, allowing plenty more runners to claim glory. Be warned though, it's an off-road run that can be very muddy.

180
COASTAL TRAIL SERIES
PEMBROKESHIRE, WALES
Trail
April/Various

Set in the UK's only coastal National Park, the choice of 10K, half-marathon, marathon and 55-km (34-mile) ultra offers runners the chance to take part in one of the very best scenic trail runs in the UK. With fabulous wild headlands, views of sandy bays and the sea, as well as undulations that result in outstanding views, runners taking part in any of the four distances will experience nature at its wildest.

181 | **Sea, mountains and rainbows on the Worms Head 10K**

181
WORMS HEAD 10K
RHOSSILI, WALES

Trail/Coastal

January/10 km

Few races offer such amazing views of rugged, spectacular coastline and can claim to run next to one of the top ten beaches in the world. For the race, you'll stick to the trails, but below you are 6.5 km (4 miles) of superb beach that will entice you to return for another day, while Worms Head Island out to sea provides a spectacular backdrop.

182
LOVE TRAILS
GOWER PENINSULA, WALES

Festival/Trail

July/Various

With four marked runs, guided runs, inspirational talks, film screenings, fitness sessions, wild swimming and three nights of live music and DJ sets, this is a vibrant celebration of trail running. The festival has quickly become one of the summer destinations for runners keen to immerse themselves in their sport. It also hosts the World Beer Mile Relay Championships, billed as an 'unmissable spectacle'.

183

THE BLACK MOUNTAINS
BRECON BEACONS, WALES
Running route/Mountain
All year round/Various

The Black Mountains are a collection of hidden gems on the eastern edge of the Brecon Beacons, offering superb views of the stunning Welsh countryside. Keep an eye out for all manner of wildlife, including red kites, as you make your way up Table Mountain followed by Pen Twyn Glas. For anyone wanting to race, there are events from 14 to 50 km (8.6 to 31 miles) every June.

184
TAFF TRAIL
WALES
Running route/Trail
All year round/89 km

Run this route in either direction from the northern point of Brecon or the southern city of Cardiff. The 89-km (55-mile) route is popular among cyclists aiming to tackle it in one day, but walkers usually enjoy the route over a period of time, picking up where they left off. The trail passes through the stunning Brecon Beacons National Park, with outstanding views at the top of some seriously tough climbs. Luckily, there are plenty of picturesque villages with warm, welcoming tea rooms and pubs to help runners refuel along the way.

185
RABBIT RUN
BRIDGEND, WALES
Trail/Coastal
June/12 km

In the not so distant past, Steve Ovett, an icon of middle-distance running, used the Big Dipper sand dune as part of his training regime on Merthyr Mawr beach. Of course, the beach is open to all any time of year, so you too can experience the pain that dune can inflict, or, if you prefer, enter the Rabbit Run, a 12-km (7.5-mile) trail race that goes down the Big Dipper as part of its course. There is also a Bunny Run and Toddler Dash for kids to enjoy.

186
THE NATIONAL
VARIOUS, UK
Trail
February/11 km

To compete in the national championships is always special, and this one, with its fabulous history, especially so. Dating back to 1876, it is traditionally the highlight of the English cross-country season, and still sees thousands tackle the 11 muddy kilometres (7 miles) it invariably provides. It's not about being the champion, this is all about taking part, and every club member in Britain proudly recalls their National. Join a club and you're eligible to participate. Simple.

187
GILSLAND CHASE
NORTHUMBERLAND, ENGLAND
Running route/Trail
All year round/Various

The Northumberland countryside makes for perfect fell running. Club runners use it as a base for winter training, staying in the historic Gilsland Hall Hotel. Back in the 1800s the area was popular for Victorians seeking health benefits by drinking and bathing in the natural spa water. Today the health benefits are earned by jumping through muddy puddles, racing down gorges and sprinting up steep hillsides. Take any path out from the Gilsland Hotel and you won't be disappointed.

188

GREAT NORTH RUN
NEWCASTLE, ENGLAND

Road/Urban

September/21 km

If you love big events, this one is for you. The GNR is the largest half-marathon in the world, and almost 60,000 competitors enter it every year. Held in Newcastle at the start of autumn, conditions are usually good, and competitive runners either see it as an end to their summer season or the start of their winter one. Anybody can take part, but entry is by ballot system with deadlines to be met, so get in early to not miss out.

189

DURHAM HERITAGE COAST TRAIL

SEAHAM TO CRIMDON, ENGLAND

Running route/Coastal

All year round/17.5–21 km

A 17.5-km (11-mile) section of the England Coast Path National Trail, this walking route from Seaham to Crimdon is practical as well as spectacular, with permanent markers for a half-marathon that you can run at any time, at no cost. Following the decline of mining in the area, you can see for yourself the return to nature. Look out to sea and you might spot a seal or even a basking shark.

190

HUTTON ROOF FELL RACE

CUMBRIA, ENGLAND

Mountain/Trail

June/11 km

Fell running in Britain sums up what running is all about. The short but demanding trail across the top of Hutton Roof, a local landmark fell, is just part of the day. As for the rest of the run, it's about 11 km (7 miles), and compared to other fell races, very beginner friendly – you'll only have to walk a little! The race starts and finishes in a country fair with local livestock on show and stalls selling traditional homemade cake and biscuits.

191

BRAMPTON TO CARLISLE 10

CUMBRIA, ENGLAND

Road

November/16 km

A race with a wonderful history, this is the oldest 10-mile (16-km) road race in the UK. With winners including mile world record holder Steve Cram and Boston Marathon winner Ron Hill, it has attracted many big names over the half century and more that it has been in existence. The race is also quick, with the course record for men standing at 45:50; the women close behind with 51:50.

192

LAKELAND 50 OR 100

LAKE DISTRICT, ENGLAND

Ultra/Trail

July/80 & 160 km

This ultra is held in beautiful national parkland and crosses many of the Lakeland fells. Only the toughest runners try the challenging 160-km (100-mile) trail and manage to complete it as the race winds through jagged, rough terrain in darkness through night and, possibly, sun during the day. Much of the race is off the beaten track, and is superbly organised, with fully stocked checkpoints and strict cut-off points to ensure safety.

192 | Tackling the fells and valleys of England's Lake District

195 | **Festivals bring extra fun to races**

193
GRASMERE GALLOP
LAKE DISTRICT, ENGLAND
Trail
May/Various

Starting at Grasmere Sports Ground in the heart of the Lake District, it is no surprise that these 5.7, 10 and 17 km (3.5, 6.2 and 10.5 miles) are all hilly races. Taking in many local landmarks that include Loughrigg Fell and Loughrigg Tarn, runners will return to the village of Grasmere by running alongside Grasmere Lake and Rydal Water, areas synonymous with the famous poet William Wordsworth.

194
HAWKSHEAD 16K
LAKE DISTRICT, ENGLAND
Trail
August/16 km

When a hill is named 'the coffin trail', that probably should be the clue you need to know this 16 km (10 miles) will be a tough run. However, getting to the hill is such an amazingly scenic affair – through Coniston Hills, the Langdales and most of the Lakeland fells, not to mention the rural country pubs and a lakeside run along the shores of Lake Windermere – you tend to forget how hard it might be. The hill itself is about 1.6 km (1 mile) long, so be ready. The reward is that the race finishes in the wonderfully picturesque village of Hawkshead.

196 | Run to the top of England on Scafell Pike

195
KESWICK MOUNTAIN FESTIVAL
LAKE DISTRICT, ENGLAND
Festival/Mountain
May/Various

There are several races on offer at the Keswick Mountain Festival, which caters to all outdoor-sports enthusiasts. Choose from a nice 5K that takes in a few of the surrounding hills, a challenging 10K or a much longer 50K, which takes you around the back of Buttermere, Crummock Water and Newlands Valley, making it one of the most scenic races in the Lake District – which says a lot.

196
PIKES PEAK
LAKE DISTRICT, ENGLAND
Running route/Mountain
All year round/Various

Scafell Pike, England's highest mountain, sits proud at 978 m (3,209 ft) high. There are optional routes to scale the mountain, ranging in difficulty and length. The most popular route starts from Wasdale and follows the path to the summit. Other routes from Langdale are longer and more challenging. You can run these paths any time of year, but be careful, as it can get misty at the summit. Whichever route you take, be sure to reward yourself at one of the many watering holes with some quality pub grub and a pint at the bottom.

197
BLACKPOOL 10
LANCASHIRE, ENGLAND
Road/Coastal
November/16 km

The traditional seaside town of Blackpool features the Tower and its world-famous ballroom, the seafront and its amusements, trams, donkeys and the traditional hotels so enjoyed by millions for more than a century. The superquick promenade 16 km (10 miles) offers all of the above and more. Expect a great time, even though there are one or two sharp climbs to test out, and seek out a stick of Blackpool rock candy at the end for a sugar fix.

197 | **Runners flock to the seaside for this 10-miler**

198
MAD DOG 10K
SOUTHPORT, ENGLAND
Coastal/Novelty
May/10 km

Held along the shoreline in Southport, Lancashire, this popular event normally attracts around 3,500 runners – including chariot racers, fancy-dress runners and children – who are encouraged by large crowds and on-course entertainment, with live bands at each kilometre. A race for both serious athletes and fun-runners, it has often been voted 'Best 10K in the UK'.

199
RIVINGTON PIKE
LANCASHIRE, ENGLAND
Running route/Trail
All year round/Various

Situated in the west Pennines, Rivington Pike is a popular spot for those escaping the surrounding cities for a rewarding day out. For this reason, it is advised to go early in the morning if going on a weekend or during the holidays. There are various routes to the summit, and several fell races are held here throughout the year. Pick a clear day for extra-special views reaching as far as the city of Manchester to the south and the Irish Sea to the west.

200
GREAT MANCHESTER 10K
ENGLAND
Road/Urban
May/10 km

The biggest 10K in Europe makes way for the elite international athlete, experienced club runner and enthusiastic fun-runner. The atmosphere in this northern England city is incredible, as crowds, bands, dancers and DJs line the course to cheer on participants through the streets. The race starts and finishes in the city centre, and takes a relatively flat course out to Manchester United's Old Trafford Football Stadium, past Salford Quays, before runners collect their well-deserved medal.

201
MANCHESTER MARATHON
ENGLAND
Road/Urban
April/42 km

If you want a fast marathon in the UK, this is the one to aim for. While Manchester is surrounded by hills, the city itself is relatively flat and makes for a great PB course. It is also one of the largest marathons in the UK, so the atmosphere on the course is terrific, and you can be sure the hardy Mancunians will line the streets whatever the weather. Football fans may love or hate the fact that Old Trafford Stadium is the backdrop for the start and finish.

203 | **No need for the ferry when you can run under the Mersey**

202
RUN FOR THE 96
LIVERPOOL, ENGLAND
Road/Urban
May/5 km

Held to honour the 96 supporters who were killed while watching Liverpool Football Club's FA Cup semifinal at Hillsborough Football Stadium in 1989, this 5K brings together football supporters from all over the world. Held in Stanley Park, next to Liverpool's Anfield Stadium, there is also a virtual option for runners that cannot make it to the event, who can still run at the same time and upload their time and evidence of completing the distance to claim the event medal.

203
MERSEY TUNNEL 10K
LIVERPOOL, ENGLAND
Road/Urban
April/10 km

This unique race starts in the centre of Liverpool and finishes on the Wirral Peninsula. In between is the River Mersey, which runners cross by descending gently into the Wallasey Tunnel, followed by 2.5 km (1.5 miles) underground, before slowly ascending onto the Wirral. The race ends close to the Mersey Ferry terminal, making it easy for runners to take a ferry across the Mersey, back to the start.

205 | Tough but fun at Mr Mouse's Tough Guy

204
ROUND SHEFFIELD RUN
YORKSHIRE, ENGLAND
Urban/Novelty
June/24.5 km

This is a unique event where the 24.5-km (15-mile) route is broken down into eleven individually timed stages that make up 20 km (12.5 miles) of the total distance. Between stages the competitors are free to relax and walk or jog to the next stage. After the race is over, runners receive their results for each stage, as well as a combined overall result, so there's plenty of opportunity for competition, albeit friendly.

205
TOUGH GUY
WOLVERHAMPTON, ENGLAND
Obstacle course race
February/13+ km

Held on Mr Mouse's farm, the aptly named and totally original Tough Guy will test and strain your every sinew. Barbarians, Spartans and masochists unite to put themselves through veritable hell over 8 'country' miles (13+ km) – expect kilts, mud, ice-cold water, electric shocks, barbed wire, pain, laughter, tears but, above all, comradeship and a massive sense of achievement (if you manage to dodge the hypothermia).

206 | The Wrekin dominates the Shropshire skyline

206
THE WREKIN
SHROPSHIRE, ENGLAND
Running route/Trail
All year round/6.4 km

This 6.4-km (4-mile) run is best completed on an out-and-back basis, starting from the parking lot at the base of the Wrekin, near Telford. With volcanic origins, the Wrekin is a prominent feature and can be seen from miles around, rising to a height of 407 m (1,350 ft). From the car park, simply follow the clearly marked but occasionally very steep trail to the summit, taking in the views of Shropshire, the Welsh Borders and the West Midlands on the way, before following the same route back down.

207
HECKINGTON 10
LINCOLNSHIRE, ENGLAND
Road
July/16 km

The fact this race sells out more or less instantly should be a clue to just how enjoyable it is. It's over the classic distance of 10 miles (16 km), but what really makes it stand out is the finish – right in the middle of a country show. Traditional in every way, there's even grass-track cycling to watch after you've finished, not to mention a wander through the show, devoted to displaying the latest tractor machinery and farming equipment.

209 | Runners rev up for the Silverstone Half-marathon

208
BURGHLEY HOUSE
LINCOLNSHIRE, ENGLAND

Running route/Park

All year round/Various

If you fancy following in the steps of Lord Burghley in the movie *Chariots of Fire*, then you have to run around this park. Rolling, magnificent scenery and a wonderful Elizabethan prodigy house, built and still lived in by the Cecil family, provides the backdrop, while the mental image of Lord Burghley hurdling on the pristine lawns as he prepared to compete in the 1924 Olympic 400 m hurdles is all the inspiration you'll need.

209
SILVERSTONE HALF-MARATHON
NORTHAMPTONSHIRE, ENGLAND

Track

November/21 km

Zooming around this motor-racing circuit is not just for Formula 1 drivers, as every November the famous track plays host to a fantastic half-marathon. You too can corner at speed – sometimes in excess of 19 km/h (12 mph) – and you can also take the chequered flag, having stormed along the Stowe Circuit and raced up Copse Runway. It may look flat on TV, but there are some surprisingly tough inclines that might slow your speed a little.

210 | **In sooth, 'tis a long way around the Shakespeare Marathon**

210
SHAKESPEARE MARATHON
STRATFORD-UPON-AVON, ENGLAND
Marathon/Road
April/21 & 42 km

One lap for the half-marathon, two for the marathon, enables runners to experience the historic town of Stratford-upon-Avon, home to one of the world's greatest ever playwrights. Both races start in the town centre, before heading towards the town's outskirts, with much of the course held on the Greenway, a flat, firm, traffic-free trail that follows the route of a former railway line.

211
CAMBRIDGE HALF-MARATHON
ENGLAND
Road
March/21 km

The first few kilometres of this popular half-marathon will explain why this event sells out more or less within a week. You'll pass though King's and Jesus colleges, savouring their incredible architecture, before you head out onto a superfast out-and-back course. Experience incredible culture as you're treated to a possible PB, and afterwards, why not take a punt on the River Cam?

SOUTH WEST COASTAL PATH
ENGLAND
Running route/Coastal
All year round/1,014 km

This undulating route, which has the Atlantic Ocean as its backdrop, is one for geologists and lovers of ancient history. It's a mighty 1,014 km (630 miles) long, and you can run along the coastline of Exmoor, Devon, Cornwall and Dorset. Of course, you don't have to run it all in one go – although some do – as any section will provide a fascinating glimpse into life in ancient Britain, with Bronze and Iron Age burial features as well as rock formations that are 185 million years old.

213

JURASSIC COAST CHALLENGE

WEYMOUTH, ENGLAND

Trail/Coastal

June/Various

The spectacular Jurassic Coast is a UNESCO World Heritage site, with plenty of undulations and incredible scenery along England's south coast. Starting in Poole Harbour, runners have a choice of 100 km (62 miles), 50 km (31 miles) and 25 km (15 miles), and can even choose to complete the ultra over two days as a 'daylight only' option, with an overnight camp. The routes pass sites such as Lulworth Cove, Chesil Beach and Portland Bill, with fantastic views across the English Channel.

215 | **Runners and ponies roam the fells of Exmoor**

214

TEIGNMOUTH SEAFRONT
DEVON, ENGLAND
Running route/Coastal
All year round/6.4 km

Starting at Teignmouth's Lower Point car park, opposite the Ness cliffs on the other side of the Teign Estuary, runners keep the sea to their right and follow the seafront past the pier until the railway line merges from the left. As the beach narrows, you can run alongside one of the most spectacular sections of railway in the UK, with trains emerging or disappearing into the tunnel ahead as they travel to and from London and the West Country. When you reach the end of the path by the entrance to the railway tunnel, simply turn round and run the 3 km (2 miles) back to the car park.

215

EXMOOR FELLS
ENGLAND
Running route/Trail
All year round/Various

Exmoor National Park is trail running at its best. It's an absolute paradise for the endurance runner, with extensive, different trails to choose from, all with a backdrop of breathtaking scenery across hilly moorland. Unsurprisingly, there are many running events held here, but to really feel like you are running in the wilderness, head out at dawn, any time of the year, and enjoy it all to yourself.

217 | **Getting motivated for the Great South**

216

JAMAICA INN
CORNWALL, ENGLAND
Running route/Trail
All year round/8 km

Readers of classic literature who like a testing hill or two will be drawn to the inn featured by Daphne Du Maurier in her 1936 novel about rum smuggling in the 1820s (also an Alfred Hitchcock film). The inn itself is popular, but runners will appreciate the beauty of Exmoor. Head across the road and up the famous Brown Willy tor, survey the vast expanse of the moors, and return – an easy but rewarding 8 km (5 miles).

217

GREAT SOUTH 10-MILE
PORTSMOUTH, ENGLAND
Road/Coastal
October/16 km

One of the fastest 10-mile (16-km) races in Europe, the highlight (not including crossing the finishing line in an amazing time) has to be passing HMS *Victory*, the flagship from which Lord Nelson led the British navy to victory over the Spanish at the Battle of Trafalgar in 1805. This course is flat and, as long as the wind isn't too keen off the sea, very fast. Full of history, Portsmouth is a typical British seaside town.

218
PORTSMOUTH COASTAL HALF-MARATHON
HAMPSHIRE, ENGLAND

Multi-terrain/Coastal

February/21 km

The English beach can be chilly in February, so what better way to keep warm than to keep running, for 21 km (13.1 miles), to be exact. This half-marathon incorporates beach, grass, road, mud and trail to keep the route interesting. Add to that the beautiful views of the sea and the Isle of Wight, and you certainly won't get bored. The event is well organised and inclusive of all abilities.

220 | Go with the flow and follow the water in Oxford

219
RIDGEWAY RUN
TRING, ENGLAND

Trail

October/14 km

This (approximately) 14-km (9-mile) race starts on a lane just outside the town, before quickly crossing farmland to enter the historic Ashridge Forest. Runners climb steadily up to the Ashridge Monument, and then run on a trail through the forest to emerge into glorious countryside overlooking the Vale of Aylesbury. After a sharp climb up Pitstone Hill, it's time to descend back to the finish in Tring.

220
OXFORD RIVER RUNNING
OXFORDSHIRE, ENGLAND

Running route

All year round/Various

Oxford conjures up images of a picturesque, inspiring city full of historic university buildings and cosy pubs on a riverside setting. In addition to cycling, rowing and traditional punting, it's also the perfect place to head out for a run. Start at Folly Bridge and run towards Port Meadow, a beautiful section of countryside just minutes from the city. There are many excellent routes along the River Thames and its tributaries, but other good spots include the Oxford University Parks, the city centre and Christ Church Meadow.

221 | **Running history beckons at Iffley Road**

221
OXFORD UNIVERSITY'S IFFLEY ROAD TRACK
ENGLAND
Running route/Track
All year round/Various

On a breezy day in May 1954, Roger Bannister ran four laps of the track at Iffley Road in less than four minutes – securing him running immortality. The cinders he ran on are long gone, replaced by today's all-weather surfaces used by modern athletes, but the venue, complete with the church tower he looked up at to see if the flag blowing in the wind had dropped, is still there. Run a lap, run four, just to say you've been there.

222
CLIVEDEN CROSS COUNTRY 10K
BERKSHIRE, ENGLAND
Trail
January/10 km

A runner's winter in the UK has to include cross country. Often events are club only, but this exception is well worth a look thanks to the scenic but testing terrain in the beautiful grounds of Cliveden House. The course is rolling parkland, and you should make time to check out the house and its 350 years of history. Indeed, you could even stay for the weekend – the food and accommodation are superb.

223
BEAT THE BOAT
ETON, ENGLAND
Trail/Novelty
August/10 km

This is a 10K trail race on the footpath that runs alongside the River Thames. It's as it sounds: you decide the pace you're likely to run and race the boat closest to your precited time: 40, 50, 55, 60 or 70 minutes. Of course, friends and family can buy tickets for the boats so they can watch you in action, or maybe they'll prefer to visit Windsor Castle, which sits royally alongside the route.

224
RUNFESTRUN
WINDSOR GREAT PARK, ENGLAND
Festival/Multi-terrain
May/Various

This three-day event features eleven different runs throughout the festival weekend. It's here that the music world meets running head on, as each night of the festival sees headline acts take to the stage after thousands have spent the day racing, running and talking all things fitness related. Invented by radio celebrity Chris Evans, you'll have the chance to meet superstars from the running world, camp in a royal park and enjoy some superb food.

225
DOWN TOW UP FLOW HALF-MARATHON
WINDSOR, ENGLAND
Multi-terrain
July/21 km

Following the towpath of the River Thames, this is a scenic, flat multi-terrain half-marathon. The race takes its name from the fact that the route is reversed each year, alternating between starting in Windsor and finishing in Marlow ('up flow'), then starting in Marlow and finishing in Windsor ('down tow') the following year. With plenty of spectator points along the route, it is a popular family event.

226

LONDON MARATHON
ENGLAND

Road/Urban
April/42 km

If you're a marathon runner, you'll be wanting to tick this one off your bucket list. Part of the World Marathon Majors for elite athletes, the London Marathon has seen the world record broken on several occasions. It's also home to world records for many a fancy-dress runner. Thousands of Londoners and tourists from around the world line the streets to cheer on every participant. At mile 6 (9.7 km), the 150-year-old clipper *Cutty Sark* is the first major landmark on the route and a popular viewpoint for spectators. The race culminates with a thundering atmosphere on The Mall to finish outside Buckingham Palace.

227 | **The London Color Run is a run to dye for**

227
LONDON COLOR RUN
ENGLAND
Novelty
September/5 km

Dubbed 'the happiest 5K on the planet', this is certainly a run with a difference. Participants are handed colourful paint packs that they can use to throw at one another during the event. The race feels more like a celebration than a competitive event, so take your time to soak up the atmosphere – and the paint – while you navigate Crystal Palace as a rainbow of happy, healthy people. Top tip: don't wear your best running gear for this one!

228
MIDNIGHT 2 MIDNIGHT
LONDON, ENGLAND
Night/Novelty
August/Various

This epic 24-hour running event features a series of 5–10K runs that set off on the hour every hour from a specified basecamp in East London. With stretching sessions, yoga classes, refreshments and fun in between, runners pay for their ticket and then choose how many of the runs they want to take part in. A non-competitive and inclusive event, all proceeds go towards environmental causes, so it's a win–win.

228 | Midnight 2 Midnight – an ideal race for insomniacs

229

GREENWICH FOOT TUNNEL & PARK
LONDON, ENGLAND
Running route/Park
All year round/Various

If you're in the relatively unspectacular surroundings of East London and the Docklands area, head for this tunnel, which is 371 m (1,217 ft) long. In just a few minutes you'll pass under the River Thames and find yourself at the gates of the 74-acre (30-hectare) Greenwich Park, home of the Royal Observatory, not to mention the line that is used to indicate Greenwich Mean Time. Oh, and there's the odd hill to enjoy. Get to the top and enjoy spectacular views.

230

BRIGHTON BEACH
EAST SUSSEX, ENGLAND
Running route/Coastal
All year round/Various

The pavements and paths that line the magnificent beach of Brighton provide a great environment for running, with the sea to one side and the historic and varied buildings of the seafront to the other. With hardly any inclines, but with a regular sea breeze, you can run as far as you want on paths that stretch from Rottingdean in the east to Shoreham-by-Sea in the west.

232 | **Beware of polar bears in the Spitsbergen Marathon!**

231
ORION 15
ESSEX, ENGLAND
Trail/Forest
March/24 km

Hilly, muddy and boasting a history that dates back more than 60 years, this testing 24-km (15-mile) run through the magnificent Epping Forest always appears on quite a few bucket lists. Things have advanced slightly since finishers washed the mud off in tin baths, but not much! This is very much a traditional club-type event that is open to all. Be warned though: if you think Essex is flat, you'll discover it most definitely is not.

232
SPITSBERGEN MARATHON
NORWAY
Road/Snow
June/42 km

Running in Norway always has the ability to surprise and delight; after a kilometre you'll understand why there have been so many incredible Norwegian runners. The scenery makes you want to get out and be one with nature. Few marathons can conjure up that feeling, but if you want wilderness, in a controlled way, then this is the one for you. Complete with snow and reindeer, you'll fall in love with this race.

233
MIDNIGHT SUN MARATHON
TROMSØ, NORWAY
Night/Snow
June/42 km

The inspiration of the marathon distance and the mystical magic of the longest day are the perfect combination. The best place to experience both is in Tromsø, high up in the Arctic Circle, where more than 6,000 runners enjoy Norwegian hospitality and a stunningly scenic course. Be ready for snow-capped mountains and hours of sunlight.

235 | **The notorious 1,000 Sherpa Stairs**

234
POLAR NIGHT HALF-MARATHON
TROMSØ, NORWAY
Road/Night
January/21 km

The polar opposite to its summer cousin, the Midnight Sun Marathon, this half-marathon provides all you would expect from an Arctic winter. It's dark and cold, but what a great way to start the year. If the sun never sets in Tromsø in June, you can imagine it's going to be dark in January. Yet, fear not, this is a quick half-marathon that allows you to experience the Arctic in perfect safety.

235
TROMSØ MOUNTAIN CHALLENGE
TROMSØ, NORWAY
Trail/Mountain
August/Various

If trail running is your thing, this has to be on your list of must-run races. The weekend has something for everyone, from a super-tough 50-km (31-miles) ultra to an easier view-friendly 25 km (15.5 miles) complete with serene mountain lakes. How tough? To get you in the mood, kick off with the uphill race that takes you up 1,000 'Sherpa Stairs', built by Sherpas from Nepal.

236

ARCTIC TRIPLE LOFOTEN TRAIL

LOFOTEN ISLANDS, NORWAY
Trail/Ultra
May/80 & 160 km

Runners are faced with three choices of distance: 80 or 160 km (50 or 100 miles) or a 160-km (100-mile) relay, all of which are held in the stunning setting of the Lofoten Island archipelago inside the Arctic Circle. The picturesque setting results in runners experiencing a series of beaches, ridges, hills and cliffs, with all three races finishing in the stunning setting of Svolvær Harbour.

238 | **Lake reflection in Østre Anlæg public park**

237
PALACE PARK
OSLO, NORWAY
Running route/Park
June/Various

For some, this might seem a bit standard. A nice park in Oslo. Nice but ordinary. However, it's all about the timing. Run it in June when the Bislett Games are taking place and you could well meet a world record holder, Olympic champion or an international superstar, as the greats always run a lap or two the day after competing in the Diamond League.

238
PARKS AND LAKES
COPENHAGEN, DENMARK
Running route/Park
All year round/7 km

This 7-km (4-mile) parks run starts in Østre Anlæg. By following the perimeter paths through some of Copenhagen's most picturesque parks, runners have the chance to exercise in a mainly traffic-free area that passes through lakes, parkland, ancient streets and alongside the modern Danish National Stadium.

239
SUNDSVALL TRAIL RACES
SWEDEN
Trail/Coastal
May/3–35 km

Swedish trail races are all about one thing: the incredible scenery. Nolbykullen, a mountain located right at the outlet of the river Ljungan in the Bothnian Sea, provides the backdrop as you make your way along the riverside route for any one of four distances from 3–35 km (2–22 miles). Expect rocky ascents that require some concentration, but above all, expect cool, fresh Scandinavian air, pristine forests and crystal-clear water (it's cold!) to make this a weekend to remember.

240

GÖTEBORGSVARVET HALF-MARATHON
GOTHENBURG, SWEDEN
Urban
May/21 km

This Swedish event has one claim to fame – and it is a big one at that – as with an enormous total of 62,000 entrants it is quite simply the biggest running event in the world. Not an event for those who prefer to run alone, then, the race starts outside and finishes inside the athletics arena, and in between it follows the banks of the Göta älv River.

241

KUSTMARAN AND KRISTIANOPEL RUNT
SWEDEN
Road/Coastal
July/Various

This event offers a choice of a marathon, half-marathon, 10K or 5K, all of which run along the scenic coastal road between the towns of Kristianopel and Torhamn in the south-west corner of Sweden. All on roads that are fast and flat, the races offer a chance for fast times – as long as the weather is kind and the wind is blowing in the right direction.

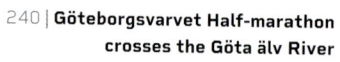

240 | **Göteborgsvarvet Half-marathon crosses the Göta älv River**

242
NUTS YLLÄS PALLAS
LAPLAND, FINLAND
Trail
July/Various

Despite the midnight start for one of the races, you'll need sunglasses here, as truly the sun never sets in Lapland in the summer. Expect long rolling hills, the odd sharp climb, amazing trails that are superbly marked and, of course, plenty of reindeer wandering freely. There are four distances to choose from, including 58 km (36 miles), 107 km (66.5 miles) with a midnight start time, 160 km (99.5 miles) and the popular 37 km (23 miles).

243
CROSS LAPLAND MARATHON/ HALF-MARATHON
TERVOLA, FINLAND
Road
June/21 or 42 km

The marathon and half-marathon are held on alternate years, so check which event is taking place if you are considering entering: years ending in an odd number host the full marathon; even-number years host the half-marathon. The routes are alongside the Kemijoki River, starting from the town of Tervola, and the organisers boast of abundant, varied scenery.

242 | **NUTS Ylläs Pallas runners can expect to spot reindeer**

EUROPE 169

244
NAKUKYMPPI
FINLAND
Novelty/Trail
September/10 km

In the pristine forests of Finland, participants of this 10K race can run, walk or Nordic walk at their own pace – naked. Equipped with only shoes, socks and hats (women can wear a little something up top, although most don't), the 150 or so nudes can enjoy a welcoming, warming sauna at the finish line.

245
MYRSKYLÄ
FINLAND
Running route/Trail
Spring, Summer, Autumn/Various

Distance-running legend Lasse Virén, the Flying Finn, used this forest in a sleepy village outside of Helsinki when he was preparing to win four gold medals over 5,000 m and 10,000 m at the 1972 and 1976 Olympic Games. It's wonderfully peaceful as you make your way along the pristine forest paths that roll through the Finnish countryside, imagining world records and Olympic glory.

246
HELSINKI CITY RUNNING DAY
FINLAND
Festival/Novelty
May/Various

More than 15,000 runners take part in this event, which combines six running events (including the 1K mini-marathon, marathon relay and a combination of the full and half-marathons) in one day, the odd dedicated athlete completing the full and half-marathons. For running fans, this is all about one thing: the Olympic Stadium, where, in 1952, the legendary Emil Zátopek won the 5,000 m, 10,000 m and marathon. You can feel the history as you run through the wonderful park that forms part of the route.

247
PENICHE
PORTUGAL

Running route/Coastal
All year round/8 km

Situated on Portugal's west coast, and exposed to the winds and waves of the Atlantic Ocean, the small town of Peniche is a great base for a fantastic coastal run. There is a runners' pavement that follows the beach, with an outdoor gym and obstacles to spice up your run should you wish to. It's possible to run for up to 8 km (5 miles), taking in views of the ocean, beach and crashing waves.

248
THE ROCK
GIBRALTAR

Running route/Coastal
All year round/Various

This small British territory on the southern coast of Spain is dominated by the Rock of Gibraltar, which rises 426 m (1,398 ft) from the sea. This makes a run to the top of the rock a must-do challenge for runners, but be warned that it can get hot, so set off early from the town and take plenty of water. There are various routes to the top that are well signposted, but all are steep and have steps in places. Watch out for the Barbary macaques, which have a habit of stealing anything edible from unwary visitors.

249
BILBAO NIGHT MARATHON
SPAIN

Road/Night
October/42 km

Fans of this night race in Spain enjoy the pleasant temperature and amazing atmosphere, running past cheering, light-waving spectators. There are three distances to choose from – 42, 21 and 10 km (26, 13 and 6 miles) – as well as fireworks that light up the sky and live bands dotted around the city's streets, providing all the inspiration you'll need.

250
ULTRA PIRINEU
CATALONIA, SPAIN

Ultra/Trail
October/94 km

Wind, spectacular views above the clouds and alpine mountain paths – complete with bell-wearing cows chewing the cud in the meadows – are all on the agenda for this ultramarathon. The village start is amazing, as, for this weekend at least, you'll take on the mantle of a superstar with adoring fans seeing you on your way. They're also out in huge numbers at the ski station, which sits high above the clouds in Cadí-Moixeró Natural Park. There are four distances to choose from including the Sky 36 km (22 miles) and the Ultra 94 km (58 miles).

251
SEVILLE
SPAIN
Running route/Urban
All year round/Various

This is one of those runs that has an open door to when and where you do it. The route may vary depending on your hotel's location, but you must go through the Moorish palace grounds, Palacio de los Marqueses de la Algaba, and experience the orange trees, part of the city's rich history. There are some fabulous festivals to enjoy once your run is over, and the weather is usually superb.

253
SKYRACE COMAPEDROSA
ANDORRA
Mountain/Trail
July/21 km

This is a challenging race that ascends and descends 2,300 m (7,550 ft) in just 21 km (13 miles). The race starts and finishes at the small town of Arinsal, in the heart of the Pyrenees, passing lakes and crossing high, narrow rides before reaching the highest point in Andorra, Coma Pedrosa, at 2,942 m (9,652 ft). The final mile to the summit involves a vertiginous climb of 1,000 m (3,280 ft), much of which is on rocky terrain and narrow tracks. Once at the top, the runners follow a circular high-altitude route back to the finish.

252
WORLD'S FASTEST MARATHON
SIERRA NEVADA, SPAIN
Marathon/Mountain
October/42 km

With a total descent of nearly 2,000 m (6,500 ft), on a course that is almost continuously downhill, this is truly a marathon for fast times. Starting in the Sierra Nevada mountains, runners head to the historic coastal city of Grenada, helped all the way by gravity, and the race is popular with those who are trying to gain qualifying times for marathons such as Boston and Fukuoka. The downhill running will mean that those muscles and joints will get even more of a workout than usual, so post-race rehabilitation will be much needed.

248 | The macaques will be looking out for your snacks

254

PARIS MARATHON
FRANCE

Road/Urban

April/42 km

The first marathon held in Paris was the Tour de Paris in 1896, which attracted 191 entrants. The modern version of the race was introduced in 1976 and today attracts around 50,000 entrants. Starting on the iconic Avenue des Champs-Élysées, the route passes many of the city's most famous landmarks, including the Place de la Concorde, the Place de la Bastille, the Île de la Cité and the Eiffel Tower. The route also runs alongside the bank of the River Seine before finishing in front of many thousands of spectators on Avenue Foch.

EUROPE

255

PARIS TO VERSAILLES 16 KM
FRANCE

Urban
September/16.2 km

Running narrow city streets is always fun – more so when it's in a race heading to the grand Château de Versailles. Approximately 20,000 runners toe the line underneath the Eiffel Tower before heading along the Seine and through the André Citroën tunnel on the way to the final few kilometres through forest. The notorious Côte des Gardes section is a punishing 7 per cent gradient on cobblestones. The race is 16.2 km (10 miles), the exact distance from the base of the Eiffel Tower to Château de Versailles. Finish under the twin arches and celebrate with a vino.

256

MARATHON DU MEDOC
MEDOC, FRANCE

Novelty/Marathon
September/42 km

Running and wine, wine and running – not the most natural of partners, but in this world-famous race, costumed runners can literally drink in the delights of the Bordeaux region, with 23 wine-swilling posts and plentiful food stops offering the Medoc runner's staple sustenance of foie gras, oysters and cheese. Sick bag, anyone?

256 | Marathon du Medoc runners need strong legs and a stronger stomach

257 | **Step back in time through the historic streets of Lyon**

257
LYON URBAN
FRANCE
Urban/Trail
November/40 km

Trail running usually involves mud, tracks and the odd hill, while urban trails like this one provide the same excitement using back allies, courtyards, riverside paths and streets that are hard to find on the map. If there's a better way to explore Lyon we haven't heard of it. More than 8,000 runners experience the amazing 40 km (25 miles), which take you into the heart of historic Old Lyon, listed as a UNESCO World Heritage site.

258
LA SAINTÉLYON
FRANCE
Night/Snow
December/60 km

Sixty kilometres (37 miles) in the dark, in the winter, in the snow and ice. What's not to like about this classic? Fear not, you won't be alone. In fact, you'll be joined by close to 20,000 other runners keen to tackle the challenging trail route. The catch line for the event is 'for enlightened amateurs', which tells you headlamps are a must. There are eight different categories to make sure there's a challenge for everybody. Don't forget your gloves.

259 | A sea of colour and determination at UTMB

259

ULTRA-TRAIL DU MONT-BLANC
FRANCE/ITALY/SWITZERLAND
Ultra/Mountain
August/160 km

Evidence of qualifying performances in other ultras is needed before runners can even enter this gruelling two-day event. Starting at Chamonix, France, runners follow mountain trails around the perimeter of the Mont-Blanc Massif, entering Italy and Switzerland before returning to Chamonix. With a total distance of 160 km (99.5 miles) and an ascent and descent of 8,700 m (28,500 ft), the race starts at 7 p.m., and runners must have returned to Chamonix within 48 hours to officially finish.

260

CHAMONIX
FRANCE
Running route/Mountain
Summer/Various

Stand in the town square, near the railway station, and follow your nose . . . up. There are countless incredible trails in this town that, in winter is a ski hotspot, but in the summer is paradise for any trail runner. Chamonix hosts the UTMB in late August, but for easier days, there is much more on offer. Take the cable car up to 2,200 m (7,200 ft) and run the flat paths, marvelling at the mountains, and stopping for coffee at the well-spaced refuges.

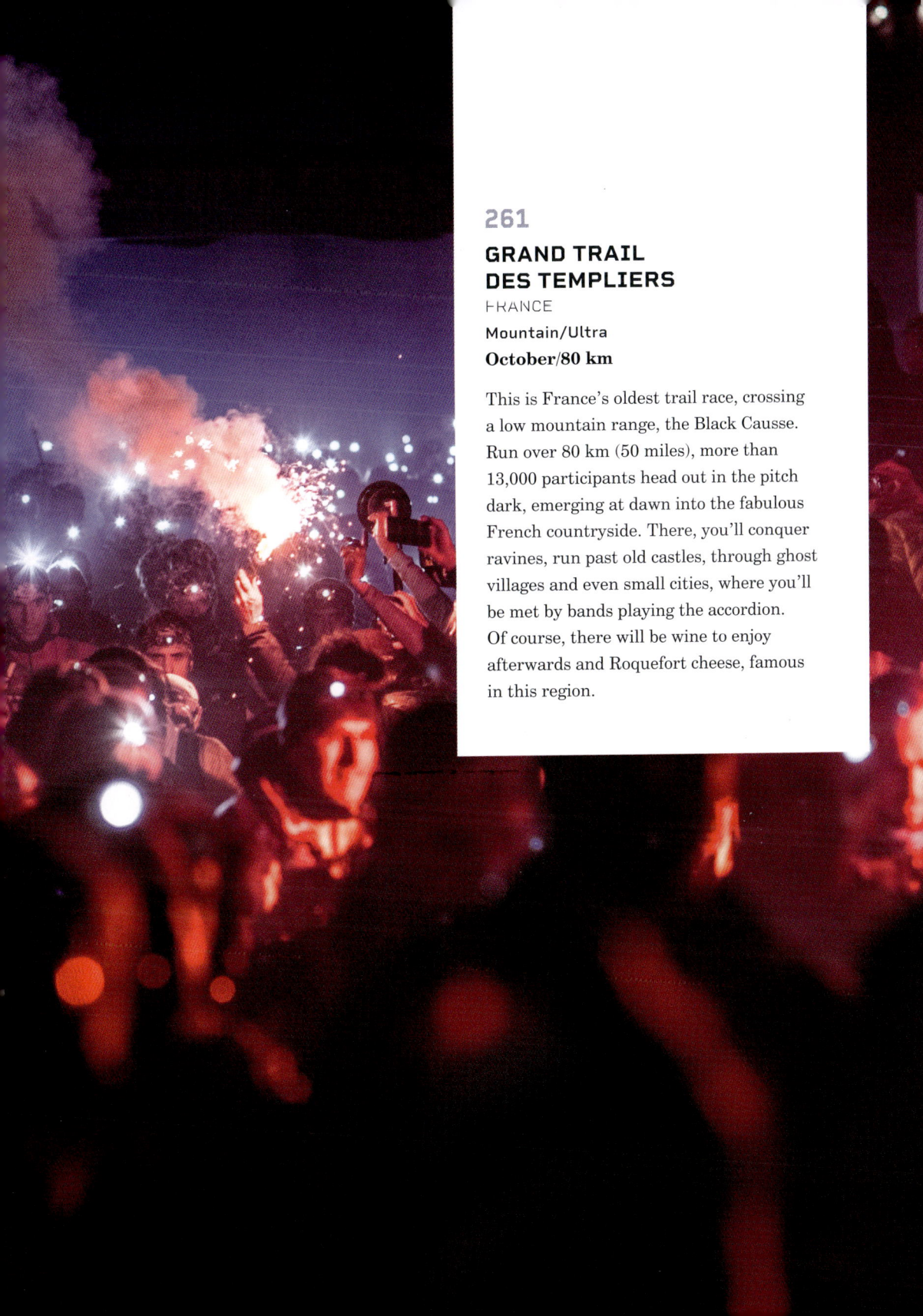

261

GRAND TRAIL DES TEMPLIERS
FRANCE

Mountain/Ultra
October/80 km

This is France's oldest trail race, crossing a low mountain range, the Black Causse. Run over 80 km (50 miles), more than 13,000 participants head out in the pitch dark, emerging at dawn into the fabulous French countryside. There, you'll conquer ravines, run past old castles, through ghost villages and even small cities, where you'll be met by bands playing the accordion. Of course, there will be wine to enjoy afterwards and Roquefort cheese, famous in this region.

262 | Join the stars at the National Centre for Altitude Training

262

THE NATIONAL CENTRE FOR ALTITUDE TRAINING
FONT ROMEU, FRANCE
Running route
May/June/Various

This is all about the location rather than any one specific route. Every superstar runner who uses the area as a training base has their favourite route. Paula Radcliffe, world champion and former world record holder for the marathon, runs a couple of kilometres around the complex before heading out for 8 tough kilometres (5 miles) through the forests. Altitude, solitude and a sense of achievement – this has it all. Go in early May and June, and take your autograph book.

263

BRUSSELS 20K
BELGIUM
Urban
May/20 km

First held in 1980 when it attracted 4,000 entrants, the Brussels 20K (12.5 miles) is now hugely popular, regularly attracting 40,000 runners from over 130 countries. Taking in many of the main monuments and parks of Brussels, runners are supported by seven drinks stations and a banana station on the course. In recent times the Race Starter has been the King of Belgium and the Belgian Prime Minister.

265 | **A stadium finish at the Amsterdam Marathon**

264
BÜTGENBACH HALF-MARATHON
BELGIUM
Festival
May/21 km

Multi-eventers, sporty families and serious half-marathoners in search of entertainment will find it here. The weekend involves just about everything from swimming and cycling to running. It'll be the half-marathon around the lake that interests you, but there's plenty to get everyone busy, including an 11.6-km (7.2-mile), a 4.9-km (3-mile) and a young athletes' 800 m.

265
AMSTERDAM MARATHON
THE NETHERLANDS
Marathon/Urban
September/42 km

Many emerge from this event with one important memory: a PB. Rated as one of the premier marathons in the world, it has plenty going for it along with that 'quick course' tag. The best bit is you start and finish in front of the grandstand in the Olympic Stadium – the very same arena where the legendary Paavo Nurmi won his ninth gold in the 10,000 m in 1928. It sends shivers down your spine just thinking of that, let alone being there.

266
LOOP DEN HAAG HALF-MARATHON
THE HAGUE, THE NETHERLANDS
Road
March/21 km

This is a popular road race, held on a fast, flat course, which is perfect for achieving a PB. First established as a 15-km (9-mile) race in 1975 before switching to the half-marathon distance just one year later, the race attracts a number of elite runners, and has been the scene of a sub-one-hour world record, set by Kenya's Sammy Wanjiru in 2007. The city itself is considered the home of international law and arbitration and, as such, has some impressive buildings and architecture.

267
ROTTERDAM MARATHON
THE NETHERLANDS
Road/Urban
April/42 km

Renowned for fast times on its flat course, the Rotterdam Marathon has been held since 1981 and regularly attracts a large field of runners from around the world. Being in April, it promises cool conditions that are ideal for fast times, although famously in 2007, the race had to be stopped after 3 hours 30 minutes, when temperatures reached an unseasonal and dangerous 34°C (93°F). The course finishes on the Coolsingel, one of the most famous streets in Rotterdam, which was a canal until 1922.

268
BAMBÉSCH FOREST
LUXEMBOURG
Running route/Forest
All year round/4.8–7.5 km

Bambésch Forest has a variety of marked trails and paths that offer a choice of distances from 4.8 to 7.5 km (3 to 4.5 miles). Located just 4.8 km (3 miles) from the centre of Luxembourg City, the forest's trails are popular with walkers, cyclists and runners, so at times the paths can become crowded. By linking routes together there is an option to extend the marked trails into a longer run, and while gently undulating, there are no steep ascents or descents.

269
SERENGETI PARK RUN
HODENHAGEN, GERMANY
Park
September/10 km

The clue is in the location. This is an adventure run in every sense, and it's all about getting muddy – very muddy. But this run also involves wildlife, being in one of the best animal parks in Germany. Treat yourself to a lodge the night before and this will complete your safari experience, all within commuting distance of Hamburg.

EUROPE 183

270 | **Pass through the Brandenburg Gate on the Berlin Marathon course**

270
BERLIN MARATHON
GERMANY
Road/Urban
September/42 km

This superfast World Major course was instantly the recipient of iconic status in 1990 thanks to its journey through the Brandenburg Gate shortly after the infamous Berlin Wall came down. The event has it all: history, culture, incredible architecture, but more importantly, a course record that is as close to 2 hours as you can get. Quick doesn't do the route justice: it's the best.

271
THE GREAT 10K
BERLIN, GERMANY
Urban
October/10 km

Any run that includes the world-famous Tiergarten is worthy of inclusion, but when it also takes in Berlin Zoo, the Grosser Stern Siegessäule – the column built in 1864 to celebrate victory in the Danish-Prussian War – and Schloss Charlottenburg, one of the premier sights in Berlin, well, then you have it all and more. Berlin always offers quick courses, so you should have no problem posting a memorable run for all the right reasons.

272

AIRPORT NIGHT RUN
BERLIN, GERMANY
Night
April/10 & 21 km

This unusual but exciting race circulates the illuminated southern runway of Berlin's Brandenburg Airport. There is a choice of distances that include a half-marathon, 10K and 4 x 4-km (2.5 x 2.5-mile) relay, with all of the races starting in daylight at around 7 p.m., but finishing in the dark later in the night. All the courses are fast and flat, giving a great opportunity for PB times.

273
KREISSPARKASSEN TRAIL
HERRENBERG, GERMANY
Trail/Forest
April/Various

There are two things you can count on for this race: it will be superbly organised and, with its 42.2 km (26.2 miles) of forest paths, the route will be wonderfully groomed. Forests in this region are always the best places to run, and this is no exception. There's a fair bit of climbing, so be ready for a challenge! Afterwards, enjoy the amazing medieval city of Herrenberg.

275 | **It's tough underfoot on Hochstaufen**

274
BAVARIA RUN
MUNICH, GERMANY
Multi-distance
July/Various

The annual Bavaria run offers a choice of 5, 10 and 15 km (3.1, 6.2 and 9.3 miles) distances, all of which follow an undulating 5-km (3-mile) route through the Olympic Park, which was created for the 1972 Olympic Games. Runners will pass many of the venues used for the Games, including the Olympic Stadium and the Olympic Village, scene of the Israeli hostage crisis, which remains as one of the darkest times in the history of the Olympics.

275
HOCHSTAUFEN/ BAD REICHENHALL
BAVARIA, GERMANY
Running route/Trail
All year round/9.5 km

Hochstaufen is a mountain in the Bavarian Alps that provides a popular but tough out-and-back trail run that includes a leg-burning ascent of over 1,000 m (3,500 ft). The 9.5-km (5.9-mile) trail and the mountain offer spectacular views and a chance to experience nature at its very best. Runners will find themselves sharing the trail with hikers who are also making their way to the summit, where there is a welcome cafe that offers the chance for a spot of mid-run refuelling.

276
TOUR DU LAC DE JOUX
SWITZERLAND
Trail
July/12 & 24 km

The two routes follow hiking trails along the side of, or overlooking, picturesque Lac de Joux, which lies in the Vallée de Joux. The longer distance (24 km/15 miles) involves a complete circuit of the lake, while the shorter distance (12 km/7.5 miles) starts at Lac de Joux's north-eastern end and finishes with the longer race at the lake's south-western tip. Nordic walking and children's races are also on offer.

277
CHRISTMAS MIDNIGHT RUN
LAUSANNE, SWITZERLAND
Night/Novelty
December/2.8 km

Christmas in Switzerland is as special as it sounds. Be prepared to race a fair few Santas in this city-centre burn-up that is more about the evening than the short distance (2.8 km/1.7 miles). Santa uniforms are compulsory, as runners entertain the crowds. Lights, sausages sizzling in the market – it has everything a night race should offer in December. Plus, of course, snow!

278
GRAND PRIX OF BERN
SWITZERLAND
Urban
May/4.7 & 16 km

Attracting a field of 16,000 runners, the 16-km (10-mile) race starts at the unusual time of 4 p.m., and takes runners past all of the main sights of the historic city of Bern. A great atmosphere is guaranteed from 100,000 spectators and on-course musical entertainment. The shorter 4.7 km (3 miles) is aimed at younger runners and novices, but still takes in many parts of the Old Town.

279
SURVIVAL RUN
THUN, SWITZERLAND
Mountain/Novelty
March/Various

For a controlled adventure complete with mountains and after-event catering, this Survival Run will test you, but also reward. Thun, after all, is a superb city offering plenty of hospitality after you've tackled the obstacles – including Heart Attack, Dead Marshes and Crocodile Swamp – and their onslaught of mud, water, ice and, in all probability, a sprinkling of snow.

Even if you survive the Survival Run, your kit may not

280 | **High-altitude running at Monte Rosa**

280
ULTRA TOUR DU MONTE ROSA
SWITZERLAND/ITALY
Ultra/Mountain
September/170 km

A 170-km (100-mile) loop around the mighty Monte Rosa, visiting both Italy and Switzerland, this ultra can be tackled as a single race (the Ultra Tour) or as a four-day stage race. Either way, be ready for wild countryside, stunning views, technical terrain, high mountain passes and around 11,500 m (37,700 ft) of climb and descent in the shadow of the Matterhorn. With a route that is 85 per cent on mountain trails, the UTMR is widely considered to be tougher but quieter than the more famous UTMB.

281
SILVESTERLAUF
ZURICH, SWITZERLAND
Road/Mountain
December/8.8 km

Winding through the medieval streets of Zurich, the route twists and climbs around an 8.8-km (5.5-mile) multi-lap circuit in front of an enthusiastic, bell-ringing crowd. Races take place the whole day for all age groups, from under 11s and mother and child races to the Happy Runs, for slower and happier athletes. Christmas in Zurich is as you'd expect, with chocolate available at every opportunity.

283 | A 'mountain piper' welcomes runners in a snow flurry near the Eiger glacier

282
BISSE DU TORRENT NEUF
SWITZERLAND
Running route/Multi-terrain
All year round /Various

An hour or so running on this trail will involve wooden paths bolted to the mountain side, metal suspended bridges and/or a superbly groomed dirt track. And that's just the running surfaces. Perhaps one of the most scenic routes in all of Switzerland, the setting is simply stunning. Make sure you stop and take it all in, or take a lunch to eat outside the small chapel on the trail. This route is all about taking your time and enjoying the atmosphere.

283
JUNGFRAU MARATHON
ALPS, SWITZERLAND
Mountain/Festival
September/4.2 & 42 km

The Swiss Alps rise up in front of you as you climb from 500 to 2,100 m (1,640 to 6,890 ft) through the Kleine Scheidegg mountain pass. This isn't about fast times; it's about soaking up the amazing atmosphere as the Jungfrau, Mönch and Eiger all provide an iconic backdrop. Alphorn players, bell ringers and bagpipers will help make your day even more memorable, while the event itself includes a 4.2-km (2.6-mile) mini-marathon and plenty of family events to keep everyone entertained.

284
EIGER ULTRA TRAIL
ALPS, SWITZERLAND

Ultra/Mountain
July/101 km

Offering a range of routes, from a 101-km (63-mile) ultra to a 16-km (10-mile) 'pleasure trail', all of the routes include some of the most spectacular scenery that the Swiss Alps has to offer. The ultra is an iconic race in the annual calendar of mountain running, and includes a huge ascent and descent of 6,700 m (22,000 ft). It also has a Couples category for those who wish to compete in teams of two.

286 | **Spartacus Runs are always muddy affairs**

286
SPARTACUS RUN
LUGANO, SWITZERLAND
Obstacle course race
October/3–10 km

Lugano hosts one of a series of Spartacus runs held in cities throughout Europe. Spartacus runs are gruelling events of between 3 and 10 km (2 and 6 miles), where competitors have to cope with obstacles either running as a team or individually. Mud, water, rope nets, barbed wire, log carrying, climbing, crawling and occasionally crying are an integral part of the events.

285
SIERRE-ZINAL
ALPS, SWITZERLAND
Mountain
August/31 km

A mountain race like no other, situated in the Valais Alps, this 31-km (19-mile) race is picture-perfect. It's not an easy ride though, with a long mountainous trail up at least 2,200 m (7,200 ft). You'll certainly break a sweat, and it's not just the going up you need to worry about – there are some steep declines, too. The race is superbly organised, with parallel events for juniors and children to keep them occupied.

287
SWISS SNOW RUN
AROSA, SWITZERLAND
Snow
January/1–21 km

If this race took place in August, it'd be all about the spectacular mountain scenery, the Alpine village start and the climbs. This, however, is a winter race, so the scenery is still there – the village is most definitely present, complete with its heady, aromatic winter ambience – and the climbs are there, too, covered in snow. There's a lakeside start and finish, and while you won't go all the way to the mountain summit, this is a challenge that will leave your legs feeling like they did. The race distances vary from 1 to 21 km (0.6 to 13.1 miles).

288
SWISSALPINE RACE WEEKEND
DAVOS, SWITZERLAND

Mountain/Festival

July/Various

First held in 1986, this race weekend offers runners a choice of five events, alongside one for children. The longest is the K68 (covering 68 km/42 miles), and the shortest is the K10 (10K). All of the routes include high-Alpine running through valleys and over mountain passes. The races are just part of an annual gathering of Alpine runners that has become a major feature in the calendar of Swiss mountain running.

288 | **Runners pass through stunning Alpine scenery**

289
LEMA TRAIL
SWITZERLAND

Trail/Mountain

April/7.2 km

This 7.2-km (4.5-mile) race is all about the trail. If racing isn't your thing, instead stay in a mountain refuge hut and explore the scenic route between the village of Miglieglia in the Malcantone to the summit of Monte Lema. Most take the cable car, but runners will love the feeling of achievement this run or race gives as they take on the vertical kilometre that follows the path of the cable car.

290
MALTA MARATHON
MALTA

Marathon

March/42 km

Definitely one of the must-run marathons for this time of year, given the mild climate runners will enjoy. This is always popular with the in-crowd and more than 1,000 runners take part in what is a largely flat course. There's plenty to see, the highlight being the section of the route that follows the seventeenth-century aqueducts from Mriehel to Birkirkara, or maybe it's the fact that it's predominately downhill.

291

ORTLER SKY TRAILS
SOUTH TYROL, ITALY

Trail/Mountain
July/Various

Offering distances of 80, 45, 31, 22 and 2.5 km (50, 28, 19, 14 and 1.5 miles), these races take place in the South Tyrol area of northern Italy. All of the races start in Sulden Am Ortler and are set in magnificent Alpine scenery, with the longer distances reaching altitudes of over 3,000 m (9,800 ft). Don't be fooled into thinking that the shortest route is an easy option – it is called the 'Ortler Vertical' and involves a climb of over 850 m (2,800 ft).

292

BRIXEN DOLOMITEN MARATHON
ITALY

Mountain/Festival
July/42 km

This historic mountain marathon has recently grown into a running festival with the addition of an 84-km (52-mile) ultra and a shorter 29-km (18-mile) race, and, consequently, attracts runners from all over the world. The marathon starts in the town of Brixen and finishes on the Plose, Brixen's local mountain, at a height of 2,450 m (8,000 ft). The ultra starts and finishes in Brixen and has an altitude gain of over 4,700 m (15,000 ft); the shorter race climbs 1,850 m (6,000 ft) before dropping 545 m (1,800 ft) to the finish at Plose.

291 | **Magnificent scenery dominates all distances of the Ortler Sky Trails**

293

JESOLO MOONLIGHT HALF-MARATHON

ITALY

Night/Festival

May/10 & 21 km

As the name suggests, this nighttime half-marathon and 10K start at 7.30 p.m. on a Saturday, guaranteeing a party atmosphere from the supporters lining the route. This is enhanced with on-course bands and market stalls, as the runs wind along the shoreline and river. The revelry continues after the finish line has been crossed, with a post-race beach party into the early hours of Sunday morning.

295 | Pisa's most famous landmark leans over the city's marathon

294

ECOMARATONA DEL VENTASSO

ITALY

Marathon/Trail

July/42 km

A marathon that aims to put nature and the environment at its heart, this is a challenging off-road course that reaches a high point of over 1,700 m (5,500 ft). The course is in the Italian Apennine mountains, and passes through villages along a ridge that separates Tuscany from the territory of the Lunigiana. The route is safe and does not include dangerous or exposed areas.

295

PISA MARATHON

ITALY

Road/Marathon

December/42 km

Italians know a thing or two when it comes to putting on memorable events. This is a marathon that takes you along flat and fast tree-lined avenues, out to the coast, before returning to where it all began – the leaning tower. What a sight to encourage you to pick up the pace in those final kilometres. This is a race where history meets culture, and you're the winner!

296 | Dark, quiet streets beckon runners of the Roma by Night

296

ROMA BY NIGHT
ROME, ITALY
Night/Urban
October/21 km

Imagine the streets of Rome closed to traffic in the cool of an evening. Magical is the only way to describe this superb event. The race starts and finishes at Ponte della Musica, the Music Bridge that spans the Tiber. Be ready for a fast, flat and illuminated course that takes you on a journey through history, all under the stars.

297

SENTIERO DEGLI DEI
AMALFI COAST, ITALY
Running route/Coastal
All year round/8 km

Anything that translates to 'The Path of the Gods' should be enough of a clue as to the views and history you'll experience on this comfortable 8 km (5 miles). Hugely popular with walkers, runners can also experience stunning views of the Amalfi Coast and the island of Capri on their morning run. You'll be high up on the clifftop before dropping back down to the beach, where you can kick back with a celebratory cocktail.

298 | Runners in Prague cross the Vltava River

298

PRAGUE HALF-MARATHON
CZECH REPUBLIC

Road/Urban

March/21 km

Described by the organisers as beautiful, funny and fast, the Prague Half-marathon was first held in 1999, and starts and finishes in the centre of the historic city. The fast course often attracts a strong field of elite runners and is ideal for anyone seeking a PB, as the conditions are often perfect for distance running. Its status as a world-leading event is confirmed through its recognition by World Athletics as a 'Gold Label' race.

299

BRNO HALF-MARATHON
CZECH REPUBLIC

Road/Urban

April/21 km

European city-centre road races are always memorable, as you are immersed in amazing history. This half-marathon is no exception, as you'll love the vibe this former Communist country provides. Head off from Svobody Square for flat, fast 21 km (13 miles), and return to an appreciative crowd keen to celebrate your run with a local brew.

300
SILVRETTARUN 3000
ISCHGL, AUSTRIA

Mountain

July/Various

This Alpine running event starts in Ischgl and finishes in the village of Galtür, with a choice of four different routes: Small, Light, Medium and Hard. The Small route is 11 km (7 miles), with an altitude gain of 300 m (900 ft); the Light route is 19 km (12 miles), with 870 m (2,900 ft) of climbing; the Medium route climbs 1,480 m (4,900 ft) over a distance of 30 km (18.5 miles); while the mighty Hard route climbs 1,800 m (5,900 ft) to the 3,000-m (9,800-ft) summit of Kronenjoch, and covers a distance of 42 km (26 miles).

301
OSSIACHER SEE NACHTHALBMARATHON
AUSTRIA

Multi-terrain/Night

July/21 km

Held at Lake Ossiach, this is a point-to-point half-marathon between the villages of Bodensdorf on the lake's north shore and Ossiach on the south shore. The route is largely asphalt and gravel roads, and fortunately for those who like their sleep it starts at 7 p.m., and even the slowest runners should cross the finish line before bedtime.

302
BLED NIGHT RUN
SLOVENIA

Road/Night

June/10 km

Starting at 10 p.m., the 10K race starts on the promenade of Bled, adjacent to the picturesque lake, and runners complete two laps of the lake in ever-increasing darkness. With shorter distances of 800 and 1,200 m (0.5 and 0.75 miles) for less serious runners and children, the race is popular with runners and families of all abilities. Finishers receive a medal, t-shirt and goody bag, and late-night childcare is provided for runners with children.

302 | A picturesque lakeside setting for the Bled nighttime run

304 | Elite runners head the field in Bratislava

303
LOKRUM ISLAND
CROATIA
Running route/Coastal
All year round/7 km

The small island of Lokrum is located just 600 m (650 yards) from Dubrovnik, and can be reached by taking a short ferry journey. Once there, the island has a network of paths that total around 7 km (4 miles), including the Celestial Way, which leads to the island's highest point, Fort Royal, 84 m (277 ft) above sea level. Many of the paths offer great views back to the city and over the sea.

304
BRATISLAVA HALF-MARATHON
SLOVAKIA
Road/Urban
September/21 km

Held in the beautiful capital of Slovakia, this half takes you on a wonderful tour of the city's best-known historic sites. Participants will feel like superstars for a day as the Bratislava Half is part of Slovakia's biggest running event, which includes plenty of action for all the family. This fast race attracts runners from around the world, including elite athletes from Europe and Africa, so be prepared for a PB.

306 | Crossing the Danube River is part of the Budapest Half-marathon

305
PRESOV NIGHT RUN
SLOVAKIA
Night/Novelty
March/5 & 10 km

Be prepared for a unique 5K or 10K of music, lights and special effects if you enter this unusual race. Starting in darkness at 7 p.m., accompanied by a DJ and street musicians, it's easy to forget this is a race. Yet the accurately measured courses give runners the opportunity to set a good time in a great atmosphere during the cool conditions of a spring evening.

306
BUDAPEST HALF-MARATHON
HUNGARY
Urban/Road
September/21 km

Running through the heart of Budapest, the course crosses several bridges over the Danube River and provides an opportunity to sightsee the capital city's most famous landmarks, including Buda Castle and the Parliament Building. It's possible to run the race as an individual or as part of a team of two or three. Although the half-marathon attracts more than 10,000 entrants, they are started in waves, which reduces overcrowding, and the race has become a popular attraction for runners from many nations.

307
LAKE BALATON 26
HUNGARY
Multiday adventure/Relay
March/196 km

Hungary's biggest lake plays host to a very special event that is perfect for any runner looking for a challenge. This four-day-long event will see you running about 48 km (30 miles) each day, 196 km (122 miles) in total, along the shores of this amazingly beautiful lake. Do it on your own, as part of a relay team, or even just take part in the final two days.

308
BRASOV HALF-MARATHON
ROMANIA
Road/Urban
October/21 km

Clearly, a run in the heart of Transylvania will have a definite vibe to it. This event starts and finishes in Brasov's city centre, which offers everything from Gothic spires to medieval gateways and even Soviet blocks. Few races cover such a diverse history in such a relatively short distance. While the Count himself won't be there in person, he'll be with you in spirit.

309
TIRANA HALF-MARATHON
ALBANIA
Road/Urban
October/10 & 21 km

This is the city's largest sporting event, regularly attracting a field of around 2,500 runners, many of whom travel from overseas. There is a cut-off time of 2 hours for the 10K, 4 hours for the half-marathon, and both routes wind their way through Albania's capital city and old town. Runners who have completed the events regularly praise the organisation and the route, and the races offer a chance to visit a country that was once isolated and difficult to access.

310
ATHENS CLASSIC MARATHON
GREECE
Road/Marathon
November/42 km

Claiming to follow the original course taken by the unfortunate Greek runner Pheidippides, from the ancient battle town of Marathon to Athens, this is a very popular race attracting runners from all over the world. Pheidippides was bringing news of victory in the Battle of Marathon, but despite the final 11 km (7 miles) of the run being downhill, exhaustion got the better of him and, after announcing victory, he died. The highlight of the race, for those who are hopefully in much better shape than Pheidippides, is the finish in Athens' Ancient Olympic Stadium.

310 | **Try to finish the Athens Classic Marathon in better shape than Pheidippides**

312 | **Roman history lines the route of the Paphos Marathon**

311

SKIATHOS 10K TRAIL RUN
GREECE
Trail/Coastal
May/10 & 21 km

Fans of *Mama Mia!* will love this trail (there's also a half-marathon distance available), which, for the first couple of kilometres, runs through traditional cobbled Greek island streets – truly, you're as good as on set. You'll climb up high above the village, wind your way through a forest and finish in the harbour area. Then, of course, you could jump on a local ferry and check out that church. Or slip into a local bar to celebrate.

312

PAPHOS MARATHON
CYPRUS
Road/Coastal
March/42 km

Anyone who likes a bit of Roman history must do this race – if nothing else, the mosaics on the route are considered among the finest in the world and serve as a stunning record of Greco-Roman daily life. But that's just half of it. The race itself starts at Aphrodite's birthplace, Petra tou Romiou, and follows the sparkling Mediterranean coastline. Along the route, you'll be able to soak it all up, from typical Cypriot village life to the bustling town of Paphos.

314 | **The Galata Bridge opens up to marathon runners**

313
VITOSHA 100K
BULGARIA
Ultra/Mountain
June/100 km

Although run mainly on trails and footpaths, this popular and friendly 100-km (62-mile) ultra starts on the outskirts of Bulgaria's capital city, Sofia, and follows an anticlockwise loop around the Vitosha Mountain. The high point of 1,351 m (4,432 ft) is reached just before 70 km (43 miles), after which runners have a long but steady descent back to Sofia. None of the ascents or descents are overly challenging, so this is a good race to try if you are after a first experience of a mountain ultra.

314
ISTANBUL
TURKEY
Running route/Urban
All year round/Various

There are not many places where you can run across a bridge to go from Europe to Asia without a passport, but Istanbul is one of them. The Bosphorus River is opened to runners each October for the Istanbul Marathon, but at other times of the year the Galata Bridge will take you from one continent to the other, with various choices of runs around the coastline or busy cobbled streets, soaking up the atmosphere and sights of this unique city.

317 | **The rolling forest trails of the Beskidy Ultra**

315
PIRITA PATH
ESTONIA
Running route/Coastal
All year round/4 km

This flat waterfront run from the capital, Tallinn, to nearby Pirita is 4 km (2.5 miles), or double if run out and back. There are great views of the Tallinn Bay and the large ferries and ships that have arrived from the Baltic Sea. Although the run is alongside a road, there is a pathway that makes this a safe running route, and, as a result, it is popular with runners and cyclists, so can get busy at times.

316
WARSAW HALF-MARATHON
POLAND
Urban
May/21 km

Starting in the New Town, the race soon crosses the Vistula River for the first time as runners pass over the Gdanski Bridge. Running through the historic UNESCO World Heritage areas of Warsaw, with views of the city and Royal Castle, the Vistula River is crossed for the second time before finishing the race in Multimedia Fountain Park.

EUROPE 207

318
VILNIUS CHRISTMAS RUNS
LITHUANIA

Novelty
December/Various

These festive races have a long tradition, and runners are encouraged to dress as Christmas characters or movie superheroes. Held through the historic streets of Vilnius Old Town, families are encouraged to run together. The large crowds and narrow streets help to create a great atmosphere and a Christmas spirit along the 3, 6, or 12 km (2, 4, or 7.5 miles).

317
BESKIDY ULTRA
POLAND

Trail/Forest
September/30–100 km

Runners can choose from five different races, ranging from 30 km (19 miles) all the way to 100 km (62 miles), in which they'll experience the rolling forest trails for which this region is so well known. The ever-changing scenery is tough in places – technical, even – but for most of it, all you'll need to worry about is how to edit down the collection of stunning pictures you'll accumulate on any of the runs.

319
KULDIGA HALF-MARATHON
LATVIA

Urban
August/21 km

Held since 2006, this tough, often hot half-marathon is held in the city of Kuldiga. The course is renowned for its many twists and turns, and much of the route is on cobbled roads through the old town. It also includes the Latvian half-marathon championships, so attracts both serious and recreational runners.

320

VELODOROZHKA

MINSK, BELARUS

Running route/Park

All year round/up to 25 km

Although Velodorozhka means 'bike path', this paved path alongside the Svislach River is great for running, too. The path is 25 km (15.5 miles) long, from Dradzy Forest Park in the north to the Chyzhowskae Reservoir in the south, and can be run in full or in shorter sections. Highlights of the route include Gorky Park, Victory Park, Lošycki Park and the area through the waterfront. Both Gorky Park and Victory Park offer the chance to add on extra distance through their own network of paths.

321

MILESTII MICI WINE RUN

MOLDOVA

Novelty

February/10 km

This is a 10K through the world's largest wine cellar. Yes, really! The cellar boasts more than 200 km (125 miles) of passages and more than a million bottles of wine. The footing is a little uneven and it is a little dark, but the heady aroma of wine makes it all worthwhile. Of course, it's not a fast course, but, as you'd expect, there's plenty of celebrating to be done afterwards, as you'll be rewarded with a glass or two.

320 | **The Velodorozhka is a popular run in Belarus**

322 | **See the sights of Moscow during the half-marathon**

322

MOSCOW HALF-MARATHON
RUSSIA

Urban
May/21 km

The largest half-marathon in Russia takes in all of the main sights of the city as runners cover the distance. Starting at the Olympic Park used for the 1980 Olympic Games, runners cross the Krymsky Bridge and pass the Kremlin and St Basil's Cathedral in Red Square. The race starts in waves based on predicted finish time, and chip timing ensures that all runners receive an accurate time.

AFRICA AND THE MIDDLE EAST

AFRICA AND THE MIDDLE EAST

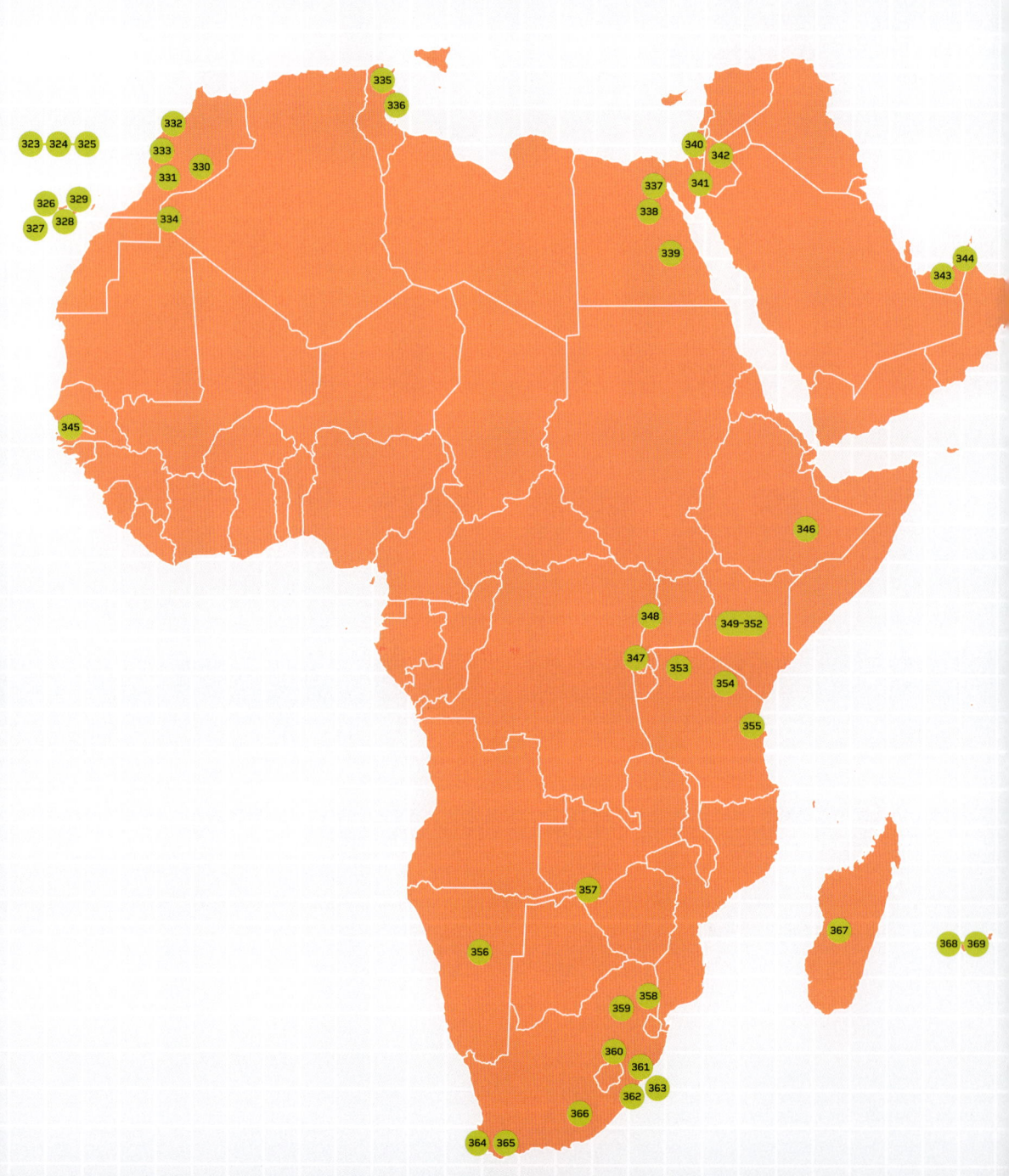

AFRICA AND THE MIDDLE EAST: ENTRY LIST

JANUARY
339 Egyptian Marathon, Egypt

FEBRUARY
334 Sahara Marathon, Algeria
347 Rwamagana Marathon, Rwanda

MARCH
340 Jerusalem Marathon, Israel
354 Kilimanjaro Marathon, Tanzania
365 Two Oceans Marathon, South Africa

APRIL
323 Madeira Island Ultra-Trail, Madeira
330 Marathon des Sables, Morocco
336 Sfax International Half-marathon, Tunisia
342 Dead Sea Ultra, Jordan
345 Great Gambia Run, The Gambia
355 Heart Half-marathon, Tanzania
365 Two Oceans Marathon, South Africa

MAY
324 Madeira Sky Race, Madeira
326 Transvulcania, Canary Islands
367 Ultra Trail des ô Plateaux, Madagascar

JUNE
327 Tenerife Blue Trail Night Challenge, Canary Islands
356 Citidash 5K & 10K, Namibia
360 4Peaks Mountain Challenge, South Africa
362 Comrades Marathon, South Africa

JULY
335 Zriba Night Trail, Tunisia
357 Victoria Falls Marathon, Zimbabwe
363 Durban 10K, South Africa
368 Mauritius Marathon, Mauritius

AUGUST
358 Skukuza Half-marathon, South Africa
361 Mandela Day Marathon, South Africa

SEPTEMBER
325 Fanals Vertical Kilometre, Madeira

OCTOBER
369 Avalon Trail, Mauritius

NOVEMBER
338 Pharaonic Race 100K, Egypt
346 Great Ethiopian Run, Ethiopia
348 Rift Marathon, Uganda
352 Masai Mara Half-marathon, Kenya
353 Serengeti Safari Marathon, Tanzania

DECEMBER
329 Lanzarote Marathon, Canary Islands
351 Baringo Half-marathon, Kenya

ALL YEAR ROUND
328 Jinama Trail, Canary Islands
331 Toubkal Circuit, Morocco
332 Casablanca Waterfront, Morocco
333 Menara Gardens, Morocco
337 Gezira Island, Egypt
341 Timna National Park, Israel
343 Yas Marina Circuit, United Arab Emirates
344 Dubai Marina, United Arab Emirates
349 Nangili Road, Kenya
350 Iten, Kenya
359 Faerie Glen Nature Reserve, South Africa
364 Table Mountain, South Africa
366 Tsitsikamma Trail, South Africa

324 | The steep and challenging route of the Madeira Sky Race

323

MADEIRA ISLAND ULTRA-TRAIL
MADEIRA
Ultra/Coastal
April/115 km

Portugal's green and rugged island in the North Atlantic has many trails. The MIUT races 115 km (71 miles) (with 7,100 m/ 23,000 ft total gain) north-west to south-east, from ocean to summit, through forests, along levadas (traditional water canals) and seaside cliffs to finish on a beach. The changing views and terrain mixed with floral and eucalyptus fragrance make this challenging trail well worth it. It's a destination with friendly people, good food and reasonable prices.

324

MADEIRA SKY RACE
MADEIRA
Ultra/Coastal
May/55.6 km

Part of the sky-running festival taking in Santana on the north coast of the island, the Sky Race covers 55.6 km (34.5 miles), with over 4,000 m (13,000 ft) of ascent and descent. Runners tackle the via *ferrata* – a series of iron steps and ladders – that line this part of the route. Starting in the town, the race climbs to the summit of Pico Ruivo, at 1,861 m (6,106 ft) the highest mountain on the island, before plunging down a technical trail to sea level on the way back to the finish. You'll see spectacular mountain and coastal scenery on the way.

325

FANALS VERTICAL KILOMETRE
MADEIRA
Novelty/Coastal
September/4 km

The climb of 1,000 m (3,280 ft) is achieved after just under 4 km (2.5 miles) of running, with an average gradient of 26 per cent. This energy-sapping event takes place on the western tip of the island, starting 78 m (256 ft) above sea level from the town of Ribeira Funda, before climbing steeply along trails. Due to the narrow nature of the course, runners are started one at a time to avoid overcrowding.

326

TRANSVULCANIA
LA PALMA, CANARY ISLANDS
Ultra
May/Various

The Transvulcania offers a choice of distances from the leg-burning Vertical Kilometre to the 74-km (46-mile) Ultra. The terrain is volcanic, and with spectacular, steep ascents and descents – a total climb of over 4,400 m (14,500 ft) – so it is no surprise that the ultra is considered to be one of the toughest races of its kind in Spain, and attracts a top-quality field from all over the world.

326 | **Above the clouds on the Transvulcania**

AFRICA AND THE MIDDLE EAST

327
TENERIFE BLUE TRAIL NIGHT CHALLENGE
CANARY ISLANDS
Festival/Mountain
June/Various

Offering a range of race distances and endurance challenges, this race festival takes place within Teide National Park. The race surfaces are mainly dirt roads and tracks, and pass through a volcanic landscape rich with rock formations and barren mountain scenery. The feature race is the 101-km (62.8-mile) ultra, which climbs from sea level to an altitude of 3,550 m (11,600 ft) as runners cross from one side of the island to the other, with a cut-off time for completion of 24 hours.

328
JINAMA TRAIL
EL HIERRO, CANARY ISLANDS
Trail/Coastal
All year round/16 km

This 16-km (10-mile) trail runs along the middle of the El Golfo valley, and contains 1,500 m (4,900 ft) of ascent and 1,300 m (4,300 ft) of descent. Starting in the village of Frontera, there is a tricky climb up to Mirador de Jinama, followed by magnificent views over the valley and the sea as the trail crosses the hillside and the top of the cliffs. After passing through forests, fields and meadows, the trail descends to the village of Villa de Valverde.

329
LANZAROTE MARATHON
CANARY ISLANDS
Marathon/Coastal
December/42 km

All the races (there's also a half-marathon and 10K) take place along a coastal road that runs alongside the south-east side of this popular tourist island. The course is fast even though it can be breezy and there are some slight undulations. The runners in the marathon and half-marathon are supported by pacemakers running at a variety of different speeds. There is a cut-off time of 6 hours for the marathon, and 3 hours 30 minutes for the half.

330

MARATHON DES SABLES
SAHARA DESERT, MOROCCO

Multiday adventure/Desert
April/251 km

Marathon des Sables (that's French for 'Marathon of the Sands') is a six-day ultra covering 251 km (156 miles) across the Sahara. In temperatures that can top 49°C (120°F). Oh, and you have to carry your own gear, including food. This self-sufficiency aspect, in the midst of such a hostile environment, takes the event into a life-changing realm that transcends running, which is, no doubt, at the crux of its appeal. Hardy participants speak of an immersive experience, as far removed from modern life as is possible.

332
CASABLANCA WATERFRONT
MOROCCO
Running route/Coastal
All year round/21 km

With great views over the Atlantic Ocean and the constant surf breaking onto the beaches, a 21-km (13-mile) path along the waterfront is certainly the place to run in Casablanca. The paved path is not as flat as you would expect for a waterside run, although the reasonably firm sand of the beaches does provide another running option. As time goes by on the route, runners pass historic landmarks that include mosques and the El Hank Lighthouse, which is the tallest in Morocco.

331
TOUBKAL CIRCUIT
ATLAS MOUNTAINS, MOROCCO
Running route/Mountain
All year round/72 km

With arduous scree and rock underfoot, and likely some ice, runners would be wise to take their pick from the full 72-km (44.7-mile) trekking trail, perhaps circuiting (rather than summiting) the high-altitude mountain through the Berber villages and verdant, mule-strewn valleys.

333
MENARA GARDENS
MARRAKESH, MOROCCO
Running route/Park
All year round/7 km

The inner alleys and courtyards of central Marrakesh are certainly not conducive to running, but the Menara Gardens, built in the twelfth-century BCE, provide a tranquil oasis to run around. There are approximately 4 km (2.5 miles) of paths, which all interlink between olive groves, gardens and a lake. To lengthen the run, add on the nearby Oliveraie Park to provide a total combined loop of around 7 km (4 miles).

334 | Sand, sweat and supporters on the Sahara Marathon course

334
SAHARA MARATHON
ALGERIA
Festival/Desert
February/42 km

This race festival (also a half-marathon, 10K and 5K) was established to support the many people in the area living in refugee camps, and since it was first held in 2001, many hundreds of thousands of dollars have been raised for humanitarian projects. The terrain is on packed earth tracks, with sand and rocks, and is fairly flat. There are regular drink stations, and the course is marked with flags and piles of stones. The sun, sand and wind are potential hazards, so runners are recommended to wear head scarfs or hats for protection.

335
ZRIBA NIGHT TRAIL
TUNISIA
Night/Trail
July/17 km

Starting at 7.45 p.m. from the Berber village of Zriba, the 17-km (10.5-mile) looped trail of this nocturnal nature race follows a purely natural route though wooded and agricultural land, passing wadis, lakes and through olive, thyme and rosemary trees. The route is marked with ecologically sound lime symbols on the ground as well as reflective posts. With the start taking place just after sunset, runners need to use a headlamp to help negotiate the sometimes steep climbs and technical descents.

336

SFAX INTERNATIONAL HALF-MARATHON
TUNISIA
Coastal
April/21 km

Often referred to as the second city of Tunisia, Sfax is a Mediterranean port that was established in AD 849 on top of the ruins of the ancient Roman city of Taparura. There is a cut-off time of 3 hours, with the run winding through the ancient city streets and alongside the port. Drink stations are provided regularly to keep runners refuelled and refreshed.

337

GEZIRA ISLAND
CAIRO, EGYPT
Running route
All year round/8.8 km

Amid the hustle and bustle of one of Africa's busiest cities, Gezira Island provides one of the top places to run in Cairo. The best running spot is alongside the River Nile on the island's western side, following the pavement and pathway for 4.4 km (2.7 miles) before turning round to run back. The route can be made longer and more interesting by including some of the island's inner streets, particularly those in the northern residential area. There is also the option of including the horse track in the Gezira Sporting Club, which is open for runners, except on race days.

336 | **The ancient walls of the medina in Sfax**

338 | Members of the Egyptian team in the Pharaonic Race

338
PHARAONIC RACE 100K
CAIRO, EGYPT
Ultra
November/100 km

The idea for this race came about in 1977, when an Egyptian Egyptologist discovered a piece of rock telling a story of Pharaonic soldiers who, in 680 BCE, were ordered to run in a 100-km (62-mile) race by their king (who also took part). The present-day race starts at 6 a.m., with a challenging cut-off time of 11 hours, and, partly as a result of this, the number of official finishers is often low. The race is held over what is believed to be the original route, and passes many ancient relics, monuments and pyramids.

339
EGYPTIAN MARATHON
LUXOR, EGYPT
Road/Marathon
January/42 km

Starting in the shadow of the Temple of Queen Hatshepsut, the Egyptian Marathon passes through a plethora of ancient locations that include the Temple of Habou, the Temple of Amenophis and the Colossi of Memnon, before reaching the finish line back at the Hatshepsut temple. The race was first held in 1995 and has become the oldest marathon in Africa and the Middle East.

340

JERUSALEM MARATHON
ISRAEL

Road/Marathon
March/42 km

The marathon starts in front of Israel's parliament building, the Knesset, in the western part of the city, before looping through the Hebrew University of Jerusalem and through the biblical Valley of the Cross. Competitors experience a welcome descent into the Old City, then through the ancient Zion Gate, one of the Old City's eight gates, before finishing in Sacher Park. The route is challenging and undulating, but has grown in popularity since its inception in 2011, and regularly attracts more than 25,000 entrants.

AFRICA AND THE MIDDLE EAST

341 | Discover unique geology from the Jurassic era

341
TIMNA NATIONAL PARK
ISRAEL

Running route/Desert
All year round/Various

This is a great chance to try some desert trail running in an environment that is safe, easy to navigate and spectacular. The National Park is located 20 km (12 miles) north of Eilat and contains over 80 km (50 miles) of trails, many of which are part of marked routes that offer a choice of distances. Solomon's Pillars and Mount Timna are the standout geographical features that make this a never-to-be-forgotten spot for running.

342
DEAD SEA ULTRA
JORDAN

Ultra/Road
April/50 km

Although the distance is a gruelling 50 km (31 miles), the highlight (or lowlight) of this race is that it is downhill and finishes beneath sea level. Starting at an altitude of 900 m (2,950 ft) above sea level in the highlands of Amman, the course drops continuously to finish at the Earth's lowest land point, the Dead Sea, 400 m (1,310 ft) below sea level, resulting in a total descent of 1,300 m (4,265 ft). Don't be fooled into thinking that downhill running makes the race easy – the hot tarmac and relentless sunshine offer little protection and lots of heat.

343
YAS MARINA CIRCUIT
ABU DHABI, UNITED ARAB EMIRATES
Running route/Track
All year round/5.5 km

If you are a fan of Formula 1, this run is for you. On a 5.5-km (3.4-mile) circuit more used to the speed and noise of some of the fastest racing cars in the world, the pace slows somewhat on Tuesday evenings, when runners (and cyclists) are permitted to use the circuit. After a free registration, runners lap in a clockwise direction (cyclists lap anticlockwise), and it is certainly worth posing for a selfie on the start and finish line, beneath the towering grandstands that line both sides of the track.

344
DUBAI MARINA
UNITED ARAB EMIRATES
Running route/Urban
All year round/8.5 km

Known locally as the Marina Walk, the 8.5-km (5.3-mile) loop around the marina is a favourite of Dubai runners. One of the most scenic runs in this ultra-modern city, the palm tree-lined route contrasts soaring skyscrapers on one side with yachts bobbing in sparkling blue waters on the other. Three road crossings mean shorter loops are easily achieved, while the Palm Jumeirah Park provides additional waterfront running. Best done as an early morning run to avoid the crowds.

345
GREAT GAMBIA RUN (BAJANA INTERNATIONAL MARATHON)
THE GAMBIA
Road/Marathon
April/42 km

This race is held every Easter Sunday, attracting an international field of more than 2,000 runners. They have the chance to experience many areas of remote rural Gambia, including villages where the locals line the course to cheer you on. Fund-raising for local charities is a key aim of the event, which is organised by the Gambia Volunteers Trust, and the money is used to support disadvantaged rural communities.

346

GREAT ETHIOPIAN RUN
ADDIS ABABA, ETHIOPIA
Road
November/10 km

One of the biggest races in Africa, with around 45,000 participants, this 10K regularly attracts an international field and has been called 'the most exciting race in the world'. The huge number of runners and the watching crowds create an unforgettable atmosphere, but don't expect a fast time as the roads are crowded, and at 2,400 m (7,870 ft) above sea level, the lack of oxygen will slow down many runners. The inaugural event in 2001 was won by Haile Gebrselassie, one of the world's greatest ever distance runners.

347

RWAMAGANA MARATHON
RWANDA
Trail
February/42 km

Held in the Rwandan Eastern Province of Rwamagana, these marathon, half-marathon and 10K races are on a tricky, tough course that largely consists of dirt tracks. Attracting serious runners and fun-runners alike, the highlights of the race are the stunning scenery and the vocal encouragement from the many locals who line the route. There are frequent drink stations offering water and bananas.

348 | **The Rwenzori Mountains of the Rift Marathon**

348

RIFT MARATHON
UGANDA
Marathon/Trail
November/42 km

Described as both brutal and beautiful, the dirt trail of the Rift Marathon loops through villages and banana plantations, all in the shadow of the spectacular Rwenzori Mountains, located where the Rift Valley meets the Congo Basin. Starting and finishing at an altitude of 1,513 m (4,964 ft), with climbs and descents of over 16 per cent, marshals, medics, and water and electrolyte stations are present to support the runners. The race can be experienced as part of a six-day trip staying at the Kyaninga Lodge, with all profits going to the Kyaninga Child Development Centre.

349

NANGILI ROAD
ELDORET, KENYA
Running route/Road
All year round/22 & 40 km

One of the most famous, and notorious, training runs in Eldoret, the Nangili Road has been used by scores of elite Kenyan runners refining their training under the watchful eye of their coaches, driving alongside in their 4x4s, as they prepare for major marathons around the world. Beginning at the Maili Tisa safari park, with an altitude of 1,955 m (6,414 ft), after a flat start being watched by the local giraffes, the road heads upward through tea plantations, with locals cheering on the runners. Whether you decide to do 22 km (14 miles) or the popular 40-km (25-mile) version, it is a major challenge.

AFRICA AND THE MIDDLE EAST 229

350 | A high-altitude training group in Iten

350
ITEN
KENYA
Running route/Trail
All year round/Various

Iten is not a race nor a run: it's a mythical place for those who want to run fast, with thousands of runners making the pilgrimage to train on its dirt roads and often severely rolling countryside at an altitude of 2,400 m (7,900 ft). Home to the iconic St Patricks School and the High Altitude Training Centre, Iten hosts the largest women-only race, on Christmas Eve over 5K, and is the regular training base of many of the best Kenyan runners, as well as hosting a number of commercial training camps.

351
BARINGO HALF-MARATHON
KENYA
Trail
December/10 & 21 km

Located in the Rift Valley, at an altitude of just under 2,500 m (8,200 ft), the Baringo Half, with its twisting, undulating course, is for the more hardy runner, winding through local countryside before dropping over the last mile to finish in Kabarnet, the largest town of the province. Established in 2001 by local runner and multiple world champion Paul Tergat, to help find and develop talented local runners, winning times are fast, but for those who prefer something shorter there is also a 10K race and a fun-run for kids.

352

MASAI MARA HALF-MARATHON
KENYA

Trail

November/21 km

Set within the spectacular Masai Mara National Reserve, expect to have zebra and wildebeest cutting across the marked dirt trail loop, which runs through some of the most mind-blowing scenery you can imagine. Held in the stunning Lemek Conservancy, one of the best game-viewing areas, the race attracts an international field and raises money to support conservation projects in the reserve.

354 | **Job done: a Kilimanjaro Finisher's Medal**

353
SERENGETI SAFARI MARATHON
TANZANIA
Multi-terrain
November/42 km

Held in the western part of Tanzania's Serengeti National Park, the marathon, half-marathon and 5K races are a mixture of rough trails and roads. Starting inside the park, the run passes through the vast Serengeti Plains, with a chance to spot wildlife that, in many cases, is likely to be far faster and much hungrier than the runners. Cut-off times are imposed of 4 hours for the half and 6 hours for the marathon, but booking a safari package will ensure you can stay for longer.

354
KILIMANJARO MARATHON
TANZANIA
Road
March/42 km

The Kili, as it is known locally, annually attracts some 12,000 runners to Moshi to race in the shadow of the majestic Mount Kilimanjaro, which towers over the town at 5,895 m (19,300 ft). The influx of runners creates a lively buzz around the town as people take time to relax and enjoy the local cuisine and the jacaranda tree scent. All three events – marathon, half-marathon and 5K – after winding through small-holder farms, villages, banana and coffee plantations, patches of forest and Moshi itself, finish in the MoCU Stadium.

355
HEART HALF-MARATHON
DAR ES SALAAM, TANZANIA
Coastal/Road
April/21 km

Located on Tanzania's Indian Ocean Coast, the city of Dar es Salaam is now a major commercial port as well as home to the Heart series of races – half-marathon, 10K and 5K – all held to raise awareness about preventable chronic diseases. All three races start and finish at the north of the city near Coco Beach, making it perfect for post-race relaxation, and, if the tide is in, a recovery dip as well.

356
CITIDASH 5K AND 10K
WINDHOEK, NAMIBIA
Road/Urban
June/5 & 10 km

This event has been designed to showcase the best running talent in Namibia, while also aiming to become the largest mass-participation sporting event in the country. There are two 10K races: an elite event with a cut-off time of 50 minutes and a fun event for those aiming to run at a steadier pace. The 5K is also promoted as the fun event, and all of the races give runners the chance to see the sights of Namibia's capital city.

357
VICTORIA FALLS MARATHON
ZIMBABWE
Road
July/42 km

All the routes – marathon, half-marathon and 7.5-km (4.7-mile) fun-run – encompass incredible scenery close to the iconic Victoria Falls. The race starts with a bridge crossing over an international boundary in the spray of the falls, then cuts through a World Heritage Site, and provides the chance of seeing big game such as elephants – all of which certainly caters to the adventure sports tourist.

358
SKUKUZA HALF-MARATHON
KRUGER NATIONAL PARK, SOUTH AFRICA

Trail
August/21 km

Promoted as a unique race in a unique place, the Skukuza Half is held in the heart of Kruger National Park, and regularly attracts more than 1,500 runners. The race takes place in and around the staff village that is linked to the Skukuza Tourist Rest Camp, and is started from the 'village green' by the (recorded!) sound of a lion's roar. In case any of the lion's relatives or other big game have ventured onto the undulating course, runners are accompanied by teams of rangers to keep them safe.

359
FAIRIE GLEN NATURE RESERVE
PRETORIA, SOUTH AFRICA

Running route/Trail
All year round/Various

Close to the city of Pretoria, this nature reserve includes an area declared a critically endangered ecosystem in 2011. However, a series of carefully constructed paths and walkways provide runners with a choice of three short trails. It is possible to combine these for runs of differing lengths, but each trail offers the chance to catch a glimpse of the reserve's wildlife that includes zebra, impala and red hartebeest – fortunately for runners, all of which are vegetarian.

358 | A local resident inspects the Skukuza route

360
4PEAKS MOUNTAIN CHALLENGE
SOUTH AFRICA

Mountain
June/24 km

The 4Peaks covers a distance of 24 km (15 miles), along with an impressive gain in elevation of 1,800 m (5,900 ft), which turns a modest distance into a demanding race. Held in the Moolmanshoek Private Game Reserve, the circular race encompasses four peaks along the ridges of the Witteberg mountain range, combining steep ascents and descents on tricky terrain. Runners self-navigate with the help of marshals, and are required to carry their own safety kit and water.

Climbing the hill towards Pietermaritzburg

361

MANDELA DAY MARATHON

IMBALI, SOUTH AFRICA

Road

August/42 km

With a route of profound cultural significance, the Mandela Day Marathon celebrates the 'triumph of the human spirit'. Starting at Manaye Hall, where Nelson Mandela made his last speech as a free man in 1962, the race finishes 42 km (26.2 miles) later in Howick, where he was arrested by apartheid police soon after, a spot now known as the Nelson Mandela Capture Site. Both the marathon start and finish form part of the Freedom Route, designed to promote the history of the heroes who helped shape the Rainbow Nation.

362

COMRADES MARATHON

PIETERMARITZBURG/DURBAN, SOUTH AFRICA

Ultra

June/92 km

A hugely popular event that is televised nationally and named after the comradeship at the heart of the race, runners need to qualify by posting a time in one of a series of qualifying races. First held in 1921, the Comrades is approximately 92 km (57 miles), alternating on a yearly basis from a 'Down Run' between Pietermaritzburg and Durban to an 'Up Run' in the opposite direction the following year. The race has strictly enforced cut-off points, and runners who fail to make them in the required time have to board the infamous 'bailer bus' to be taken to the finish. Supporters line the route, cooking on braais and cheering on the runners in the world's oldest and largest ultramarathon.

AFRICA AND THE MIDDLE EAST

363
DURBAN 10K
SOUTH AFRICA
Road/Urban
July/10 km

Known as the City Surf Run, this race starts at Blue Lagoon Beach, passing through the heart of the city, past historical landmarks and back along the open coastline to finish on the beachfront precinct. Be inspired as elite and masses alike are supported by raucous encouragement from radio and the best local entertainment groups – dancers, drummers and more – creating a vibrant atmosphere as runners are encouraged to live up to the event slogan: 'Run Durban your way'.

364
TABLE MOUNTAIN
CAPE TOWN, SOUTH AFRICA
Running route/Mountain
All year round/Various

A run to the 1,000-m (3,500-ft) summit of Table Mountain will provide amazing views on the way up, and again when you catch your breath at the top. Starting from the car park near the cable car station, there is a gentle jog to the start of the trail, then a 3-km (2-mile) uphill section that is steep but runnable, especially if you take time out for photos as the views unfold. The last section to the summit is steep and best suited for a fast walk. Either run back down or catch the cable car for a much quicker descent to the bottom.

365
TWO OCEANS MARATHON
CAPE TOWN, SOUTH AFRICA
Road/Ultra
March or April/21 & 56 km

The Two Oceans is a 56-km (35-mile) ultra and a half-marathon, which is held over the Easter weekend. Both races start in Newlands, close to Cape Town, and follow routes that have a backdrop of spectacular scenery through the Cape Peninsula, before finishing at the campus of the University of Cape Town. As the name suggests, the race passes both of the oceans that surround the Peninsula – the Indian Ocean to the east and the Atlantic Ocean to the west.

366 | Incredible gorges are part of the Tsitsikamma Trail

366

TSITSIKAMMA TRAIL
SOUTH AFRICA
Running route/Trail
All year round/62 km

Located near the southern tip of the country, the Tsitsikamma Trail is a truly unique 62-km (39-mile) adventure through indigenous Afromontane forest and mountain fynbos. Designed for hikers to take six days, the trail's overnight huts make it a flexible journey for those travelling at a faster pace, although one that is likely to be slowed by having to clamber over the roots of the Real Yellowwood, South Africa's national tree, as well as admiring the stunning river gorges and streams.

367

ULTRA TRAIL DES Ô PLATEAUX
MADAGASCAR
Ultra/Mountain
May/126 km

The 126-km (78-mile) ultra starts at 2 a.m. and involves at least one, possibly two, nights on the course. The terrain is entirely off-road trails and very mountainous, with significant ascents and descents. A total of over 5,000 m (16,000 ft) is climbed by the ultra runners, who have to complete the race within 36 hours. Only 100 runners are allowed to enter each race (also includes 70-, 40- and 30-km/ 43-, 25- and 19-mile options), which take place in the central highlands area of Madagascar.

AFRICA AND THE MIDDLE EAST 239

368
MAURITIUS MARATHON
MAURITIUS
Road
July/42 km

The Mauritius Marathon is held close to the spectacular south-west coastline of the island, and ticks the box for runners who are seeking exotic locations for their marathons. The course runs through traditional fishing villages, alongside the lagoon and past the foothills of Le Morne mountain. Finishing on the beach of Saint Felix, the marathon is held on roads, in a friendly atmosphere with plenty of local support.

369
AVALON TRAIL
MAURITIUS
Trail
October/Various

The Avalon is one of several races organised to promote the sharing of the remarkably beautiful trails in Mauritius. They provide something for everyone: from a 4-km (2.5-mile) fun-run held on rolling hunting trails, through the 11-km (6.8-mile) Lancelot Trail race mixing forest and open terrain, to Arthur's Trail – 18 km (11 miles) of extremely technical, undulating hunting trails, which the organisers warn feels more like double the distance.

368 | **Journey to Mauritius for an exotic marathon**

ASIA
AUSTRALASIA AND THE SOUTH PACIFIC

ASIA, AUSTRALASIA AND THE SOUTH PACIFIC: ENTRY LIST

JANUARY
- 390 Hong Kong 100 Ultra Trail Race, Hong Kong
- 402 Khon Kaen Marathon, Thailand
- 405 Ultra Trail Angkor, Cambodia
- 409 Ho Chi Minh City Marathon, Vietnam
- 449 North Shore Run Series, New Zealand
- 457 Tussock Traverse, New Zealand
- 461 Wine Run, New Zealand

FEBRUARY
- 446 Cradle Mountain, Australia
- 455 Tarawera Ultra, New Zealand
- 464 Shotover Moonlight Adventure Run, New Zealand

MARCH
- 393 Nagoya City Marathon, Japan
- 398 Tokyo Marathon, Japan
- 404 Vientiane Half-marathon, Laos
- 433 Six Foot Track Marathon, Australia
- 437 Australian Alpine Ascent, Australia
- 463 Macpac Motatapu, New Zealand

APRIL
- 394 Sakura Michi Nature Run, Japan
- 410 2XU Compression Run, Singapore
- 415 Moon Shadow Night Run, Australia
- 420 Kangaroo Island Marathon, Australia
- 424 Five Peaks SA Trail Running Festival, Australia
- 427 Gold Coast Running Festival, Australia

MAY
- 379 Everest Marathon, Nepal
- 381 Thunder Dragon Marathon, Bhutan
- 386 Great Wall Marathon, China
- 434 SMH Half-marathon, Australia
- 441 Puffing Billy Running Festival, Australia
- 452 Waiheke Half-marathon, New Zealand
- 458 Hawke's Bay Marathon, New Zealand

JUNE
- 384 Lanzhou Marathon, China
- 396 Ohme Road Race, Japan
- 412 Borneo Marathon, Malaysia
- 465 Mount Difficulty Ascent, New Zealand
- 471 Aitutaki Pursuit in Paradise Marathon, Cook Islands

JULY
- 371 The Great Tibetan Marathon, India
- 378 Longrun Marathon, Maldives
- 395 Fuji Mountain Race, Japan
- 417 Australian Outback Marathon, Australia
- 470 Savai'i Marathon, Samoa
- 472 Tahiti-Moorea Marathon, French Polynesia

AUGUST
- 377 Arugam Bay Half-marathon, Sri Lanka
- 383 Mongolia Sunrise to Sunset, Mongolia
- 408 Da Nang Marathon, Vietnam
- 416 City to Surf, Australia
- 419 Alice Springs Running Festival, Australia
- 426 Challenge the Mountain, Australia
- 431 Dubbo Stampede, Australia
- 435 City2Surf, Australia
- 445 Flinders Island Running Festival, Australia
- 453 Mount Maunganui Half-marathon, New Zealand

SEPTEMBER
- 372 Ladakh Ultra, India
- 375 Satara Hill Half-marathon, India
- 382 The Gobi March, Mongolia
- 422 Adelaide City to Bay, Australia
- 432 Backyard Blister, Australia
- 438 Surf Coast Century, Australia
- 442 Phillip Island Running Festival, Australia
- 462 4 Paws Marathon, New Zealand

ASIA, AUSTRALASIA AND THE SOUTH PACIFIC

OCTOBER
- 373   Delhi Half-marathon, India
- 376   Himalaya 100-mile Stage Race, India
- 385   Beijing Marathon, China
- 430   Byron Bay Lighthouse Run, Australia
- 439   Melbourne Marathon Festival, Australia
- 448   Great Barrier Island Wharf to Wharf, New Zealand
- 450   Auckland Marathon, New Zealand
- 456   Taupo Ultra, New Zealand
- 459   Abel Tasman Coastal Classic, New Zealand
- 460   Aoraki Mount Cook Marathon, New Zealand

NOVEMBER
- 373   Delhi Half-marathon, India
- 376   Himalaya 100-mile Stage Race, India
- 380   Everest Trail Race, Nepal
- 400   Bagan Temple Marathon, Myanmar
- 407   Halong Bay Heritage Marathon, Vietnam
- 428   Ultra Trail Gold Coast, Australia
- 444   Summit Survivor, Australia
- 447   Point to Pinnacle Half-marathon, Tasmania
- 454   Rotorua Running Festival, New Zealand
- 468   Queenstown Marathon, New Zealand

DECEMBER
- 391   Fukuoka Marathon, Japan
- 469   Kepler Challenge 60 km, New Zealand

ALL YEAR ROUND
- 370   Baku Boulevard, Azerbaijan
- 374   Mumbai, India
- 387   The Bund, China
- 388   Sai Van Lake, Macau
- 389   Victoria Peak Circle Run, Hong Kong
- 392   Kyoto, Japan
- 397   Imperial Palace Loop, Japan
- 399   Arakawa Trail, Japan
- 401   Lumpini Park, Thailand
- 403   Patong Beach to Kalim Hill, Thailand
- 406   Hoang Lien National Park, Vietnam
- 411   Lambir Hills National Park Summit Trail, Malaysia
- 413   Manila Baywalk, Philippines
- 414   Kokoda Trail, Papua New Guinea
- 418   Uluru Base Trail, Australia
- 421   Elder Park, Australia
- 423   Mount Lofty Climb, Australia
- 425   Cairns, Australia
- 429   Snapper Rocks, Australia
- 436   Bondi Beach, Australia
- 440   Albert Park, Australia
- 443   Portsea, Australia
- 451   One Tree Hill, New Zealand
- 466   Routeburn Track, New Zealand (summer)
- 467   Milford Track, New Zealand (summer)

ASIA, AUSTRALASIA AND THE SOUTH PACIFIC 245

SAMOA   COOK ISLANDS   FRENCH POLYNESIA

370 | A straight section of the Baku Boulevard

371 | Sharing stories after the Tibetan Marathon

370
BAKU BOULEVARD
AZERBAIJAN
Running route/Track
All year round/7.4 km

Fancy running on the famous Baku Formula 1 track? Well, you can on the long Baku Boulevard, which runs alongside the city on the coast of the Caspian Sea. Azerbaijan is known as the land of carpets, wind and fire, and you'll get a taste of all three as you make your way past the carpet factory and the flame towers, all while facing an incredibly strong headwind at most times of the year. Incorporating a lap of the second-longest Formula 1 track will add 6 km (3.7 miles) to the distance.

371
THE GREAT TIBETAN MARATHON
TIBETAN PLATEAU, INDIA
Multi-terrain/Mountain
July/42 km

Taking place at an average altitude of 3,600 m (12,000 ft), this has been described as one of the world's most extreme marathons. The altitude means that runners are required to spend five days acclimatising in Ladakh prior to the race. On race day, runners are set on their way from Hemis Monastery by the sound of Buddhist horns and a blessing from the monks. They follow a route mixing tarmac, gravel and small wooden bridges, all under the awesome vista of the Stok Kangri mountain range, to the finish at Spituk Monastery, with a Buddhist celebration.

372 | Mountainous scenery dominates the Ladakh Ultra

373 | Young and old alike compete in Delhi

372

LADAKH ULTRA
LEH, INDIA
Ultra/Mountain
September/72 km

These high-altitude races place an extreme physiological demand on the runners, particularly those taking part in the 72-km (45-mile) ultra and the marathon. With most of the running taking place at an altitude of 3,500 m (11,500 ft), the organisers advise runners to arrive two weeks before race day to acclimatise. Despite the tough nature of all the distances (half-marathon and 7 km/4.3 miles are also available), more than 6,000 runners regularly take part. They are all treated to stunning vistas of mountains, rivers and valleys, during a real test of human endurance.

373

DELHI HALF-MARATHON
INDIA
Road/Urban
October or November/21 km

At the front end the World Athletics Gold Label, this half-marathon attracts some of the best runners in the world, lured by the possibility of quick times on the superfast out-and-back course – also an incentive for the 30,000 others who take part in the event's four races. The course starts in the Nehru Stadium, and the organisers work hard to ensure the race is held at the best time for the lowest possible air pollution.

375 | The twisting route of the Satara Hill Half

374
MUMBAI
INDIA

Running route/Urban
All year round/Various

The heat and humidity of India's Arabian Coast makes early morning running the best option, and remember to stay hydrated both during and after your run. The best running spot is the Marine Drive seawall, which stretches for just over 4 km (2.5 miles). This coastal run has a mystical feel to it, as well as epic views across the sea and the city. Don't expect to see too many other runners out at the same time – running is not yet as popular in India as it is in many other countries.

375
SATARA HILL HALF-MARATHON
SATARA, INDIA

Road/Mountain
September/21 km

Held in the capital of the Maratha Kingdom, the Satara Hill Half is popular with runners from around the world. Running through picturesque, undulating countryside, past waterfalls and the nearby Satara Mountains, runners will gain 420 m (1,380 ft) in elevation and will often find themselves running in clouds, which only adds to the magical feeling that this race generates. It's not one that will get you a fast time, but it certainly is one that will remain long in your memory.

376
HIMALAYA 100-MILE STAGE RACE
DARJEELING, INDIA

Multiday adventure/Mountain
October/November/161 km

Run in Tour de France style, this is a stage race, at a high altitude of 3,000 m (9,800 ft) to more than 5,000 m (16,400 ft), with a significant backdrop looming large every day. You'll see an iconic mountain range that includes Lhotse and Everest. There are five very achievable daily stages of 39, 32, 42, 21 and 27 km (24, 20, 26, 13 and 17 miles), and you'll stay overnight in tents or lodgings such as local monasteries.

377
ARUGAM BAY HALF-MARATHON
SRI LANKA

Road/Coastal
August/21 km

These events are held with the aim of supporting children's educational charities in Sri Lanka. Starting and finishing at Al Aqsa School, the runs (also 10K and 5K) are held along roads near to beautiful Arugam Bay, and as a result the course is largely flat. Runners are supported with drink stations, and the road to recovery starts with a post-race food pack for all finishers.

376 | Majestic Mount Everest overlooks the Himalaya Stage Race

Even local runners have weary legs towards the end of the Everest Marathon

378
LONGRUN MARATHON
MALDIVES

Road

July/42 km

Unusually, the marathon is a night race, starting at 2.20 a.m., but the half-marathon and 10K are also races for early starters, as they begin at 5.20 a.m. and 6.20 a.m. respectively. All the races are held on a beautiful 7-km (4.3-mile) loop, and regularly attract an international field of more than 2,000 runners. The races start and finish at Hulhumalé Park, in the centre of Male, the capital city, and there is plenty of music and entertainment to keep runners – and the local residents – awake.

379
EVEREST MARATHON
KHUMBA VALLEY, NEPAL

Mountain

May/Various

Fear not, you don't have to retrace those famous steps from 1953, but you do get to experience Everest base camp as you run in one of three events: a full-on, tough-as-you-like 60 km (37 miles), the classic marathon distance (billed as the 'highest and most adventurous marathon in the world'), or the challenging half-marathon. Truly, this is a once-in-a-lifetime event, in which you'll be treated to the most spectacular scenery on the planet.

381 | The Thunder Dragon Marathon promotes running in Bhutan

380
EVEREST TRAIL RACE
SOLUKHUMBU, NEPAL
Multiday adventure/Mountain
November/160+ km

A six-day, semi-self-supported epic requiring runners to cover over 160 km (100 miles) with a height change of 26,000 m (85,000 ft), the Everest Trail Race is based in the Solukhumbu region, at an altitude of between 2,000 and 4,100 m (6,600 and 13,500 ft). The beautiful remoteness of the daily stages means runners are required to carry clothing, sleeping bag, plus survival and medical kits, as they tackle this most demanding of trails over snow and different types and colours of rock, set against a panorama of some of the world's highest mountains.

381
THUNDER DRAGON MARATHON
PARO VALLEY, BHUTAN
Trail
May/21 & 42 km

With an entry field of less than 200 runners, this marathon may not yet be a big event in the international calendar, but it has provided a boost to running in Bhutan, with many locals encouraged to enter. The races start in the shadow of the famous Tigers Nest, before roads and farm tracks take runners past rice fields and local villages, and the final 10 km (6 miles) is a steady climb to the finish. Not a race for a fast time, as the starting elevation is at 2,400 m (7,900 ft) and there is a climb of 995 m (3,250 ft) for the marathon, and half of that for the half-marathon.

382

THE GOBI MARCH
MONGOLIA

Multiday adventure/Multi-terrain
September/250 km

Sleeping sometimes in traditional Mongolian gers or in the race-tented village, competitors in the Gobi March spend seven days covering 250 km (155 miles) in stunning central Mongolia. Taking place on tracks and off-road trails, over grassland, fields, soft sand and dunes, rocky terrain, riverbeds and river crossings, the route climbs and descends from its start at the Khar Bukh Balgas fortress to the finish in Karakorum. You'll pass numerous stupas and temples, traditional villages, the UNESCO World Heritage Centre of the Orkhon Valley Cultural Landscape and Genghis Khan's battlefields.

382 | The Gobi March attracts an inquisitive onlooker

383 | It's easy to see why the MS2S is called the world's most beautiful race

383
MONGOLIA SUNRISE TO SUNSET
MONGOLIA
Trail/Mountain
August/42 & 100 km

The MS2S offers a choice of two distances, 42 and 100 km (26 and 62 miles), both of which require an overnight stay in a Mongolian ger. Starting in Lake Khövsgöl National Park, runners follow specific trails through spectacular scenery of mountains and lakes, with a total ascent and descent of over 2,500 m (8,200 ft) for the marathon, and over 3,300 m (10,800 ft) for the ultra. Be warned: there are cut-off times during the race for both distances.

384
LANZHOU MARATHON
CHINA
Marathon
June/42 km

Awarded China's 'Best Marathon' status by the Chinese Athletics Association, the highlight is the spectacular setting alongside the banks of the Yellow River. The out-and-back route crosses the river, and provides runners with continuous mountain scenery close to Lanzhou City, the capital of Gansu Province, and on the ancient Silk Road.

385

BEIJING MARATHON
CHINA

Road/Marathon
October/42 km

Touted as China's top road race, and a World Athletics Gold Label event, the marathon starts in the historic Tiananmen Square and, after touring through the city's financial, cultural and technology centres, finishes in the Olympic Sports Center, next to the iconic Bird's Nest stadium. Held in autumn, it's a good time of year for both fast times and seeing the city at its best, with golden leaves falling from the gingko trees.

386
GREAT WALL MARATHON
TIANJIN, CHINA
Marathon/Novelty
May/42 km

Run in waves starting at 10-minute intervals, this has to be one of the most iconic and challenging marathons in the world. Starting and finishing in the Yin and Yang Square in the fortress of Huangyaguan in Tianjin, the route then loops on and off the Great Wall itself. Be prepared for steps and more steps, compensated for by breathtaking views as you head through open fields and built-up conurbations, sharing the journey with runners of all nationalities.

387
THE BUND
SHANGHAI, CHINA
Running route/Urban
All year round/Various

The cosmopolitan city of Shanghai delivers a skyline of high-rise contemporary buildings and skyscrapers that is like no other in the world. Mixed in with these are much older colonial buildings that are a reminder of the city's long heritage as a trading post. A wide path along the banks of the Huangpu River can be crowded with tourists, but is the best place in Shanghai to combine a run with some serious sightseeing.

388
SAI VAN LAKE
MACAU
Running route
All year round/2.6 km

In the densely populated independent state of Macau, often referred to as the gambling capital of the world, there are not too many quiet and relatively peaceful places to run. However, the 2.6-km (1.6-mile) loop of the man-made Sai Van Lake is one of them, and the wide, flat path that surrounds the lake is understandably popular with runners. The loop includes a short tunnelled section that runs underneath the 338-m (1,109-ft) high Macau Tower.

389
VICTORIA PEAK CIRCLE RUN
HONG KONG
Running route/Mountain
All year round/Various

Victoria Peak is one of Hong Kong's main physical landmarks, reaching an elevation of 552 m (1,811 ft). The roads and trails that wind from the base to the summit offer runners a choice of routes, but the easiest and most popular is to take the Peak Tram to the summit, then follow the well-signposted road back to the base. This offers the chance to circle the entire peak, so the views are ever changing and fantastic in all directions. Runners looking for something more challenging can start from the base and run up to the summit.

390 | A rewarding view during the Hong Kong Ultra

390
HONG KONG 100 ULTRA TRAIL RACE
HONG KONG
Ultra/Trail
January/103 km

The HK 100 covers 103 km (64 miles) of the best bits of the region's famous MacLehose Trail. Starting on the Sai Kung Peninsula, runners can except to experience the best scenery Hong Kong has to offer – unspoilt remote beaches, nature trails through ancient forests, past reservoirs, and up and down steep hills – none more profound than the race finale, from Hong Kong's highest peak, Tai Mo Shan, with a 4-km (2.5-mile) descent to the finish.

391
FUKUOKA MARATHON
JAPAN
Marathon/Urban
December/42 km

The Fukuoka Marathon has a long and famous heritage, having first been run in 1947. Normally held on the first Sunday in December, its prestige in the marathon running calendar is emphasised by its Gold Label status awarded by World Athletics. Unusually, it is a male-only event, and runners are only allowed to take part if they have achieved qualifying times or have been invited to run by the organisers. During the race, failure to meet strictly enforced cut-off times at various parts of the course results in elimination.

393 | The fast, flat Nagoya City Marathon

392
KYOTO
JAPAN
Running route
All year round/20 km

Cultural Kyoto is the former capital of Japan and is situated on the island of Honshu. Running through the city is the Kamogawa River, which provides a chance for long, flat runs away from the high volumes of traffic and fumes that running elsewhere in Japan can bring. An out-and-back run along the river will yield a distance of just over 20 km (13 miles), probably best run in the spring months, when the spectacular cherry blossom is in bloom.

393
NAGOYA CITY MARATHON
JAPAN
Road/Festival
March/42 km

Held on the same day as the longstanding and iconic Nagoya Women's Marathon, a World Athletics Gold Label event, the Nagoya City Marathon features half- and quarter-marathons open to both men and women. All the races start from the Nagoya Dome, with the marathon finishing in the same place. The fast and flat courses cater to some 40,000 runners on race day, creating a true festival of running in this marathon-mad country.

394

SAKURA MICHI NATURE RUN
JAPAN

Multi-terrain/Ultra

April/250 km

Established and named in honour of Ryoji Sato, who dreamed of establishing a tunnel of cherry trees across the length of Japan connecting the Pacific Ocean to the Sea of Japan, this 250-km (155-mile) ultra follows that route as some 2,000 trees he planted are in awe-inspiring pink blossom. Supported by more than 1,000 volunteers and held over three days, the route from Kanazawa to Nagoya is on good, firm surfaces.

395

FUJI MOUNTAIN RACE
JAPAN

Mountain

July/42 km

From the centre of Fujiyoshida to the summit of Mount Fuji and back, the Mountain Race ascends and descends 3,000 m (9,800 ft) over 42 km (26 miles). After a fast, slightly uphill 10 km (6 miles) on closed roads, runners turn onto the Yoshida Trail, often described as a vertical staircase, where runners use hands and knees to reach the top. The volcanic earth provides for fast descending for those who manage to achieve the 4.5-hour cut-off time.

395 | **Some steep climbing during the Fuji Mountain Race**

397 | **The Imperial Palace is a popular location for exercise in Tokyo**

396
OHME ROAD RACE
OME, JAPAN
Road
June/10 & 30 km

This historic race has been an important part of the Japanese road-running calendar since it was first held in 1967, attracting an entry field of 182. Today, the race regularly attracts more than 16,000 runners of varying abilities, and is held entirely on-road in Ome, a town close to the outskirts of Tokyo. The course is 30 km (19 miles) out and back, with runners turning halfway to retrace their steps along the same route to the finish, and a 10K distance is also available.

397
IMPERIAL PALACE LOOP
TOKYO, JAPAN
Running route
All year round/5 km

Turn up outside Tokyo's impressive Imperial Palace day or night and you might think there is an organised race taking place. In fact, it is runners from across the city of 30 million people turning up for their daily exercise. Somehow everyone knows to run or walk in the same direction around the 5K loop; it's not signposted, but it's difficult to get lost – just follow the runners and count how many you can overtake!

398

TOKYO MARATHON
TOKYO, JAPAN
Road/Urban
March/42 km

One of the iconic six World Marathon Majors, the Tokyo Marathon attracts some 38,000 runners from all over the world. Snaking through the city on a course that symbolises the past, present and future of the city, the race finishes in the splendour of the Imperial Palace, the primary residence of the Emperor and Imperial family. For those with energy, the relaxed Friendship run and Tokyo Family run take place the day before.

399

ARAKAWA TRAIL
YAKUSHIMA, JAPAN

Running route/Trail
All year round/21 km

Those wishing to travel the full length of the A1, or Arakawa Trail, either need to take the special Arakawa bus or a prearranged taxi to the start at the old railway terminal or be on a guided tour; arrangements are in place to ease the environmental impact on the most used trail in Yakushima. From the start, the trail follows old railway tracks through forests, over bridges and past settlements, until you reach the most notable of all the trees en route, the Jomon Sugi, a giant cedar tree that scientists estimate to be 2,000 to 7,200 years old. From there, follow your tracks back to the start.

400

BAGAN TEMPLE MARATHON
MYANMAR

Multi-terrain
November/42 km

The ancient site of Bagan is in central Myanmar, and is the site of more than 2,000 ancient temples and pagodas, which line the routes of all three races – the marathon, half and 10K. Held on a combination of roads and dirt tracks, the races pass through a mystical landscape of ancient monuments and flat plains. There are plentiful aid stations providing water and bananas, and at two of them runners can also leave their own personal refuelling supplies.

400 | Temples and pagodas are an integral part of the Bagan Temple Marathon

401

LUMPINI PARK
BANGKOK, THAILAND
Running route/Park
All year round/Various

Bangkok is renowned as a city of noise, fumes and crowds. Lumpini Park, in the centre of the city, is an oasis of calm that gives runners the opportunity to enjoy a green environment, with trees that provide welcome shade from the heat of the sun. The sounds of the city fade away, and there are many paths crisscrossing the park that offer the chance to run at any chosen distance or pace.

402

KHON KAEN MARATHON
THAILAND
Road/Marathon
January/42 km

Started in 2004 to celebrate the fortieth anniversary of the Cities University being formed, the AIMs-accredited Khon Kaen Marathon has steadily grown to become one of the largest marathons in Thailand, with more than 40,000 runners taking part in the events. The marathon itself is a scenic looped course passing through cultural and ethnic, as well as academic, communities. Pre-event sightseeing tours to either Joyful Farm and Fascinating Village or Dinosaur Planet are put on by the organiser on Saturday.

403

PATONG BEACH TO KALIM HILL
PHUKET, THAILAND
Running route/Trail
All year round/15 km

Starting off with suspicious ease along the beachfront in Phuket, the oft-described running capital of Thailand, there are certainly easier trails than the 15 km (9 miles) up and around Kalim Hill. If done as a clockwise loop, the first 4 km (2.5 miles) provide flat running with views across the water. From there, it's a strenuous climb to 532 m (1,745 ft) – worth it for the views across the town and beach. A final steep descent drops you back onto the beach and an easy jog to the finish. Given the heat and humidity, take plenty of water.

ASIA, AUSTRALASIA AND THE SOUTH PACIFIC 265

404 | The Vientiane races promote running to families in Laos

404
VIENTIANE HALF-MARATHON
LAOS
Road/Urban
March/21 km

The historic city of Vientiane is the capital of Laos and hosts these races on the first weekend of March each year. The inclusive event is used to promote exercise throughout the country, and children and their families are encouraged to take part in the 5K. The routes all pass through the ancient streets of the capital and alongside the banks of the famous Mekong river. There is a cut-off time of 3 hours 30 minutes for the half-marathon, and medals are awarded to half-marathon and 10K finishers.

405
ULTRA TRAIL ANGKOR
ANGKOR, CAMBODIA
Ultra/Trail
January/Various

This weekend of running offers something for everyone, from a tough 100-km (62-mile) ultra, to an 8-km (5-mile) Elephant Trail. Other races include a marathon, a 16-km (10-mile) Temple Run and a 32-km (20-mile) Jungle Trail. The Angkor Region, situated in the province of Siem Reap, is a source of national pride to the Cambodian population, as its rich array of temples and monuments makes it one of the main archaeological sites in Southeast Asia. All of the races make the most of the area's attractions, passing rice fields, local villages and temples.

406

HOANG LIEN NATIONAL PARK
SA PA, VIETNAM

Running route/Trail

All year round/Various

Named after the highest mountain range in Vietnam, the Hoang Lien National Park is a vibrant and wild home to over 50 per cent of the species of flora and fauna in the country, many of which are extremely rare. The uncultivated nature of the national park makes for true trail running, in terrain that includes the country's highest peak, Mount Fansipan (3,143 m/10,311 ft), lush forests and Heaven's Gate, the summit of Quan Ba Pass, which connects Lao Cai with Lai Chau.

407

HALONG BAY HERITAGE MARATHON
HANOI, VIETNAM

Marathon/Coastal

November/42 km

These marathon, half-marathon and 10K races offer runners a unique chance to see the stunning attractions of the World Heritage Centre that is Hanoi. The route crosses Bai Chay Bridge, the longest single-span bridge in Southeast Asia, which provides stunning views of Halong Bay and the nearby mountains and coast. Beware an early pre-sunrise start time of 5.30 a.m., chosen to avoid the worst of the heat.

406 | **Hoang Lien National Park is home to incredible trails and summits**

408
DA NANG MARATHON
VIETNAM
Road/Coastal
August/42 km

Also featuring a half-marathon, 10K, 5K and a 'kids' dash', this is a popular event for runners of all abilities. The route includes coastline and views of the mountains, as well as bridge crossings of the famous Hàn River. With plenty of local tourist attractions nearby, this is a great race to combine with a holiday to see the sights of Vietnam.

409
HO CHI MINH CITY MARATHON
VIETNAM
Road/Urban
January/42 km

This marathon is Vietnam's biggest, and with the climb up to the turnaround point in the middle of the iconic Phu My Bridge, over the Saigon River, it's a race very much about the journey rather than the times. It's a journey that will enable runners to experience the contrasts of old Saigon and modern Ho Chi Minh City. For those wanting something a little less demanding, there are also 5K, 10K and 21-km (13-mile) races on the same day.

410
2XU COMPRESSION RUN
SINGAPORE
Road/Festival
April/Various

With a half-marathon, 10K and 5K, the 2XU is one of a series of three similar events in south Asia. Roving spotlights, music and entertainment all help create a buzzing atmosphere for the predawn half-marathon start. The vibe is maintained along the route with bands and feed stations, as runners pass by the Esplanade theatre, one of Singapore's iconic buildings. For those with energy aplenty, there are post-race activities, massages and more entertainment in the race village at the F1 Pit Building, built especially for the annual Grand Prix.

410 | **The sun starts to rise at the beginning of the 2XU Compression Run**

411

LAMBIR HILLS NATIONAL PARK SUMMIT TRAIL
BORNEO, MALAYSIA
Running route/Trail
All year round/12.6 km

A 30-minute drive from Miri makes the natural wonderland of the Lambir Hills National Park easily accessible. The Summit Trail, at 6.3 km (3.9 miles) each way, is not quite the longest trail in the park, but it will take the most time, due to its steepness in parts as it climbs to the top at 456 m (1,496 ft). Having experienced the transition from dipterocarp to heath forest and the visual splendour of wild orchids, you'll be rewarded further by stunning views from the top. If warm, take a refreshing dip in the Dinding Waterfall on the descent.

413

MANILA BAYWALK
PHILIPPINES
Running route/Coastal
All year round/3 km

Although only stretching for about 1.5 km (1 mile) from north to south, the Baywalk is a popular spot for runners (and pedestrians). The wide concrete path is flat and keeps runners separated from the nearby traffic. Coconut trees line the route and offer some welcome shade during the hottest parts of the day, but the best time to run it is at sunset, when the views over the ocean are superb.

412

BORNEO MARATHON
MALAYSIA
Marathon/Night
June/42 km

Since it was first held in 1984, this race has grown in popularity and now regularly attracts an entry field of 10,000 runners from approximately 50 countries. Due to Borneo's heat and humidity, it is a night race, starting at 2 a.m., and the organisers raise funds for many local charities. The course is undulating, but the early start means that runners are treated to stunning views of the sunrise over Mount Kinabalu and the islands of the South China Sea.

414

KOKODA TRAIL
PAPUA NEW GUINEA
Trail/Multiday adventure
All year round/96 km

The towering Owen Stanley Range divides Papua New Guinea in two; crossing it is the wild and remote Kokoda Trail – 96 km (60 miles) of a muddy single track. The site of bitter fighting between the Japanese and Australians in 1942, the trail may only reach a height of 2,190 m (7,200 ft), but the mountainous nature of the terrain means a total of over 6,000 m (19,700 ft) climbing and descending, with frequent river crossings. Tackle it as a multiday trip and stay in rural guest huts dotted along the route. You could also hire a guide or go on an organised trip.

ASIA, AUSTRALASIA AND THE SOUTH PACIFIC

415
MOON SHADOW NIGHT RUN
PERTH, AUSTRALIA

Trail/Night
April/Various

Perth Trail Series offers a huge selection of races throughout the year, but it's the Moon Shadow Night Run that stands out from the rest. Starting at dusk, runners take to the trails with their headlamps and fairy lights at the ready. There are three distances to choose from – 4, 7 and 12 km (2.5, 4.5 and 7.5 miles) – and all abilities are welcome. As night draws in, you're treated to views of Perth's twinkling lights while you speed to the finish line of these unique races.

416
CITY TO SURF
PERTH, AUSTRALIA

Road/Urban
August/Various

This mass participation event caters to everyone from elite athletes to families and young children. From 4 km (2.5 miles) to the marathon, the races start and finish in the magnificent 60,000-seater Optus Stadium, once voted the 'most beautiful stadium in the world'. The routes are all on road, and on fast, flat courses, with plenty of running alongside the scenic Swan River. The potential for PBs is helped by perfect running conditions and a great atmosphere in the Perth sunshine.

417
AUSTRALIAN OUTBACK MARATHON
NORTHERN TERRITORY, AUSTRALIA

Marathon/Desert
July/42 km

Expect to get covered in red dust whichever distance you choose. there are also half-marathon and 6- and 11-km (3.5- and 7-mile) options. Following bush roads and bush trails, runners will mainly run on red earth and sand, which can get soft in places. Spectacular views of Uluru (formerly known as Ayers Rock) and Kata Tjuta (previously known as The Olgas) make this a race where you will find yourself in a location that you may only ever visit once in a lifetime.

418 | Uluru dominates the desert

418

ULURU BASE TRAIL

NORTHERN TERRITORY, AUSTRALIA
Running route/Desert
All year round/10 km

This 10-km (6.2-mile) trail is a dedicated flat trail for walkers and runners to enjoy the beauty and spirituality of Uluru. You can no longer hike to the top of the sacred rock, but you can certainly take it all in from below, appreciating its sheer size. The trail is well signposted, and it is recommended to head out in a clockwise direction. If you're keen for more exploring afterwards, there are plenty of trails throughout the national park – just remember to bring plenty of water and start early in the morning, as some trails close in the heat of the day.

419

ALICE SPRINGS RUNNING FESTIVAL

NORTHERN TERRITORY, AUSTRALIA
Festival
August/Various

Starting and finishing in Alice Springs, the cosmopolitan Red Centre town, the Running Festival consists of three events – a 10K walk/jog, a half-marathon and a full marathon. Renowned for its friendliness and professional organisation, the marathon typically has fields of well under 100 runners, creating a feeling of wonderfully supported solitude as runners make their way on roads through the local bush. The early winter start in the dark is compensated for by stunning views of the sun breaking over the West MacDonnell mountain range.

420
KANGAROO ISLAND MARATHON
SOUTH AUSTRALIA, AUSTRALIA

Marathon/Coastal

April/42 km

Many see Kangaroo Island as a mini Australia, home to everything Aussie – beaches, mountains, native bushland, animals, sea life, boutique wineries and distilleries. Understandably, it's a popular spot for tourists, and due to its large size it's never overcrowded. The devastating bushfires of 2020 destroyed so much of its stunning landscape and wildlife, but the island is determined to recover and thrive once again. And so, the Kangaroo Island Marathon runs on, to serve distance runners seeking a race like no other.

422
ADELAIDE CITY TO BAY
SOUTH AUSTRALIA, AUSTRALIA

Road/Urban

September/12 km

Adelaide's biggest fun-run sees thousands of people on the streets supporting both the elite and casual runner racing their way along a 12-km (7.5-mile) route from the city centre to the popular beachside suburb of Glenelg. Runners head down the flat Anzac Highway to try and beat their time from last year. Afterwards, hang around the Jetty Road area or head back to the city on a free bus or tram.

421
ELDER PARK
ADELAIDE, AUSTRALIA

Running route/Park

All year round/Various

Perched on the southern bank of the Torrens Lake, Elder Park is a beacon of green beauty. Numerous walking and running trails provide visitors with quality views across city and water, as well as the iconic Rotunda, constructed in 1882 using ironwork from a Glasgow foundry in Scotland, where there is also an Elder Park. The park is a popular spot for runners of all abilities, but the trails can become crowded with hikers and cyclists at peak times.

423
MOUNT LOFTY CLIMB
SOUTH AUSTRALIA, AUSTRALIA

Running route/Mountain

All year round/4 km

Mount Lofty is located in the beautiful Adelaide Hills and is the biggest peak in the region. There is a strenuous 4-km (2.5-mile) route from Waterfall Gully to the summit, where you can enjoy coffee and cake overlooking the pretty city and bay. It's a popular route for the citizens of Adelaide, some of whom walk it every day. Only the very fit would tackle this as a run, however, as it's steep in parts. Take a few breaks on the way down to spot koalas, kangaroos, bandicoots and some amazing birdlife.

424

FIVE PEAKS SA TRAIL RUNNING FESTIVAL
SOUTH AUSTRALIA, AUSTRALIA
Festival/Mountain
April/Various

Set in the beautiful Mount Lofty ranges, this multi-distance event has a great local feel to it, organised by Trail Running South Australia. If you fancy a practice run, or if 58 km (36 miles) isn't long enough for you, the group also does four training runs of the peaks at various stages in the lead up to the event. The full ultra takes in five peaks, with some seriously steep inclines and declines. Not for the fainthearted!

425

CAIRNS
QUEENSLAND, AUSTRALIA
Running route/Multi-terrain
All year round/Various

Known as the gateway to the Great Barrier Reef, Cairns is also a runners' paradise. Whether it's a flat run along the esplanade admiring the yachts large and small in the marina, running under the mangrove leaves on boardwalk paths, or tackling the steeper, more rugged climbs of the Red and Blue Arrow Circuits in Mount Whitfield Conservation Park with rainforest and eucalyptus, there are runs to suit everyone from close to the city centre.

426

CHALLENGE THE MOUNTAIN
QUEENSLAND, AUSTRALIA
Road/Mountain
August/5 km

One of the best mountain races in Australasia, this must-do event in Mount Archer is open to both runners and cyclists to tackle the 5K route at a punishing 10 per cent gradient. It's possible to run it solo or in a team, with generous cash prizes up for grabs in all age categories. At the top, participants are rewarded with a party atmosphere of food, drinks, bonfires, music and an amazing view to soak it all up. Bring something warm for the often-chilly summit.

427
GOLD COAST RUNNING FESTIVAL
QUEENSLAND, AUSTRALIA
Festival
April/Various

This family festival goes all out to attract runners of all abilities, with a choice of five different distances, from 1 km (0.6 miles) to a half-marathon, which are all held on a Sunday in April. All the races start just outside the Gold Coast's main stadium, then follow a similar out-and-back course, with the turn-back point dependent on the distance that is being run. The highlights are the finish back inside the stadium and, of course, the sunshine.

428
ULTRA TRAIL GOLD COAST
QUEENSLAND, AUSTRALIA
Ultra/Trail
November/up to 300 miles

A range of distances are available at this extreme event, with many courageous athletes choosing to run 160, 320 or 480 km (100, 200 or even 300 miles)! Runners start at the crack of dawn and run multiple 25-km (15.5-mile) loops night and day to reach the finish line up to six days later. Meanwhile, at the start of each loop, base camp provides a festive atmosphere, with barbecues, camping and music giving much-needed support for the runners.

429
SNAPPER ROCKS
GOLD COAST, AUSTRALIA
Coastal
All year round/Various

Famous for its outstanding surfing conditions, the beach at Snapper Rocks has been shaped by a sandbar, formed from sand artificially pumped from the nearby Tweed River to prevent the river from silting up. The result is a beach that stretches for a mile along the coast, offering runners the chance to experience the sounds, sights and smell of the ocean waves. Choose to run on either the hard-packed sand or the beachside footpaths, with outdoor gym equipment for cross-training.

430
BYRON BAY LIGHTHOUSE RUN
NEW SOUTH WALES, AUSTRALIA
Road/Coastal
October/10 km

Byron Bay's coastal location overlooking the warm Pacific Ocean makes it a perfect spot for surfers, backpackers, couples and families alike. The friendly town hosts an annual 10K around Australia's most eastern point, the Cape Byron Lighthouse. The fun-run is organised for charity and offers road, beach, hills and, above all, good food at the finish line. If you can't make it in October, it's still worth running on your own, and if you're an early riser, why not be the first person in Australia to watch the sun come up that day?

431
DUBBO STAMPEDE
NEW SOUTH WALES, AUSTRALIA
Road/Novelty
August/Various

Taronga Western Plains Zoo is the spot for this Stampede. Here, among the animals, there are a variety of races to enter, including the Dingo Dash (5K), the Cheetah Chase (10K) or the Rhino Ramble (marathon). The event is attended by charity fun-runners and serious athletes, most with the aim of securing a fast time on this relatively flat course. Once runners have finished, they have a free pass to explore the zoo, at a more leisurely pace.

432
BACKYARD BLISTER
NEW SOUTH WALES, AUSTRALIA
Trail/Ultra
September/Unlimited

Held in September on the Hells Gate river flats, the Backyard Blister is a 'last person standing' event. Runners are required to complete a 6.7-km (4-mile) loop at the start of every hour, and must complete the loop within the hour to avoid elimination, with the next lap starting on the hour of each consecutive hour. Held on single-track trails and with a total elevation of 147 m (482 ft) per lap, this event is both a physical and mental challenge.

433
SIX FOOT TRACK MARATHON
NEW SOUTH WALES, AUSTRALIA
Trail
March/45 km

It might be called a marathon, but the Six Foot Track race is longer, at 45 km (28 miles), covering the complete distance of the trail it is named after, from the Explorers Marked Tree near Katoomba to the finish at the Jenolan Caves. As it crosses the Blue Mountains, the route has a hefty total climb of 1,528 m (5,010 ft) and a 1,788-m (5,866-ft) descent, taking in dirt trails, open plains, forest and river crossings. With a 7-hour time limit, it's not one for the inexperienced.

434
SMH HALF-MARATHON
SYDNEY, AUSTRALIA

Road/Urban
May/21 km

Fancy speeding round the streets of Sydney before the world awakes on a Sunday morning? Set your alarm clock for this one as it starts early, so you can enjoy the city without traffic. The undulating course is a fabulous way to see the sights, as you run through Darling Harbour, under the Sydney Harbour Bridge, past the Opera House and through the central business district. You can run solo or in relays, and everyone gets a finishers' medal, before heading to one of Sydney's many cafes for breakfast.

435

CITY2SURF, SYDNEY

NEW SOUTH WALES, AUSTRALIA

Road

August/14 km

Since it started in 1971 with an entry field of just over 2,000 runners, the City2Surf race has become one of the most popular fun-runs in the world, and now regularly attracts more than 85,000 runners. This 14-km (9-mile) race commences next to Hyde Park in Sydney's central business district, and after a downhill start, runners are faced with a tough climb at halfway as they ascend Heartbreak Hill. The course gradually descends from the top of the hill, with great views of the ocean before competitors reach the finishing line at the iconic Bondi Beach.

437 | **The Snowy Mountains dominate the Alpine Ascent**

436

BONDI BEACH
NEW SOUTH WALES, AUSTRALIA
Running route/Coastal
All year round/Various

The surfers' paradise of Bondi Beach is also a great place for running, with a choice of distances that could start and finish on the famous beachfront. A mixture of beach, paths, trails and some road allows runners to get as far from the beach as they wish, and the further you go, the more the crowds are left behind.

437

AUSTRALIAN ALPINE ASCENT
NEW SOUTH WALES, AUSTRALIA
Festival/Mountain
March/25 & 50 km

This sell-out event is part of a multi-event festival set in exquisite alpine scenery. Take on the 25- or 50-km (15.5- or 31-mile) road/trail run and rub shoulders with some of the world's best endurance athletes as you cross the Kosciuszko National Park, taking in the iconic Snowy Mountains. As you will probably guess from the name, these events feature a fair bit of elevation, so start doing your hill work now!

438
SURF COAST CENTURY
VICTORIA, AUSTRALIA
Ultra/Relay
September/100 km

Victoria's surf coast is, as its name suggests, home to some of the best waves in Australia, with Bells Beach being the location of one of the oldest pro-surfing events in the world. It's also home to one of the world's most spectacular running events. Runners will navigate forest trails and beautiful beaches, and take in soaring clifftops high above the powerful Southern Ocean. Don't be put off by the 100-km (62-mile) distance; a popular and very enjoyable way to run the race is as part of a team of up to four people.

439
MELBOURNE MARATHON FESTIVAL
VICTORIA, AUSTRALIA
Festival/Road
October/Various

This popular running festival is billed as the largest event of its kind in Australia, attracting thousands of entrants that include local runners as well as many from all over the world. All of the races start at Batman Avenue in the centre of Melbourne, a road named after a long-dead Australian businessman, rather than the Caped Crusader, and ends with a lap to remember inside the magnificent 100,000-capacity Melbourne Cricket Ground.

439 | **Running along the bank of the Yarra River in the Melbourne Marathon**

441 | Wave to your supporters aboard the train

440
ALBERT PARK
MELBOURNE, AUSTRALIA
Running route/Park
All year round/4.7 km

Not too far from Melbourne's city centre is Albert Park Lake, a large lake with a well-maintained gravel running trail of 4.7 km (3 miles) on its shore. If you're into motor racing, you'll be excited to know that it doubles up as the Formula 1 track in March. Run the track on your own or as part of a Parkrun (see page 310) on a Saturday morning.

441
PUFFING BILLY RUNNING FESTIVAL
VICTORIA, AUSTRALIA
Festival/Novelty
May/up to 25 km

This is a delightfully family-friendly race against the historic *Puffing Billy* steam train travelling through the lush Dandenong Ranges rainforest. Runners can choose to run the full train line at 25 km (15.5 miles) or a shortened version, often racing their friends and family waving down at them from the train. The race finishes at the end of the line at Gembrook station, where you can hop aboard for the return to Belgrave. Race fees go towards the upkeep and restoration of the train line.

ASIA, AUSTRALASIA AND THE SOUTH PACIFIC   281

442
PHILLIP ISLAND RUNNING FESTIVAL
VICTORIA, AUSTRALIA
Festival/Coastal
September/Various

Phillip Island's main attraction might be its little penguins, but this island certainly has more to offer. Held over a spring weekend on this stunning unspoilt landscape, runners can join in various events – from 2 to 50 km (1 to 31 miles) – to explore the island on foot and meet with people from all over the world. There are plenty of accommodation options on the island itself, so participants can stay and fill up on the organised pre-race dinner the night before.

444 | **Get muddy with your mates**

443
PORTSEA
VICTORIA, AUSTRALIA
Running route/Coastal
All year round/Various

Australian Herb Elliott was the 1956 Olympic 1500 m champion, world record holder and literally unbeatable, largely thanks to his spartan lifestyle-type training schedule that saw him use the unrelenting sand dunes of Portsea beach. You too can sprint up and down the sand, perhaps camping out on the beach and eating rations-like food, following in Herb's footsteps. With the largest dune at 24 m (80 ft), with a 60-degree incline, your legs will be challenged to the max.

444
SUMMIT SURVIVOR
VICTORIA, AUSTRALIA
Obstacle course race
November/5 km

Don't expect to keep clean in this exciting 5K fun-run. Do expect to have fun though! This big-kid's playground has an enormous 40 obstacles to tackle over its muddy course. You probably won't run your PB, and there's no time limit to complete the course, but you will certainly return home happy and exhausted. At 1.5 hours from Melbourne, accommodation is available onsite, and team participation is encouraged, so why not make a weekend of it with your friends?

445

FLINDERS ISLAND RUNNING FESTIVAL

TASMANIA, AUSTRALIA

Festival/Coastal

August/Various

If you love running, you will love this festival! Flinders Island has some of the cleanest air in the world, with an amazing unspoilt landscape, making it a perfect spot for running. While this may sound like it's only for extreme enthusiasts, in fact, it's very much a community event, and any ability or interest level is welcome. Take part in the 26-km (16-mile) Pub to Pub run and/or the 5K, while enjoying good food and conversation with like-minded people.

446

CRADLE MOUNTAIN

TASMANIA, AUSTRALIA

Ultra/Coastal

February/80 km

This is a unique 80-km (50-mile) run with a maximum of 60 participants. Unsurprisingly, there is high demand for a spot in this popular event, and evidence of ability and experience must be provided in order to secure a place. A large part of the race is above the tree line and can be very exposed to the tough conditions. Keep in mind that the harder the race, the bigger the reward when you're home and dry!

447 | Enjoy the view when you get there

447

POINT TO PINNACLE HALF-MARATHON

TASMANIA, AUSTRALIA

Mountain

November/21 km

They call it 'the world's toughest half-marathon', and they're not wrong. Located up Mount Wellington, this gruelling race requires incredible endurance as you run from sea level to the pinnacle, standing tall at 1,271 m (4,170 ft). It's often wondered why people would put themselves through such a tough race, but the pain is nothing compared to the euphoria you feel on reaching the top and are treated to the stunning views of Tasmania and beyond.

ASIA, AUSTRALASIA AND THE SOUTH PACIFIC

448 | Tough climbs and terrain in a beautiful place

448
GREAT BARRIER ISLAND WHARF TO WHARF
NORTH ISLAND, NEW ZEALAND

Multi-terrain/Coastal

October/Various

Simply a must-do in the southern hemisphere, this race can be done on foot or by bike. The half-marathon and marathon distances (there are also 5K and 10K) take you south through the island's forest and bushland, with amazing views of the beautiful bays and beaches en route. Expect some hilly climbs and varying terrain.

449
NORTH SHORE RUN SERIES
AUCKLAND, NEW ZEALAND

Road/Coastal

January/Various

This race series is held in three locations along the North Shore of New Zealand, featuring races over 5, 10 and 15 km (3.1, 6.2 and 9.3 miles). As you would expect along a shoreline, each course is fast and flat, so as long as the wind isn't too strong, they're great for fast times. From the heritage streets and beautiful beaches of Devonport to the pristine trails of Hobsonville Point, walkers and juniors are also welcome.

450 | Marathon runners pass through Auckland Harbour

450

AUCKLAND MARATHON
NORTH ISLAND, NEW ZEALAND
Road/Marathon
October/42 km

Another city marathon, but this time in the far southern corner of the world. The city of Auckland sits proudly over the Tasman Sea with an iconic skyline and beautifully modernised harbour. Participants enjoy racing through the city and across the Auckland Harbour Bridge, taking in the sights, smells and sounds of New Zealand's biggest city. Healthy discounts are on offer for students, and many runners choose to race for charity.

451

ONE TREE HILL
AUCKLAND, NEW ZEALAND
Running route/Trail
All year round/About 5 km

Most cities have an iconic landmark that just calls out for a run around, and Auckland is no exception. One Tree Hill is volcanic in origin, but is much more than that. Steeped in Maori history, the mountain of the kiekie vine provides a relaxing half-hour or so run away from the noise and pace of the nearby city. Indeed, for a few kilometres it's as if you're deep in the countryside, often alone to enjoy the surrounding park, which hosts a Parkrun every Saturday.

452

WAIHEKE HALF-MARATHON
AUCKLAND, NEW ZEALAND

Festival/Multi-terrain

May/21 km

Claiming to be the fittest place in the world, Waiheke Island is a 35-km (22-mile) ferry ride from Auckland. The running festival is part of a weekend of celebration and entertainment that offers runners the chance to combine exercise with culture. The courses (also 5K and 10K) are a mix of country roads and trails, and are based on a 10-km (6.2-mile) loop that passes beaches and vineyards before finishing in Alison Park.

453

MOUNT MAUNGANUI HALF-MARATHON
TAURANGA, NEW ZEALAND

Multi-terrain

August/21 km

Despite the name, this is a surprisingly flat course, as the route runs around the base of the mountain, rather than up and down it. There are some undulations but nothing too difficult, and the route is a mix of trail and road. Chip timing offers accurate finish times, and there are six aid stations en route. The highlight is the spectacular finish on Mount Maunganui beach.

454

ROTORUA RUNNING FESTIVAL
NORTH ISLAND, NEW ZEALAND

Festival

November/Various

This festival is one of New Zealand's best running events, with something for everyone. Rotorua is a popular tourist town because of its location in a geothermal-activity area. Runners will get a once-in-a-lifetime opportunity to race across sulphur flats with steam pouring up from Earth's core. Word of warning: if you are sensitive to smell, hold your nose, as the sulphur creates a strong odour as you cross – all part of the fantastic experience!

455

TARAWERA ULTRA
ROTORUA, NEW ZEALAND

Ultra/Trail

February/161 km

Claiming to be New Zealand's most prestigious ultra, runners will pass scenic lakes and waterfalls and run through forests, over a maximum distance of 161 km (100 miles). The course is undulating but not too hilly, and is often completed by runners tackling their first ultra, who are helped by the fact that the cut-off times for finishing are more generous than those of similar races. More than half of the 3,000 field come from overseas, and the races are held over a two-day period.

456

TAUPO ULTRA

NORTH ISLAND, NEW ZEALAND

Ultra/Trail

October/100 km

Lake Taupo is actually a partially filled crater of a volcano created thousands of years ago. It's a stunning spot for a 100-km (62-mile) ultra, which is run mainly on the Great Lakes Trails. It can be run solo or in a team, but running it solo is physically and mentally challenging. Thankfully, the ultra joins up with the shorter distances, so there are people around for encouragement. Make sure to reach the final checkpoint in time, otherwise you'll have to take the shortcut route and come back next year!

457
TUSSOCK TRAVERSE
TONGARIRO NATIONAL PARK, NEW ZEALAND

Trail

January/Various

Home of the famous *Lord of the Rings'* Mount Doom, the Tongariro National Park is a sacred Maori land full of pristine rivers, lakes, mountains and active volcanoes. The Tussock Traverse offers varying distances for all abilities. The events (from 6 to 32 km/ 3.7 to 20 miles) are all weather-dependent due to the elevation and terrain, but in January you can generally expect to have the sun on your back.

ASIA, AUSTRALASIA AND THE SOUTH PACIFIC

459 | Stunning scenery awaits in the Abel Tasman Coastal Classic

458
HAWKE'S BAY MARATHON
NORTH ISLAND, NEW ZEALAND
Road/Coastal
May/42 km

The stunning setting of Hawke's Bay provides the backdrop for this event, with runners passing orchards, wineries and the coast as they head around the course. The route is predominantly flat and fast, and there are plenty of spectator spots and live entertainment to keep runners motivated. Don't miss the festival at the finish line, where you can celebrate your success, soak up the musical atmosphere and refuel.

459
ABEL TASMAN COASTAL CLASSIC
SOUTH ISLAND, NEW ZEALAND
Trail/Coastal
October/33 km

Feel free to run in Abel Tasman National Park whenever you fancy, but if you would like a superbly organised trail run, then look no further than the Coastal Classic, a 33-km (20-mile) race taking in the stunning coastline. Travel to the start is by boat, and, don't worry, your return journey is included, too. Due to the logistics of getting there, and the narrowness of parts of the course, entries are limited to 350, so get in quick!

460

AORAKI MOUNT COOK MARATHON

SOUTH ISLAND, NEW ZEALAND

Marathon

October/42 km

Held in the spectacular setting of Aoraki/Mount Cook National Park, runners have a choice of distances (including a half-marathon, 10K and 5K) that all include breathtaking scenery – if, of course, they have any extra breath left to take. The race starts and finishes in Mount Cook village, and the course follows the Mount Cook road between lakes, mountains and glaciers.

461

WINE RUN, LONE GOAT VINEYARD

CHRISTCHURCH, NEW ZEALAND

Novelty

January/5 & 10 km

This race is ideally suited to runners who are connoisseurs of wine, as there is an opportunity for wine tasting at every kilometre (0.6 mile). Runners who respect their livers can chose the one-lap 5K, while those who feel a greater need for alcohol can select the two-lap 10K. It's probably not a surprise that all finishers receive a commemorative wine glass.

460 | **Follow the trail to Aoraki Mount Cook**

462 | Run with your canine friend in the 4 Paws Marathon

462
4 PAWS MARATHON
CHRISTCHURCH, NEW ZEALAND
Multi-terrain/Novelty
September/Various

Can you outrun your four-legged friend? Test your dog's fitness in this entertaining, unconventional race. The races, set over various distances, are all off-road on trail, grass or sand, so dogs are permitted to be off the lead most of the time, giving your pooch the freedom to set the pace. Don't worry, if you don't have a dog you can still join the action.

463
MACPAC MOTATAPU
OTAGO, NEW ZEALAND
Trail/Festival
March/Various

Not just for runners, the Motatapu is a multi-sport event popular with Kiwi and international adventure enthusiasts. Six events are held across the weekend, four of which are designated for walkers or runners. Whichever distance you choose, this race will have you marvelling in awe at the spectacular mountain ranges surrounding the enormous Lake Wanaka. Make your way over the ridges from Wanaka to historical Arrowtown either solo or as a team.

464

SHOTOVER MOONLIGHT ADVENTURE RUN

OTAGO, NEW ZEALAND

Trail/Mountain

February/30 km

The Shotover River was once one of the richest gold-bearing rivers in the world. Nowadays, it's more popular for whitewater rafting and jetboating. This 30-km (19-mile) adventure run starts in Skippers Canyon and climbs 1,400 m (4,600 ft) on a variation of trails through river valleys, forest and rocky gorges. The finish line is at the beautiful Moke Lake, where you can enjoy a refreshing dip surrounded by impressive mountains. Stay in Queenstown, New Zealand's adventure capital, and treat yourself to a ride on the Shotover Jet while you're there.

465 | **It's not just the ascents that are tough on Mount Difficulty**

465

MOUNT DIFFICULTY ASCENT
OTAGO, NEW ZEALAND
Trail/Mountain
June/25 & 44 km

There's an extensive list of gear you need to have for this 25- and 44-km (16- and 27-mile) race, but you'll understand why when you're running up a mountainside in the middle of winter. Though the event is classed as a run, there aren't many people that could run the entire race – some parts are so steep that there are ropes involved for safety. The toughness of the climb is worth it, of course, for the incredible views of New Zealand. Those who like *Lord of the Rings* will really feel part of the Fellowship on this one!

466
ROUTEBURN TRACK
MOUNT ASPIRING NATIONAL PARK,
NEW ZEALAND
Running route/Trail
Summer/32 km

One of New Zealand's Great Walks, the 32-km (20-mile) Routeburn track is popular as a three-day hike, with stops in the various huts, or as a day hike, with many access points to choose from along the route. Expect glacier valleys, infinite waterfalls, towering mountains, amazing birdlife and stunning fiords.

467
MILFORD TRACK
FIORDLAND NATIONAL PARK,
NEW ZEALAND
Running route/Trail
Summer/54 km

The 54-km (33-mile) Milford Track is one of the most famous New Zealand Great Walks, extremely popular among 'trampers'. It's possible to walk or run this trail that takes you through some of the most breathtaking fiord landscapes in the world. Take your time and stay in huts along the way to get the full experience; you won't want to rush when you're in this paradise. Remember to book in advance for the summer months.

468 | **Behold the beauty of the Queenstown Marathon**

468
QUEENSTOWN MARATHON
SOUTH ISLAND, NEW ZEALAND
Multi-terrain
November/42 km

Claiming to be the world's most beautiful marathon, this race starts at Millbrook Resort and finishes at the Recreation Ground in the centre of Queenstown, with half-marathon and 10K options also available. The fast, mainly flat course takes in some of the most stunning scenery that New Zealand has to offer, passing lakeside shores overlooked by the magnificent Crown and Remarkable mountain ranges. There are four designated spectator areas and eleven aid stations along a route that is 70 per cent firm, wide trails and 30 per cent road.

469
KEPLER CHALLENGE 60 KM
FIORDLAND NATIONAL PARK,
NEW ZEALAND
Trail
December/60 km

Billed as the jewel of New Zealand's mountain running calendar, this 60-km (37-mile) race follows the famous Kepler Track in Fiordland National Park. Starting and finishing in the town of Te Anau, the track has sections of flat running, and tough ascents and descents. A total of eleven checkpoints offer refreshments, and first aid, thermals and survival blankets are included in the compulsory gear that runners must carry with them.

470
SAVAI'I MARATHON
SAMOA
Road/Coastal
July/42 km

These point-to-point races are all run on a coastal road on the eastern coast of Samoa's largest island, Savai'i. The marathon starts in the lava fields of Fagamolo, and heads towards the island's capital, Salelologa Village. The half-marathon and 10K start on the same course, but at closer points to the finishing line, and while the first half of the marathon includes a climb to around 75 m (246 ft) above sea level, the second part of the route used for the shorter distances is mostly flat and fast.

471
AITUTAKI PURSUIT IN PARADISE MARATHON
COOK ISLANDS
Multi-terrain/Coastal
June/42 km

The small South Pacific island of Aitutaki is one of the Cook Islands, and its combination of blue lagoons, coral reefs and lush countryside make it as close to paradise as you could get. The races (also a 10K and half-marathon) attract runners from all over the world, and start and finish at Ootu Beach, overlooking Aitutaki Lagoon. The routes are undulating with some tough climbs, and cross the island on a combination of roads and dirt tracks, with ever-changing views of the ocean.

472
TAHITI-MOOREA MARATHON
FRENCH POLYNESIA
Road/Coastal
July/21 & 42 km

Starting from Papetoai on the Tahitian island of Moorea, marathon runners set off at 5 a.m. in darkness, which gradually lightens as the sun begins to rise. Hardy local Polynesian runners are easy to spot as many choose to run *pied uns*, or barefoot. Passing through picturesque scenery and local villages, the races finish on the beach at Temae, where local dancers and flower garlands await the finishers.

POLES
AND BEYOND

473 | **The icy location of the North Pole Marathon**

473

NORTH POLE MARATHON
NORTH POLE
Marathon/Snow
June/42 km

Billed as the world's coolest marathon, runners must cope with extreme sub-zero temperatures to complete the distance. The race is run entirely on snow and ice, and the route varies from year to year depending on conditions. Runners are required to wear layers of clothing that cover the entire body, as well a pair of ski goggles for eye protection. Held since 2002, the runners' initial challenge is to reach the start line, which requires extensive travel arrangements and flying time. The airport runway, which is cleared of snow to bring runners to the event, often forms the only part of the course where the terrain is level.

474

ARCTIC CIRCLE TRAIL
GREENLAND
Running route/Snow
All year round/164 km

Cutting through the breathtaking Greenland wilderness, the 164-km (102-mile) Arctic Trail enables runners to enjoy a totally natural experience, untouched by man other than eight small huts strategically located en route. Open all year round, runners can choose the weather to suit – warm or cold, long days or short (although mid-June to mid-September is recommended, when the tundra comes to life) – as they make their way from Kangerlussuaq to Sisimiut on an undulating route marked by stone cairns. While the huts are free to stay in, all provisions have to be carried, and it's also recommended to take a tent.

475 | Don your layers for the Polar Circle Marathon

475
POLAR CIRCLE MARATHON
GREENLAND
Marathon/Snow
October/42 km

Surely the only race in the world where the race guidelines state that three layers of clothing on your legs may be too much, the Polar Circle Marathon is like no other. Spikes for runners' shoes are mandatory for the early short section over the icecap, before returning to the frequently snow-covered gravel road to the finish in Kangerlussuaq. The mainly downhill route passes moraine plains and glacier tongues, while reindeer and musk oxen frequently gaze back as the runners make their way to the finish at the aptly named Polar Lodge.

476
WHITE CONTINENT 50K
KING GEORGE ISLAND, ANTARCTICA
Marathon/Snow
January/Various

Before the 50K, marathon and half-marathon start, contestants camp overnight close to the start on King George Island. The island is 120 km (75 miles) from the coast of mainland Antarctica, and its population consists of inhabitants of various research stations. The races attract runners who are keen to record a 'finish' on the world's seventh continent, although their accomplishment is more likely to be witnessed by penguins and seals than it is by humans. A combination of tracks and snow means that fast times are unlikely, and runners need to wear extra layers, as even in the height of the summer temperatures are unlikely to rise much above 3°C (37°F).

477

ANTARCTICA MARATHON
ANTARCTIC PENINSULA, ANTARCTICA
Marathon/Snow
March/42 km

Are you a fan of small fields and brisk weather? Look no further than the Antarctica Marathon, with entries capped at '200 runners and their supporters' and race-day temperatures averaging -9°C to 1°C (15 to 34°F), not counting wind chill. Getting to the start is itself a bit of a marathon, entailing three nights in Buenos Aires, a flight to Argentina's southern tip, then a day-long journey by ship to Antarctica. If you're interested, plan ahead. This race routinely sells out early, and waiting lists for the following year's race, and the year after that, are common.

Participants start to run in the Wings for Life World Run in Izmir, Turkey

478
WINGS FOR LIFE WORLD RUNS
WORLDWIDE
May/No set distance

Held to raise funds for spinal cord injury research, the Wings for Life World Runs are held simultaneously in thirteen different locations around the world. They are one of the very few races that have no set distance – runners simply try to run as fast as possible and to keep ahead of the 'catcher car', as if they are overtaken, they have to drop out. Venues include Perth in Australia, Lima in Peru and Kakheti in Georgia, but even if you can't make one of the official locations, it is still possible to enter virtually using the Wings for Life app.

480
MIDNIGHT RUNNERS
WORLDWIDE
All year round/Various

Midnight Runners is a community, not just a run, offering like-minded runners the chance to come together for non-competitive runs at regular intervals in cities around the world – at night. The runs are often used as training events for competitive races, and runners are able to select a pace and distance of their choice. It is one of the largest urban running collectives worldwide, currently spanning four continents and eleven global cities.

479
RAGNAR CHALLENGES
WORLDWIDE
All year round/Various

The Ragnar Challenges are based on the assumption that, collectively, runners can achieve more than when running as individuals. The Ragnar organisation regularly identifies a series of challenges, some of which runners could not achieve on their own, such as running to the moon and back or scaling great heights in a short time. Other examples of Ragnar Challenges include running for 31 consecutive days or running through the night. Runners then sign up to be part of a team that agrees to take on the challenge, either uploading their running onto the Ragnar site or completing the challenge in person on the scheduled date and time. The concept has a strong community feel to it, with mutual encouragement helping to ensure that runners upload their mileage and help their team achieve the challenge.

VIRTUAL RUNNING

Virtual running grew rapidly in popularity following the 2020 Covid-19 outbreak, which forced the cancellation of many organised events around the world. Instead of running the London Marathon, for example, many of the entrants went for a marathon-distance run (some in their back gardens!), based on their Garmin, and achieved the 'virtual London'. Virtual running participants run a route or a race at any time, anywhere, and at their own pace, then upload evidence to an online platform. Runners can choose to enter a virtual race over a set 'route' and distance – sometimes seeing the route on a treadmill screen or through an app – upload their results once completed and receive a medal; or they can choose to cover a set distance or route that can be accomplished in one go or by running a series of self-selected stages that are added together to complete the distance. Advocates of virtual running, which use a combination of GPS, phone and online technology, claim that completing a virtual challenge acts as a great motivational tool. Some popular routes and races are listed here.

481
ROUTE 66
USA
3,670 km

This iconic route from Chicago to Los Angeles is 3,670 km (2,280 miles) long, and can be completed by uploading a series of runs to an online platform, which then plots the runner's progression along the road. As with many virtual runs, it is the gradual accumulation of distance that matters, not where or when the running takes place. Before deciding to take on the Route 66 challenge, bear in mind that even running 16 km (10 miles) a day will still require 228 days to complete the distance.

482
APPALACHIAN TRAIL
USA
3,167 km

Reputed to be the longest hiking trail in the world, in reality, the Appalachian Trail is not always the easiest terrain on which to run, as in parts it is very rocky and steep and includes high passes that are often covered in snow. So, running the virtual trail, which involves completing a total of 3,167 km (1,968 miles), could be easier, but still requires a lot of effort and a lot of running. The real trail runs from Springer Mountain in Georgia to Mount Katahdin in Maine.

483
ODDYSSEY HALF-MARATHON
USA
21 km

Originally held as a real race in Philadelphia, the ODDyssey became so popular that the organisers decided to offer a virtual alternative for runners who were unable to get a place on the real start line. Unlike virtual runs that allow the distance to be completed by adding the cumulative distance from a series of shorter runs, runners who complete the ODDyssey Half must cover the 21-km (13.1-mile) distance in one go, and are encouraged to do so on the same day as the real event in June.

484
JOHN O'GROATS TO LAND'S END ANNUAL CHALLENGE
UK
1,406 km

Although there are many different ways to get from the northernmost to southernmost points of the UK, the official distance is 1,406 km (874 miles). Runners can complete the distance at any time and by running anywhere, recording their distance on a GPS device or tracking app. Promoted as an annual challenge that needs to be completed in a calendar year, the distance can be completed by running just under 27 km (17 miles) a week.

485
RUN DOWN UNDER
AUSTRALIA
14,080 km

This 14,080-km (8,749-mile) virtual route was conceived in 2014, and involves a virtual run through 98 towns and every Australian state and territory. Starting in Canberra and heading to Sydney, the run progresses in an anticlockwise direction, reaching Brisbane, Darwin, Perth, Adelaide and Melbourne. From Melbourne, runners make a virtual leap across the Bass Strait for a loop around Tasmania, before completing the final stretch back to Sydney.

486
RUN NEW ZEALAND
NEW ZEALAND
4,710 km

Run New Zealand is a virtual journey of 4,710 km (2,927 miles) across the North and South Islands, taking in 46 towns and cities. Starting in Auckland, the run heads to Cape Reinga, New Zealand's northernmost point, then south across the North Island to Wellington, 2,651 km (1,647 miles) from the start. Heading anti-clockwise around the South Island, runners pass through Queenstown before reaching the finish in Christchurch, receiving informative emails on each place after they have reached it.

TOWER RUNNING

Normally involving running up the staircases of some of the tallest buildings in cities around the world, the earliest recorded version of tower running is from England in 1730, when a barman ran up and down the 311 steps of the Monument to the Great Fire of London in under 3 minutes. Today, there are over-160-m (525-ft) races on all continents that are used to determine the winners of the Towerrunning World Cup, with fifteen Masters Races that are recognised as the most prestigious and challenging.

487

EMPIRE STATE BUILDING RUN-UP
NEW YORK, USA
October

Claiming to be the longest continuous stair climb in the world, this event has been held for over 40 years. Seen as one of tower running's most prestigious races, entry is only available through the race's oversubscribed lottery, with runners often waiting for many years before they get the chance to take part. The race involves a leg-burning climb of 1,576 stairs to the 86th floor viewing deck, and finishes outside, if the weather permits.

488

COLPATRIA TOWER ASCENT
BOGOTÁ, COLOMBIA
December

Standing at a height of 196 m (630 ft), the Colpatria Tower is the fifth-tallest building in South America. A popular tower run has been held in the building since 2005, with runners setting off in groups of ten at 30-second intervals. For many years the runners were faced with a 980-step challenge, but from 2019, elite runners had to complete a double climb, firstly ascending half the tower, followed by a second run up the full height of the tower to the roof's helipad, with times for both runs combined to determine the winners.

488 | Colpatria Tower dominates the Bogotá skyline

489

EIFFEL TOWER VERTICAL RACE

PARIS, FRANCE

March

The first recorded stair race up the Eiffel Tower was in 1905, when a Stair Championship was held that attracted almost 300 competitors. At that first event, runners 'only' had to climb 729 steps to the tower's second stage. Today, runners are faced with a total ascent of 276 m (906 ft) and 1,665 stairs to the top. The iconic venue makes this a popular race, and its uniqueness is enhanced by the 8 p.m. start time.

490

PYRAMIDENKOGEL TOWER RUN

CARINTHIA, AUSTRIA

September

The Pyramidenkogel is a unique tower run as it is very much a sprint event, with an elevation gain of just 70 m (230 ft). Situated at the top of the Pyramidenkogel Mountain, finishers find themselves at an altitude of 851 m (2,792 ft) when they reach the top of the modern and distinctive building. Recognised as the world's tallest wooden observation tower, it offers great views of the surrounding countryside bordering Austria and Slovenia.

492 | **Menara Tower lights up for the Night Towerthon**

491
INTERNATIONAL VERTICAL MARATHON
SHENZHEN FINANCE CENTRE, CHINA
May

Opened in 2015, the Shenzhen Finance Centre is the world's fourth-tallest building, with a height of 599 m (1,965 ft). Not for the fainthearted or for runners with a fear of heights, there is an incredible total climb of 541 m (1,775 ft), which includes 116 floors and 3,201 stairs, finishing at the observation deck. Due to the altitude, don't be disappointed if the views are shrouded by clouds!

492
MENARA TOWER NIGHT TOWERTHON
KUALA LUMPUR, MALAYSIA
May

Located in the middle of the Bukit Nanas Forest Reserve, a tropical rainforest teeming with local flora and fauna, in Kuala Lumpur, the Towerthon takes place up the highest telecommunication tower in Southeast Asia. The race is a lung-busting 800 m (2,625 ft) uphill through the car park, followed by a climb of 2,058 steps to finish 288 m (945 ft) higher in the KL Tower Megaview Banquet Hall. For those so inclined, the tower is also the World BASE Jump Centre.

493
EUREKA STAIR CLIMB
MELBOURNE, AUSTRALIA
November

This event caters to stair climbers of all abilities, from elite athletes to walkers. The Eureka Tower is a 297-m (975-ft) gold-plated skyscraper, located in Southbank, Melbourne, overlooking the Yarra River. Contestants have to ascend a total of 1,642 stairs to the Eureka Skydeck on the 88th floor, which, at a height of 285 m (935 ft) is the highest public vantage in the southern hemisphere.

494
SYDNEY TOWER STAIR CHALLENGE
NEW SOUTH WALES, AUSTRALIA
August

After climbing 309 m (1,014 ft) to the top of the Sydney Tower Eye, you'll probably experience the best finish-line view in the state. Staggered starts for everyone from elite runners to social walkers ensure no one gets in one another's way. There are categories for individuals and teams in running, walking, fancy dress or a nine-person team challenge to climb the tower a total of 36 times, matching the lofty heights of Mount Everest!

PARKRUNS

From their inception at Bushy Park, London, in 2004, Parkruns have become a regular Saturday morning feature in the lives of millions of people around the world. Free to enter, and over a 5K distance, they bring together communities and attract runners of all ages and abilities. Runners don't need to pre-register, and there are no prizes – Parkruns are simply a chance to run as fast or as slow as you want, and have a great time getting fit. Runners can award themselves milestone t-shirts for completing up to 500 Parkruns, and unofficial clubs have sprung up to recognise runners who have competed in more than 100 different events, or even in Parkruns that start with each letter of the alphabet. Parkrun tourism has also emerged, as runners seek to find and take part in the best events around the world.

495

CANYON RIM TRAIL PARKRUN
IDAHO, USA

As the name suggests, this out-and-back run takes place on a fully paved flat route that runs along the top of the Grand Canyon – not the one in Arizona but the still impressive Grand Canyon of the Snake River in Idaho. As a result, there can't be many other Parkruns that offer such awesome views down into a canyon floor and over to the rim on the far side. The route starts and finishes under the Perrine Bridge, with runners heading to the east, then retracing their steps to Canyon Springs Road.

496

CAPE PEMBROKE LIGHTHOUSE PARKRUN
FALKLAND ISLANDS

Held just outside the Islands' capital, Port Stanley, this is an out-and-back Parkrun that follows the coastal path, with plenty of opportunity to admire the huge expanse of the South Atlantic Ocean. The remoteness of the start means that runners are advised to walk, cycle or jog to the start line, so be prepared to run a bit further than the standard 5K distance.

497
HAGA PARKRUN
STOCKHOLM, SWEDEN

Hagaparken, to the north of the Swedish capital Stockholm, is home to the Haga Parkrun. It is a mixed-terrain two-lap course, which varies with the seasons, from sunny and warm in the summer, to ice and snow in the middle of winter. The course is a beautiful mix of forest, lawns and lakes, and has been known to attract members of the Swedish Royal Family.

498
BUSHY PARKRUN
LONDON, ENGLAND

This is where the Parkrun phenomenon started in 2004, with a field of just thirteen runners. Bushy Park is in Teddington, south-west London, and the course is a flat figure-of-eight loop on grass at the start, then it follows paths around the park, running past Hampton Wick Royal Cricket Club and close to the grounds of Henry VIII's Hampton Court Palace.

499
EAST COAST PARKRUN
SINGAPORE

Singapore pioneered the introduction of Parkruns into Southeast Asia, and the East Coast Parkrun was the first of the three that the country now has. The route runs alongside a man-made sandy beach, and the closeness of the sea and the warmth of the water often entices finishers to take part in a quick dip once their run is over. Unlike most other Parkruns that start at 9 a.m., this one starts at 7.30 a.m. to avoid the worst of Singapore's heat and humidity.

500
CLONCURRY PARKRUN
QUEENSLAND, AUSTRALIA

Parkruns don't get much more remote than this one, held at Cloncurry, the home of Qantas, Australia's national airline, and the birthplace of the flying doctor service. As you would expect from the outback, the course is on red gravel paths that wind through the bush and scrub, with regular glimpses of the local wildlife. Runners are warned to avoid wearing light-coloured shoes, unless they want them changed to red!

BIOGRAPHIES

JOHN BREWER
John has combined a long running career with a career in sport and exercise science that has allowed him to travel the world, run in many different places and become an acknowledged expert in the science of running. He helped to establish the UK's largest independent centre for applied sports science, where he and his team provided sports science testing, training advice and support for many elite athletes and teams. John later became director of Sports Science for GlaxoSmithKline, before moving into academia as a professor of Sport and Exercise Science. John now heads the Northern Consortium UK, delivering educational courses to many thousands of students around the world. John has been competing in running races since the age of eleven, and has written many books, articles and scientific papers on the sport. From an early career as a track athlete, John is now about to enter his sixth decade as a runner and enjoys recreational running as much as racing. He completed his first London Marathon in 1983, and his twentieth 35 years later.

AMY-ROSE CAULEY, CONTRIBUTOR
A keen middle-distance runner, traveller and supporter of athletics, Amy-Rose has been involved in various sports throughout her life, but it wasn't until she ran her local Parkrun at the age of 25 when she really caught the running bug. Her newfound passion led her to Trafford Athletics Club, where she developed a love for track racing. Since then, Amy-Rose has raced in the Premier division of the UK Women's Athletics League in the 800 and 1500 metres, and she also loves the adrenaline rush of the steeplechase. Amy-Rose travels globally for work and finds running a very efficient way to sightsee. She tries to fit in a race on most holidays, but, despite travelling to more than 50 countries, there is no place like home! Amy-Rose's favourite race is the Great Manchester 10K, for the unforgettable atmosphere that the city provides.

PAUL LARKINS, CONTRIBUTOR
As a magazine editor, sub-four-minute-miler and former American collegiate champion in the mile, Paul has been lucky enough to run all over the world. As a competitor, part of his running weekend at a particular event would include a spin around the city on foot, be it Moscow or Paris. As a journalist, Paul has continued that love of exploration, crossing the Grand Canyon, taking in the midnight sun in Lapland and interviewing legends on their favourite run.

INDEX

A
Abu Dhabi 212–13
  Yas Marina Circuit 226
Albania 116–17
  Tiranan Half-marathon 202
Algeria 212–13
  Sahara Marathon 221
Andorra 114–17
  Skyrace Comapedrosa 171
Antarctic
  Antarctica Marathon 300–1
  White Continent 50K 299
Arctic 118
  Arctic Circle Trail 298
  Arctic Triple Lofoten Trail 162–3
  North Pole Marathon 298
  Polar Circle Marathon 299
Argentina
  race list 90–1
  Buenos Aires Marathon 110
  El Cruce Columbia 110
Australia
  race list 242–5
  Adelaide City to Bay 271
  Albert Park 280
  Alice Springs Running Festival 270
  Australian Alpine Ascent 278
  Australian Outback Half-marathon 269
  Australian Outback Marathon 269
  Backyard Blister 274
  Bondi Beach 278
  Byron Bay Lighthouse Run 273
  Cairns 272
  Challenge the Mountain 272
  Cheetah Chase 274
  City to Surf, Perth 269
  City2Surf Sydney 276–7
  Cloncurry Parkrun 311
  Dingo Dash 274
  Dubbo Stampede 274
  Elder Park 271
  Eureka Stair Climb 309
  Five Peaks SA Trail Running Festival 272
  Gold Coast Running Festival 273
  Kangaroo Island Marathon 271
  Melbourne Marathon Festival 279
  Moon Shadow Night Run 269
  Mount Lofty Climb 271
  Perth Trail Series 269
  Phillip Island Running Festival 281
  Portsea 281
  Puffing Billy Running Festival 280
  Rhino Ramble 274
  Run Down Under virtual run 305
  Six Foot Track Marathon 274
  Snapper Rocks 273
  Summit Survivor 281
  Surf Coast Century 279
  SMH Half-marathon 275
  Sydney Tower Stair Challenge 309
  Ultra Trail Gold Coast 273
  Uluru Base Trail 270
  Wings for Life World Run 303
Austria
  race list 114–17
  Ossiacher *See* Nachthalbmarathon 199
  Pyramidenkogel Tower Run 308
  Silvrettarun 3000 199
Azerbaijan 242–5
  Baku Boulevard 246

B
Bahamas 90–1
  Marathon Bahamas Race Weekend 93
Bannister, Roger 154
Barbados 90–1
  Barbados Boardwalk 96
Belarus 116–17
  Velodorozhka 208
Belgium
  race list 114–17
  Brussels 20K 180
  Bütgenbach Half-marathon 181
Belize 90–1
  End of the World Marathon 96
Bhutan 242–5
  Thunder Dragon Marathon 251
Brazil
  race list 90–1
  Florianópolis Marathon 103
  Ibirapuera Park 102
  Jungle Marathon 102
  Rio de Janeiro Beachfront 102
  Rio de Janeiro Marathon 102
Bulgaria 114–17
  Vitosha 100K 205

C
Cambodia 242–5
  Ultra Trail Angkor 265
Canada
  race list 22–5
  5 Peaks Trail Running Series BC 82
  Around the Bay Road Race 85
  Chilly Half-marathon 86
  Foxtail Hundred 86
  Handloggers Half-marathon 82
  Hungry Hollow 5K 86
  Itijjagiaq Trail 85
  Katannilik Territorial Park 85
  Moose Mountain Trail 84
  Ottawa Race Weekend 87
  Sea Wheeze Half-marathon 83
  Toronto Women's Run Series 87
  Vancouver 83
  Wild Pacific Trail 84
Canary Islands
  race list 212–13
  Jinama Trail 218
  Lanzarote Half-marathon 218
  Lanzarote Marathon 218
  Tenerife Blue Trail Night Challenge 218
Cayman Islands 90–1
  Seven Mile Beach 94
Cerutty, Percy 281
Chile
  race list 90–1
  Atacama Crossing 104–5
  Circuito Trail Running Races 105
  El Cruce Columbia 110
  Patagonian International Marathon 108
  Rock 'n' Roll Santiago 105
  Snow Running 106
  Vulcano Ultra Trail 106–7
China
  race list 242–5
  Beijing Marathon 254
  The Bund 255
  Great Wall Marathon 255
  International Vertical Marathon 309
  Lanzhou Marathon 253
Colombia
  race list 90–1
  Bogotá Half-marathon 99
  Colpatria Tower Ascent 207
  Grand Tour of Cartagena 98
  Salento Trail Challenge 98
Cook Islands
  Aitutaki Pursuit in Paradise Marathon 295
Costa Rica 90–1
  Costa Rica Ultra Trail 97
Cram, Steve 138
Croatia 116–17
  Lokrum Island 200
Cyprus 114–17
  Paphos Marathon 204
Czech Republic
  race list 114–17
  Brno Half-marathon 198
  Prague Half-marathon 198

D
Denmark 116–17
  Parks & Lakes 164
Dominican Republic 90–1
  Santo Domingo Marathon 95
Dubai 212–13
  Dubai Marina 226

E
Easter Island 90–1
  Marathon Rapa Nui 103

Ecuador 90–1
  Parque Metropolitano Guangüiltagua 99
  Quilotoa Loop 100
Egypt
  race list 212–13
  Egyptian Marathon 223
  Gezira Island 222
  Pharaonic Race 100K 223
Elliott, Herb 281
England
  race list 114–17
  Beat the Boat 155
  Blackpool 10 142
  Brampton to Carlisle 138
  Brighton Beach 159
  Burghley House 147
  Bushy Parkrun 311
  Cambridge Half-marathon 148
  Cliveden Cross Country 10K 154
  Down Tow Up Flow Half-marathon 155
  Durham Heritage Coast Trail 138
  Exmoor Fells 151
  Gilsland Chase 135
  Grasmere Gallop 140
  Great Manchester 10K 143
  Great North Run 136–7
  Great South 10-Mile 152
  Greenwich Foot Tunnel & Park 159
  Hawkshead 16K 140
  Heckington 10 146
  Hutton Roof Fell Race 138
  Jamaica Inn 152
  John O'Groats to Land's End virtual run 305
  Jurassic Coast Challenge 150
  Keswick Mountain Festival 140–1
  Lakeland 50 Miles 138
  Lakeland 100 Miles 138
  London Color Run 158
  London Marathon 156–7
  Mad Dog 10K 142
  Manchester Marathon 144
  Mersey Tunnel 10K 144
  Midnight 2 Midnight 158
  National championships 135
  OMM (Original Mountain Marathon) 124
  Orion 15 160
  Oxford River Running 153
  Oxford University's Iffley Road Track 154
  Pikes Peak 141
  Portsmouth Coastal Half-marathon 153
  Ridgeway Run 153
  Rivington Pike 142
  Round Sheffield Run 145
  Run for the 96 144
  Runfestrun 155
  Shakespeare Half-marathon 148
  Shakespeare Marathon 148
  Silverstone Half-marathon 147
  South West Coastal Path 149
  Teignmouth Seafront 151
  Tough Guy 145
  The Wrekin 146
Estonia 116–17
  Pirita Path 206
Ethiopia 212–13
  Great Ethiopian Run 227

F

Falkland Islands
  race list 90–1
  Cape Pembroke Lighthouse Parkrun 310
  Stanley Marathon 111
  Stone Run Half-marathon 111
Finland
  race list 114–17
  Cross Lapland Half-marathon 168
  Cross Lapland Marathon 168
  Helsinki City Running Day 169
  Lapland 168
  Myrskylä 169
  Nakukymppi 169
  Nuts Ylläs Pallas 168
France
  race list 114–17
  Chamonix 177
  Eiffel Tower Vertical Race 306, 308
  Grand Trail des Templiers 178–9
  Lyon Urban 176
  Marathon du Medoc 174–5
  National Centre for Altitude Training 180
  Paris Marathon 172–3
  Paris to Versailles 16 km 174
  La SaintéLyon 176
  Ultra-Trail du Mont-Blanc (UTMB) 177
French Polynesia 242–5
  Tahiti-Moorea Marathon 295

G

Galapagos Islands 90–1
  Galapagos Marathon 100
The Gambia 212–13
  Great Gambia Run (Bajana International Marathon) 226
Gebrselassie, Haile 227
Georgia
  Wings for Life World Run 303
Germany
  race list 114–17
  Airport Night Run 184
  Bavaria Run 185
  Berlin Marathon 183
  Great 10K 183
  Hochstaufen/Bad Reichenhall 185
  Kreissparkassen Trail 185
  Serengeti Park Run 182
Gibraltar 110–17
  The Rock 170–1
Greece
  race list 114–17
  Athens Classic Marathon 202–3
  Skiathos 10K Trail Run 204

H

Hill, Ron 138
Hong Kong
  race list 242–5
  Hong Kong 100 Ultra Trail Race 256
  Victoria Peak Circle Run 255
Hungary
  race list 114–17
  Budapest Half-marathon 201
  Lake Balaton 26 202

I

Iceland
  race list 114–17
  Grímsey Island 118
  Laugavegur Ultramarathon 119
  Ölfusá River 118
India
  race list 242–5
  Delhi Half-marathon 247
  Great Tibetan Marathon 246
  Himalaya 100-Mile Stage Race 249
  Khardung la Challenge 247
  Ladakh Ultra 247
  Mumbai 248
  Satara Hill Half-marathon 248
Ireland/Northern Ireland
  race list 114–17
  Armagh 5K 123
  Ballyliffin Coastal Challenge 120
  Cliffs of Moher 121
  Connemarathon 120
  Cork City Marathon 123
  Dublin Marathon 120
  Extreme North 119
  Giant's Causeway 123
  Great Limerick Run 122
  Phoenix Park Circular 120
  Skellig Michae 122
  Sugar Loaf 10K 121
  Valentia Island Half-marathon 122
  Wild Atlantic Way 119
Isle of Man 114–17
  Easter Festival 124
Israel
  race list 212–13
  Jerusalem Marathon 224
  Timna National Park 225

Italy
  race list 114–17
  Brixen Dolomiten Marathon 194
  Ecomaratona del Ventasso 196
  Jesolo Moonlight Half-marathon 196
  Ortler Sky Trails 194–5
  Pisa Marathon 196
  Roma by Night 197
  Sentiero degli Dei 197
  Ultra Tour du Monte Rosa 188
  Ultra-Trail du Mont-Blanc (UTMB) 177

J
Jamaica 90–1
  Reggae Marathon 94
Japan
  race list 242–5
  Arakawa Trail 262
  Fuju Mountain Race 258
  Fukuoka Marathon 256
  Imperial Palace Loop 259
  Kyoto 257
  Nagoya City Marathon 257
  Nagoya Women's Marathon 257
  Ohme Road Race 259
  Sakura Michi Nature Run 258
  Tokyo Marathon 260–1
  Yoshida Trail 258
Jordan 212–13
  Dead Sea Ultra 225

K
Kenya
  race list 212–13
  Baringo Half-marathon 229
  Iten 229
  Masai Mara Half-marathon 230
  Nangili Road 228

L
Laos 242–5
  Vientiane Half-marathon 265
Latvia 116–17
  Kuldiga Half-marathon 207
Lithuania 116–17
  Vilnius Christmas Run 207
Luxembourg 116–17
  Bambésch Forest 182

M
Macau 242–5
  Sai Van Lake 255
Madagascar 212–13
  Ultra Trail des Ô Plateau 238

Madeira
  race list 212–13
  Fanals Vertical Kilometre 217
  Madeira Island Ultra-Trail 215
  Madeira Sky Race 214–15
  Transvulcania 216–17
Malaysia 242–5
  race list 242–5
  Borneo Marathon 268
  Lambir Hills National Park Summit Trail 268
  Menara Tower Night Towerthon 308–9
Maldives 242–5
  Longrun Marathon 250
Malta 114–17
  Malta Marathon 193
Mauritius
  race list 212–13
  Avalon Trail 239
  Mauritius Marathon 239
Mexico
  race list 90–1
  Carrera D Teotihuacan (Ancient Routes) Trail Race 93
  Copper Canyon 100-Mile Ultra 92
  Half-marathon Mexico City 92
  Teotihuacan 93
Midnight Runners 303
Moldova
  race list 114–17
  Milestii Mici Wine Run 208
Mongolia
  race list 242–5
  Gobi March 252
  Sunrise to Sunset (MS2S) 253
Morocco
  race list 212–13
  Casablanca Waterfront 220
  Marathon des Sables 219
  Menara Gardens 220
  Toubkal Circuit 220
Myanmar 242–5
  Bagan Temple 10K 262–3
  Bagan Temple Half-marathon 262–3
  Bagan Temple Marathon 262–3

N
Namibia 212–13
  Citidash 232
Nepal
  race list 242–5
  Everest Marathon 250
  Everest Trail Race 251

Netherlands
  race list 114–17
  Amsterdam Marathon 181
  Loop Den Haag Half-marathon 182
  Rotterdam Marathon 182
New Zealand
  race list 242–5
  4 Paws Marathon 291
  Abel Tasman Coastal Classic 289
  Aoraki Mount Cook Marathon 290
  Auckland Marathon 284
  Great Barrier Island Wharf to Wharf 283
  Great Walk 294
  Hawke's Bay Marathon 289
  Kepler Challenge 60 km 295
  Macpac Motatapu 291
  Milford Track 294
  Mount Difficulty Ascent 293
  Mount Maunganui Half-marathon 285
  North Shore Run Series 283
  One Tree Hill 284
  Queenstown Marathon 294
  Rotorua Running Festival 285
  Routeburn Track 294
  Run New Zealand virtual run 305
  Shotover Moonlight Adventure Run 292
  Tarawera Ultra 285
  Taupo Ultra 286–7
  Tussock Traverse 288
  Waiheke Half-marathon 285
  Wine Run, Lone Goat Vineyard 290
Norway
  race list 114–17
  Arctic Circle 161–3
  Arctic Triple Lofoten Trail 162–3
  Midnight Sun Marathon 161
  Palace Park 164
  Polar Night Half-marathon 161
  Spitsbergen Marathon 160
  Tromsø Mountain Challenge 161
Nurmi, Paavo 181

P
Panama 90–1
  Ciclovía Cinta Costera Path 97
Papua New Guinea 242–5
  Kokoda Trail 268
Paraguay 90–1
  Costanera Promenade 109
Parkruns 310
  Bushy Parkrun 311
  Canyon Rim Trail Parkrun 310

Cape Pembroke Lighthouse Parkrun 310
Cloncurry Parkrun 311
East Coast Parkrun, Singapore 311
Haga Parkrun 311
Peru
  race list 90–1
  Andes 101
  Cordillera Blanca 101
  Huascarán National Park 101
  Inca Trail Marathon 101
  Wings for Life World Run 303
Pheidippides 202
Philippines 242–5
  Manila Baywalk 268
Poland
  race list 114–17
  Beskidy Ultra 207
  Warsaw Half-marathon 206
Portugal 116–17
  Peniche 170
Prefontaine, Steve 29
Puerto Rico
  race list 90–1
  El Yunque National Forest 95
  Tropikal Half-marathon 95

R
Radcliffe, Paula 180
Ragnar Challenges 303
Rodgers, Bill 70
Romania 116–17
  Brasov Half-marathon 202
Russia 114–17
  Moscow Half-marathon 209
Rwanda 212–13
  Rwamagana Marathon 228

S
Samoa 242–5
  Savai'i Marathon 295
Scotland
  race list 114–17
  Arthur's Seat 129
  Cape Wrath Ultra 124–5
  Edinburgh Marathon 129
  Falkirk Epic Trail 10K 129
  John O'Groats to Land's End virtual run 305
  OMM (Original Mountain Marathon) 124
  Ring of Steall Skyrace 126–7
  South Loch Ness Trail 128
  Tiree 10K 124

Tiree Half-marathon 124
  Water of Leith Walkway 129
  West Highland Way 128–9
Singapore 242–5
  2XU Compression Run 267
  East Coast Parkrun 311
Slovakia
  race list 114–17
  Bratislava Half-marathon 200
  Presov Night Run 201
Slovenia 114–17
  Bled Night Run 199
South Africa
  race list 212–13
  4Peaks Mountain Challenge 234–5
  City Surf Run 237
  Comrades Marathon 236
  Durban 10K 237
  Fairie Glen Nature Reserve 233
  Freedom Route 236
  Mandela Day Marathon 236
  Skukuza Half-marathon 233
  Table Mountain 237
  Tsitsikamma Trail 238
  Two Oceans Marathon 237
Spain
  race list 116–17
  Bilbao Night Marathon 170
  Seville 171
  Ultra Pirineu 170
  World's Fastest Marathon 171
Sri Lanka 242–5
  Arugam Ba Half-marathon 249
Sweden
  race list 114–17
  Göteborgsvarvet Half-marathon 166–7
  Haga Parkrun 311
  Kustmaran & Kristianopel Runt 166
  Sundsvall Trail Races 165
Switzerland
  race list 114–17
  Bisse du Torrent Neuf 189
  Christmas Midnight Run 186
  Eiger Ultra Trail 190–1
  Grand Prix of Bern 186
  Jungfrau Marathon 189
  Lema Trail 193
  Sierre-Zinal 192
  Silvesterlauf 188
  Spartacus Run 192
  Survival Run 186–7
  Swiss Snow Run 192
  SwissAlpine Race Weekend 193
  Tour du Lac de Joux 186

Ultra Tour du Monte Rosa 188
Ultra-Trail du Mont-Blanc (UTMB) 177

T
Tanzania
  race list 212–13
  Heart Half-marathon 232
  Kilimanjaro Marathon 231
  Serengeti Safari Marathon 231
Tarahumara 50, 92
Tasmania
  race list 242–5
  Cradle Mountain 282
  Flinders Island Running Festival 282
  Point to Pinnacle Half-marathon 282
Tergat, Paul 229
Thailand 242–5
  race list 242–5
  Khon Kaen Marathon 264
  Lumpini Park 264
  Patong Beach to Kalim Hill 264
Tierra del Fuego 90–1
  Tierra del Fuego National Park 111
tower running 306
  Colpatria Tower Ascent 307
  Eiffel Tower Vertical Race 306, 308
  Empire State Building Run-up 307
  Eureka Stair Climb 309
  International Vertical Marathon 309
  Menara Tower Night Towerthon 308–9
  Pyramidenkogel Tower Run 308
Trinidad and Tobago 90–1
  Trinidad and Tobago International Marathon 96
Tunisia
  race list 212–13
  Sfax International Half-marathon 222
  Zriba Night Trail 221
Turkey 116–17
  Istanbul 205
  Wings for Life World Run 302–3

U
Uganda 212–13
  Rift Marathon 228
United States
  race list 22–5
  Appalachian Trail virtual run 304
  Bad Bass Half-marathon 35
  Badger Cove Half-marathon 38
  Badwater 135 37
  Barkley Marathons 63
  Bay to Breakers 33

Big Sur Marathon 36
Bird to Gird Pathway 26
Bolder Boulder 52
Boston Marathon 70–1
Bridge Run 68
Bridgehampton Half-marathon 78
Bridger Ridge Run 47
Brooklyn Half-marathon 77
California International Marathon 32
Campion Trail 58
Canyon Rim Trail Parkrun 310
Caroler 5K 73
Central Park 76
Charles River 72
Cherry Blossom Ten Mile 79
Chester Creek Trail 26
Chicago Marathon 60–1
Chicago Spring Half-marathon 59
Chuckanut 50K 29
Covered Bridges Half-marathon 69
Dale Ball Trails 53
Diablo Trails Challenge 35
Diamond Head, Hawaii 27
Dipsea Run 32
Dirty Dozen 33
Emma Crawford Coffin Races 53
Empire State Building Run-up 307
Escalante Canyons Marathon 45
Fargo Half-marathon 54
Fargo Marathon & Festival 54
Fifth Avenue Mile 77
Florida Coast 2 Coast Relay 66
Fort Smith Marathon 58
Freeze Your Half Off 62
Golden Gate Bridge 34
Gulf Shores Beaches 64
Half Dozen 33
Hamptons Marathon 78
Hapalua half-marathon 27
Hardrock 100 48–9
Hobooken Halloween 5K 79
Honey Badger 100-Mile Ultra 55
Honolulu Marathon 29
Hood to Coast 29
Interurban Trail 29
Jackson Hole Half-marathon 47
Jackson Hole Marathon 47
Joshua Tree National Park 40
Kiawah Island Marathon 81
Leadville 100 50
Lost Man Loop 50
Madison River Run 5K 47

Maine Coast 69
Malibu Half-marathon 39
Marine Corps Marathon 80
Miami Marathon 67
Monterey Bay Half-marathon 36
Monument Valley Wildcat Trail 45
Mount Desert Island Marathon 69
Music City Half-marathon 62
New Orleans 59
New York City Marathon 74–5
Niagara Falls International Marathon 73
North Collier Regional Park 66
ODDyssey virtual Half-marathon 305
Oregon Fall Half-marathon 30
Paradise Coast Half-marathon 66
Parkway Classic 80
Peachtree Road Race 68
Pensacola Women's Half-marathon Weekend 65
Pikes Peak Ascent & Marathon 52
Pre's Trail 29
Reach the Beach 69
Resurgence Half-marathon 72
Rim to Rim to Rim 46
Rock 'n' Roll Las Vegas Marathon 43
Route 66 Marathon 56
Route 66 virtual run 304
Run Crazy Horse Marathon 54
Run Sedona 46
Run Woodstock Festival 64
Runyon Canyon Park 38
San Diego Half-marathon 42
Santa Barbara Waterfront 38
Shannon Monster 5K 58
Silver Strand Veterans Day Half-marathon 42
South Kaibab Trail 46
Space Coast Beaches 66
Spartan Race, Hawaii 28
Sri Chinmoy Self-Transcendence 3100 Mile Race 78
The Strand 39
The Strip 44
Summit Rock Half-marathon 35
Surfing Madonna Beach Run 40–1
Texas Trail Festival 58
Tony Knowles Trail 26
Trans-Pecos Ultra 57
Transrockies Run 51
Tulsa Run 55
Ukrop's Monument Avenue 10K 80

Umstead 100-Mile Ultra 81
Walt Disney World Marathon Weekend 65
Western States Endurance Run (Western Sates 100) 30–1
WW (Wounded Warrior) Military Miles 58
Yosemite Valley Loop 35
Zion Half-marathon 44
Uruguay 90–1
Rambla Waterfront 109

V
Vietnam
  race list 242–5
  Da Nang Marathon 267
  Halong Bay Heritage Half-marathon 266
  Halong Bay Heritage Marathon 266
  Ho Chi Ming City Marathon 267
  Hoang Lien National Park 266
Virén, Lasse 169
virtual running 304
  Appalachian Trail 304
  John O'Groats to Land's End 305
  ODDyssey Half-marathon 305
  Route 66 304
  Run Down Under 305
  Run New Zealand 305

W
Wales
  race list 114–17
  Black Mountains 134
  Coastal Trail Series 131
  Love Trails 132–3
  Rabbit Run 135
  Race the Train 131
  Snowdonia Race 130
  Taff Trail 135
  Worms Head 10K 132
Wings for Life World Runs 302–3

Z
Zimbabwe 212–13
  Victoria Falls Marathon 232

PICTURE CREDITS

t = top, b = bottom, l = left, r = right, m = middle

Alamy: 28 US Navy Photo; 37 REUTERS; 62 J. Carlee Adams; 74–5 Felix Lipov; 76 Cavan; 78 Trevor Collens; 82 All Canada Photos; 87 Josef Pittner; 92 Cavan; 99 Juan Tapias/VWPics; 106–7 Francisco Negroni; 110 dpa picture alliance; 122 Stephen Power; 123 David Hunter; 131 ATHENA PICTURE AGENCY LTD; 136–7 Steve Mayes; 140 Helen Audley; 142 lemonlight features; 145 James Appleton; 147 James Moy; 148 DHSP; 161 Crister Haug; 171 Jason Plews; 174–5 Hemis; 176 Serge Mouraret; 181 ton koene; 183 Panther Media GmbH; 198 Vladimir Pomortzeff; 227 Christoph Keller; 230 © Sun Ruibo/Xinhua/Alamy Live News; 234–5 Ariadne Van Zandbergen; 250 Roger Cracknell 01/classic; 253 Gonzales Photo; 279 Robert Mora; 289 Tim Cuff; 298 Jose Luis Stephens; 310–1 Peter Cavanagh

Alexis Berg: © Alexis Berg 7, 63, 162–3, 177, 178–9, 190–1, 214–5, 216–7, 219

Anna Rachel: © Anna Rachel Photography 56, 72, 149

Damian Hall: 130, 188

Getty: 27 Tom Pennington; 32 David Madison; 50 Kent Nishimura; 52 Helen H. Richardson; 65 Handout; 67 Miami Herald; 70–1 MediaNews Group/Boston Herald; 70 (inset) Boston Globe; 79 The Washington Post; 103 Ivo Gonzalez/Stringer; 143 Anthony Devlin; 152 Getty Images; 154l Bettmann; 156–7 Joseph Okpako; 160 MIREILLE DE LA LEZ; 180 RAYMOND ROIG; 184 JORG CARSTENSEN; 189 AFP Contributor; 200 SAMUEL KUBANI; 203 NurPhoto; 209 Anadolu Agency; 218 DESIREE MARTIN; 223 KHALED DESOUKI; 224 NurPhoto; 229 Franck Fife; 237 Gallo Images/Stringer; 246r Ami Vitale; 249 Simon Bruty; 254 Kevin Frayer/Stringer; 258 The Asahi Shimbun; 280 The AGE; 292 Tim Clayton—Corbis; 300–1 AFP/Stringer; 302 Anadolu Agency; back cover Alex Trautwig/Staff

Graeme Hewitson: 129 © Graeme Hewitson/Monument Photos

iStock: 43 meseberg; 53 SWKrullImaging; 86 Jun Zhang; 164 lissart; 208 Kutredrig; 220 Lukas Hodon; 225 compuinfoto, 228 Misugo; 236 ChrisVanLennepPhoto; 274 PomInOz; 278 benkrut

John Brewer: 47, 84, 223

Mark Nightingale: 111 Mark Nightingale/Roddy Cordeiro

Philipp Reiter: © Philipp Reiter 30–1, 48–9, 51, 165, 185, 194–5, 256

Shutterstock: 20–1 Andre Gie; 33 Eddie Hernandez Photos; 34 cdrin; 36 Pung; 38–9 Joshua Resnick; 42 Simone Hogan; 46 Maridav; 55 LM Gray; 59 Jfharmon; 60–1 John Gress Media Inc; 66 Mark_Sawyer; 68 BluIz60; 77 a katz; 80 Rena Schild; 81 Wileydoc; 83 Max Lindenthaler; 85l Ed Dods; 85r CJ Park; 88–9 Andrey Yurlov; 93 Dmitry Rukhlenko; 94 mikolajn; 95 Katherine Robertson; 97 Dmitriy Bryndin; 100 Ludmila Ruzickova; 112–3 lzf; 134 Raggedstone; 139 Duncan Andison; 144 Philip Brookes; 146 Daveleesuk; 153 Olga_Anourina; 154r Martin Anderson; 155 Filip Fuxa; 166–7 Kedardome; 172–3 OSTILL is Franck Camhi; 187 Tobias Klein; 192 Kertu; 193 NickyRedl; 199b canadastock; 201 iremt; 204 Alfiya Safuanova; 205 sefabarisozturk; 207 astudio; 210–1 Izf; 221 Carrastock; 222 Dmitry Chulov; 226 Emilio Pastor de Miguel; 238 Emilio JoseG; 239 Myroslava Bozhko; 240 lzf; 247r paul prescott; 257 KY CHO; 259 Guillermo Olaizola; 260–1 J. Henning Buchholz; 264 Travelpixs; 266 KritsadaPetchuay; 283 Evgeny Gorodetsky; 296–7 Blazej Lyjak; 304–5 MaxyM; 306 majeczka; 307 oscar garces; 308 Sean Pavone; 312 CrispyPork

Unsplash: 26 Jack Church; 44 Joshua Sukoff; 45 Cayetano Gil; 54 Stephen Walker; 64 NICO BHLR; 98 Christian Holzinger; 101 Tom Cleary; 109 Leandro Riviello; 118 Lachlan Gowen; 121 Saad Chaudhry; 128 Ramon Vloon; 141 www.instagram.com/thevisualiza; 150 Christopher Martyn; 151 Sam Vernon; 158 Jordane Mathieu; 168 Saad Chaudhry; 196 Alex Vasey; 197 Dylan Freedom; 231 & 232 K15 Photos; 246l Graeme Morris; 247l Chaitanya Maheshwari; 269 George Bakos; 270 Antoine Fabre; 282 Donovan Simpkin; 288 Laura Smetsers; 290 Tyler Lastovich

Wikimedia Commons: 169 JIP

Also: 108 Patricia Ainol/Patagonian International Marathon®; 40–1 Surfing Madonna Oceans Project; 57 Garrett Nasrallah/Trans-Pecos Ultra; 73 Niagara Falls Marathon; 96 End of the World Marathon; 104–5 RacingThePlanet/Onni Cao; 119 Frank Tschöpe for Laugavegur Ultramarathon; front cover, 125 © Steve Ashworth; 126–7 © No Limits Photography; 132 Activity Wales Events; 133 @ davidaltabev; 159 Daniel @ danvpix Varga; 206 Karolina Krawczyk Photography; 248 Mr Dhiraj Zanvar; 251 Thunder Dragon Marathon; 252 RacingThePlanet/Onni Cao; 262–3 Albatros Adventure Marathons; 265 Vanpheng Southichak/Vientiane Half-marathon; 272 Trail Running SA (Five Peaks); 275 & 276–7 Salty Dingo/IRONMAN Australia; 281 Summit Survivor; 284 Tim Bardsley-Smith/IRONMAN New Zealand; 286–7 photos4sale.co.nz; 291 Julia Grant/4 Paws Marathon; 293 Terryjack Davis/Mount Difficulty Ascent; 294 Tim Bardsley-Smith/IRONMAN New Zealand; 299 Albatros Adventure Marathons

All trademarks, trade names and other product designations referred to herein are the property of their respective owners and are used solely for identification purposes. This book is a publication of The Bright Press, an imprint of The Quarto Group, and has not been authorised, licensed, approved, sponsored or endorsed by any other person or entity. The publisher is not associated with any product, service or vendor mentioned in this book. While every effort has been made to credit contributors, The Bright Press would like to apologise should there have been any omissions or errors, and would be pleased to make the appropriate correction for future editions.

ACKNOWLEDGEMENTS

Much of this book was written during the period when the Covid-19 pandemic caused havoc around the world. At a time when lives, communities and countries were devastated by an unseen virus, it was strange and surreal to be writing about a much more normal world of running, often at exotic locations that seemed far removed from lockdown and social distancing. It is, therefore, only right to pay tribute to the many thousands of key workers around the world who protected and saved lives, ensuring that many millions of runners were able to return to the sport and pastime that they love.

I must also thank the team at The Bright Press, and in particular my Bright Press editor, Caroline Elliker, for asking me to write this book; it has been the most enjoyable book I have written by some way, and her help, guidance and support was invaluable. However, this book is not just about the writing, so I would also like to thank the project editor, Katie Crous, who, along with designer Paul Sloman, did such a fantastic job putting the content together and sourcing the incredible images that bring to life so many of the wonderful places around the world that runners can experience and explore.

I would also like to thank the three authors (and friends) who have contributed to this book: Amy-Rose Cauley, Paul Larkins and Dr Sarah Rowell. All are far better runners than I will ever be, and they each used their extensive knowledge of competitive and recreational running to provide fantastic insight into many great races and places to run around the world. Thanks also to Mark and Susannah Nightingale, for the advice on the Falkland Islands entries and editorial checks.

Writing this book also involved many hours of research, which helped to provide the background detail that is essential for a book such as this. However, there is one particular source of information that I found to be more valuable than any other – the fantastic website that is www.greatruns.com, which brilliantly describes running locations and routes in many cities around the world.

I have been running races for over 40 years, and none of these would have been possible without the help of the many volunteers who freely give up their time to help runners enjoy their sport. Their timekeeping, coaching, marshalling and organising have all helped runners to keep on running, and without them, the sport of running, and this book, would not exist. So thank you to every volunteer who makes running races possible.

Finally, I should like to thank my family – Caroline, Beth and Emma – who have supported my running for so many years, and who went the 'extra mile' to keep a vulnerable old runner safe during the global pandemic.